对风险说不

涉外合同关键词导读与解析

雷彦璋 著

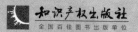

知识产权出版社
全国百佳图书出版单位

内容提要

本书通过关键词的解析，对涉外合同文本的谈判、起草与审核提供了全新的思维方式和应用技巧，通过对相同的、相似的问题进行类聚群分，让读者能够有所选择，有所侧重，并能即学即用，达到事半功倍的效果。

本书内容新颖，思维独到。通过阅读本书能够让您了解涉外合同审核的基本理念，让您了解到英文合同术语形成的历史渊源，让您很快对涉外合同文本中有关权力、义务性关键词做到准确理解。

本书还通过适当章节教您在英文合同中学会说"不"，为您对英文合同复合句的突破找到捷径，让您明白涉外合同权利义务条款约定的根据所在，让您掌握对合同约定不确定性因素的合理评估，让您懂得如何对当事人的利益进行有效保护，对您如何避免涉外合同文本冲突将有较快提升。

本书适用于企业法律顾问、涉外律师、商务合同谈判人员、合同起草与审核人员，特别适用于刚从法学院校、商务院校或英语翻译等院校毕业的大学毕业生对英文合同范本的理解与掌握。

责任编辑：蔡　虹

图书在版编目（CIP）数据

对风险说不：涉外合同关键词导读与解析/雷彦璋著. —北京：知识产权出版社，2013.4

ISBN 978-7-5130-1943-9

Ⅰ.①对… Ⅱ.①雷… Ⅲ.①涉外经济合同—法律解释—中国 Ⅳ.①D923.65

中国版本图书馆 CIP 数据核字（2013）第 050739 号

对风险说不——涉外合同关键词导读与解析

DUIFENGXIAN SHUOBU—SHEWAI HETONG GUANJIANCI DAODU YU JIEXI

雷彦璋　著

出版发行：知识产权出版社

社　址：北京市海淀区马甸南村 1 号	邮　编：100088
网　址：http://www.ipph.cn	邮　箱：bjb@cnipr.com
发行电话：010-82000860 转 8101/8102	传　真：010-82005070/82000893
责编电话：010-82000860 转 8324	责编邮箱：caihong@cnipr.com
印　刷：知识产权出版社电子制印中心	经　销：新华书店及相关销售网点
开　本：880mm×1230mm　1/32	印　张：11
版　次：2013 年 4 月第 1 版	印　次：2013 年 4 月第 1 次印刷
字　数：320 千字	定　价：32.00 元

ISBN 978-7-5130-1943-9/D·1704（4781）

前　言

　　《民商诉讼博弈与律师技能突破》、《对风险说不！非诉博弈与企业法务精要》与读者见面后，接到了知识产权出版社虹编辑的盛请约稿，希望再度合作，为读者创作更好的精神读物，并要求书中的内容尽量来自于实际，拿去能够指导实践，一下子就让我稍微放松的思绪又绷紧起来。

　　如果说《民商诉讼博弈与律师技能突破》从提升律师执业技能角度讲述了民商诉讼的技巧与素质要求的话，那么，《对风险说不！非诉博弈与企业法务精要》则侧重于提升企业法务人员或企业法律顾问处理企业非诉事务的能力，而遗憾的是这两本书很少涉及涉外法务的处理，而作为一名优秀的法务工作者或涉外律师以及涉外商务人员又不得不面对大量的涉外合同的谈判、起草与审核。

　　笔者这几年花了大量时间，对于涉外合同谈判与合同文本的起草、审核进行了细致地分类研究，并付出了很大心血，因此想通过此书将涉外合同审核、谈判与阅读中的一些体会、得失总结出来，让自己的涉外合同处理能力得到尽一步的提升。

　　为了写好本书，笔者对经手的数百份涉外合同按照关键词进行了整理、分类、总结，并逐一进行了法理分析和风险测试，认为有必要将其中的精华部分拿出来与同行分享，特别是对于有志于企业法律事务管理的同行或涉外商务合同事务的律师具有较好的提升作用。

　　本书一改前两本专著按照篇章结构的编排方式，采用了独立成章的方式对相同的、相似的问题进行了类聚群分，让读者能够有所选择，有所侧重，并能学而有用，活而用之。

本书有一些新的观点：情感类聚章，让您了解涉外合同审核的基本理念；关键词抽取章，让您掌握到英文合同起草、阅读与审核的利器；术语性关键词章，让您了解到英文合同术语形成的历史渊源；双刃性评估章，让您掌握降低法律风险的有效手段；权力把握章，让您很快理解涉外合同文本中有关权力、权利与授权性关键词；责任把握章，让您很快理解涉外合同文本中有关尽职、尽责与义务性关键词。

本书还通过适当章节教会您在英文合同中学会说不；通过关注群意章，为您对英文合同复合句的突破找到捷径；通过依照性关键词，让您明白涉外合同权利义务条款约定的根据所在；通过假设性关键词，让您掌握对合同约定不确定性因素的合理评估；通过涉外关键词，让您懂得如何对当事人的利益进行有效地保护；"让步"与"保留"条款的合理描述，对您避免涉外合同文本冲突的技巧将有较快提升。

这种编排是一尝试，也是一种创新，其目的是希望能够让读者更容易地对涉外合同进行理解，在短时间内对大量信息进行处理与吸收，并能够较快地用来指导涉外合同文本的实务应用。

本书有较高的专业学术价值，可供执业律师、法务工作人员、企业涉外商务人员、企业风险管控人员及谙熟行为经济与博弈理念的法律人士和经济学家参考；本书对涉外合同术语解释浅显易懂，特别是对于一些刚刚走出校门或还坐在课堂没有任何实践经验的法学院校、商务院校或外语学院的大学生们无不是一本有较好启发性的课外读物，能够较好地让其对涉外商务和涉外法务工作有所了解，通过学习能够使自己很快进入企业涉外法务或涉外商务工作这一角色。

雷彦璋

目 录

第1章　情感类聚：涉外合同审核必备的理念 / 1

一、类聚词的选择反映了合同起草者所关注的重点 / 3

二、意群阅读：加快涉外合同阅读与理解的有效方法 / 16

三、逻辑识别：有助于理解事项之间的关联性 / 26

第2章　关键词抽取：涉外合同起草、阅读与审核的利器 / 33

一、关键词应用的实质意义 / 33

二、关键词在涉外合同的起草、阅读与审核中的作用 / 37

三、涉外合同中关键词的具体分类 / 43

四、节点抽取：学会找到合同条款组织与思维的逻辑规律 / 54

第3章　术语性关键词：熟练阅读涉外合同的良好开端 / 61

一、路径分析：涉外合同术语形成的历史渊源 / 61

二、意思真实：术语性审核是合同审核的重中之重 / 66

第4章　基本理念：从法意性关键词入手 / 68

一、几个常用的法意性关键词理解 / 69

二、两个基于法理的重要涉外合同条款 / 80

第5章　关注群意：突破涉外合同复合句的捷径 / 85

一、思路清楚：看懂涉外合同复合句的关键所在 / 85

二、条件支撑：合同权利义务保障的有效方法 / 91

三、平行结构：简单明了的合同条款描述方式 / 93

第6章　依照性关键词：权利义务条款约定的依据所在 / 96

一、依照性关键词的常用形式 / 96

二、依照性关键词引导的内容 / 101

第7章　假设性关键词：合同约定不确定性因素的合理评估 / 109

一、假设性条款的常用关键词 / 110

二、假设性关键词在合同条款中的应用 / 115

三、假设性关键词的作用 / 118

第8章　除外关键词：协商一致的利益保护 / 121

一、除外条款的常用关键词 / 121

二、除外条款的表述方式 / 125

三、除外条款常用的条款内容分类 / 126

四、但书条款的常用关键词 / 131

五、对关键词"provided that"的重点理解 / 135

第9章　避免冲突："让步"与"保留"条款的合理描述 / 139

一、涉外合同中"让步性"条款的描述 / 139

二、对优先适用性事项或行为进行隔离 / 145

三、对"subject to"、"notwithstanding"、"without prejudice to"的区别理解 / 149

第10章　权力把握：权力、权利与授权性关键词的理解 / 153

一、涉外合同中与权利描述有关的关键词 / 154

二、涉外合同中与权利转让有关的关键词 / 161

三、涉外合同中与权利有关的类聚词 / 163

第11章　责任把握：尽职、尽责与义务性关键词的理解 / 165

一、涉外合同中关于合同各方"责任"的描述 / 165

二、涉外合同中有关义务的描述 / 173

三、涉外合同中责任义务描述的类聚词 / 176

四、涉外合同中要求"某一方有义务尽力做某事"的描述 / 177

第12章　责任追究：与违约责任相关的关键词理解 / *180*

　　一、违约责任的一般法理问题 / *180*

　　二、违约责任追究的几个法律术语 / *188*

　　三、对关键词"indemnify and hold harmless"的详细分析 / *195*

　　四、涉外合同中风险控制的基本关键词 / *201*

　　五、常用类聚词 / *206*

第13章　责任限定：涉外合同违约责任的具体描述 / *209*

　　一、违约金具体计算方式的描述 / *209*

　　二、违约救济条款的描述 / *212*

　　三、责任限额与免责约定的描述 / *219*

第14章　特殊条款：重点关注其特殊所在 / *231*

　　一、持续性条款 / *231*

　　二、完整性条款 / *233*

　　三、厘清性条款 / *235*

　　四、隔离性条款 / *240*

　　五、不放弃条款 / *242*

　　六、禁止性条款 / *244*

第15章　道不清的事：涉外合同中精确与模糊的合理并用 / *250*

　　一、必要的逻辑知识 / *250*

　　二、涉外合同中对四个模糊性关键词的理解 / *257*

　　三、条款分析：涉外合同中精确与模糊的把握 / *263*

第16章　学会说不：否定性关键词的描述与理解 / *271*

　　一、直接而明显的否定形式 / *272*

　　二、婉转而隐含的否定形式 / *283*

　　三、涉外合同中常用的正面否定实意性关键词 / *289*

　　四、双重否定的描述 / *296*

第17章　重点强调：合同条款描述形式上的多样性理解 / *299*

　　一、处于"it is …"形式表语位置的关键词 / *299*

二、主旨句的"no"表述的关键词 / 302

三、使用对副词的否定，达到对谓语的否定 / 303

四、对谓语否定的情形 / 305

五、主旨句中处于系表位置的关键词 / 307

六、主旨句中处于谓语位置的关键词 / 309

七、使用倒装句型引起重视或起到强调作用 / 312

八、采用动名词形式进行强调 / 313

九、采用无主句的形式强调行为 / 315

十、主旨句中本身含有强调、突出意思的关键词 / 316

第18章　双刃性评估：降低法律风险的有效手段 / 327

一、涉外合同阅读的思维顺序 / 327

二、涉外合同的解释原则 / 328

三、法理审核的重点是确保合同效力不被否定或撤销 / 331

四、涉外合同逻辑性审核的关注重点所在 / 333

五、特别条款审核的重点所在 / 335

六、合同风险控制的重点所在 / 337

参考文献 / 340

后　记 / 341

第1章

情感类聚：涉外合同审核必备的理念

涉外合同由于涉及法言法语，不同文化背景下的专业术语和涉外合同随着历史的变迁，又难免留下人文、社会、商贸、法律、思维发展的历史印迹，因此，我们在阅读与理解涉外合同时就不得不关注特定的语词用意与各合同条款产生的背景和各方当事人的所持立场，从而更好地把握、沟通与谈判。

笔者从一位英文的门外汉，在三五年的时间里，通过认真钻研，不仅能够熟练阅读与理解，到今天能够根据自己掌握与研究涉外合同的感受，编章成册，深深体会到只有踏准思维的节点、理清思维的顺序才能达到事半功倍的效果。

《周易·系辞上》："方以类聚，物以群分，吉凶生矣。"方：方术，治道的方法；物：事物。其原指各种方术因种类相同聚在一起，各种事物因种类不同而区分开；也可指人或事物按其性质分门别类而容易相处，并成为规律。

从上面对"方以类聚，物以群分"的解释不难理解，事物或人与社会之间的划分无不通过类聚而形成。这样不难得出结论：不同的语言之间所使用的语素、词组之间形成歧义的根本原因在于类聚的差异，即概念定义与方式、方法上的不同。笔者通过研究后发现，人类在从低级动物进化到高级动物的发展过程中，其情感与情感流无不在类聚思维中发挥着不可忽视的作用。

所谓情感流，就是个体面对决策时，在追求利益最大化的过程中形成的并与物资流、信息流、资金流既相互区别又相互联系的一种通过个体情感渗透到整体利益之中的具有积极促进作用的综合要素。情感流的存在导致人们在认识世界、改造世界的过程中逐步懂得了通过概念的划分来揭示世界与表达世界之间的差异，从而更深刻地认识世界、改造世界。

笔者在中英文涉外合同的对照研究中发现，不同民族语言与语言之间表达的异同，无不是语言在形成、分化、相互借鉴中通过人的情感类聚逐步完善而成就的。语言表达方式的差异化又无不是情感类聚的结果。诸如不同语言之间词组与词组之间表达上的不能一一对应、语言结构与表达方式上的差异等，也无不是情感类聚方式上差异的结果。为了消除差异，更好地理解不同的语言，只有通过类聚的方式、方法达到所表达思维内涵与外延的相似性、一致性和等同性。

不同语言的语素、词组与句式在表达事物之间的关系时并不能在内涵与外延上一一对应。因此，在中英文合同条款对照理解过程中难免会出现理解上的歧义。出现歧义既可能因理解人文化背景、生活习俗、专业经历不同而形成，也可能因所使用的语素、词组与句式本身出现了内涵上的差异或外延上的不周延。这就需要通过词组的类聚和句式的复杂来达到消除歧义的目的，使得对不同语言之间文本内容所理解的差异或内容在内涵上尽量保持一致，在外延上尽量达到相互周延。

情感类聚在中英文合同文本的理解中主要决定人们的以下思维方式：

（1）情感类聚决定人们对合同条款的关注点不同；

（2）情感类聚决定人们在合同条款中的选词用语习惯；

（3）情感类聚决定人们在合同条款结构描述上的差异；

（4）情感类聚决定人们对条款风险的可容忍程度；

（5）情感类聚决定人们对未来不确定因素的理解深度。

一、类聚词的选择反映了合同起草者所关注的重点

"排比"是汉语中的一种修辞手法，利用三个或三个以上意义相关或相近、结构相同或相似和语气相同的词组或句子并排，达到一种加强语势的效果。用排比来说理，可收到条理分明的效果；用排比来抒情，节奏和谐，显得感情洋溢；用排比来叙事写景，能使层次清楚、描写细腻、形象生动……总之，排比的行文朗朗上口，有极强的说服力，能增强文章的表达效果。

在涉外合同中，也时常出现相关或相近的两个或两个以上的词组或句子通过"and/or"来并列使用，但这绝不是为了达到加强语势的效果，而是为了消除用词中的歧义，确保权利义务的周延性。有的将涉外合同中的这种情况称为类义词，有的将之称为叠词，但笔者认为称之为类聚词更贴切。类聚词组的使用目的都是为了确保所描述权利义务内涵与外延的周延性保持一致，确保语词意思不出现没能涵盖之处，当然，对于合同条款来讲，无论是权利的描述还是义务的设置，似乎重复、多余不会让人厌烦，而最担心的就是有所遗漏，这也或多或少地反映了合同起草者所关注的重点所在，同时也反映了涉外合同文本类聚词出现频率较高的原因所在。

1. 类聚词的理解

所谓类聚词，就是涉外合同中有词汇并列使用的现象，即同义词、近似词或因行为连续性、一贯性而由于行文为表达类聚思想而将相关词用"and/or"（和/或）连接并列使用的一种用词习惯。例如"fair and equitable"、"final and conclusive"、"null and void"、"in full force and effect"等。这种词汇并列使用两个或多个词语的含义来共同限定其唯一词义或意思表达，以确保其要表达的思想内涵与外延上的一致，从而排除了由于一词多义可能产生的歧义，也排除了不同文化背景之间对一些特定词义赋予专业含义后出现的理解上的差异。这正是合同语言作为法律用语，必须表达严谨、杜绝语义歧义或漏洞需要

的结果。

当然，在翻译时，遇到类聚词尽量不要对所类聚的词素逐一进行翻译，而是用一最贴切、最确切的意思简略表述，或取其一，或用一最为接近的词来表达，这样才可达到类聚的目的。

EG-1-1 This contract is made by and between the Buyers and the Sellers, whereby the Buyers agree to buy and the Sellers agree to sell the under mentioned commodity in accordance with the terms and conditions stipulated below.

对句中"by"应单独理解，仅表明合同是由谁达成的；"between"单独使用，也只是对合同签约当事人范围进行了限定。而通过类聚并列为"by and between"，其含义则比单独使用的"by"或"between"更加明确、更加丰富，表明参与合同谈判全过程并最终签约的都是"the Buyers and the Sellers"，并无其他当事人。因此，将之译为"由双方……"最为贴切。

参考译文：本合同由买卖双方签订，在此依据以下条款，买方同意去买，卖方同意去卖下述商品。

EG-1-2 For and in consideration of mutual covenants and agreements contained herein, the parties hereby covenant and agree as follows.

句中"For and in consideration of"、"covenants and agreements"、"covenant and agree"三组同义词和近义词并列。"covenants and agreements"既表示了双方的约定事项，也表示了双方的协议事项，也就是说，无论是同意还是约定，都出自各方对于对价（或要因）的正确理解。"For and in consideration of"既表达了因对价（或要因）而约定，也是为了达成对价而约定，反正目的与结果保持一致，对于双方意思的表达十分精准。

参考译文：鉴于双方一致同意，特此达成如下条款。

实质上类聚词在涉外合同中产生的目的在限大程度上是起草人为防止单一语词的多义性或所表达意思与单一语词之间存在难以一一对

应或镜像，为此通过类聚这种必要的语言表达方式来排除当事人在一定语境下不必要的联想、类推及否定的推理，从而达到对事项、行为或属性的准确定义，减少当事人之间对某些特定的词义因理解上的差异所产生的纠纷。

2. 类聚词产生的原因分析

一般来讲，人的思维之所以出现歧义，往往是因为各方所表达事物及其属性要求精确、唯一，并不得通过联想、类推、否定等思维方式对此提出质疑，也就是主观意思与客观事物的一一对应或形成镜像，如同函数坐标一样可精确限定的位置。而按照爱因斯坦的理论，任何事物的存在都是相对的，即使是我们所标定的函数坐标也具有时空的相对性。因此，不难判断涉外合同中容易出现歧义也是因为时空的限定不明确所致。所以，类聚词使用的原因也主要有以下几种情况：

（1）因时间的相继性而产生。

以现代人的时空观来看，时间具有相继性，一般不应出现间隔，这样在涉外合同的表述中，如果要描述从某一时间开始、截止，以及之前、之后，为防止歧义，应明确说明是否包括某一具体的时点。如包括并从某一时间开始起计算应表述为"from and in（on）"。

EG－1－3 For value received, the undersigned does hereby sell, transfer, assign and set over to A＿ all his right, tile and interest in and to a certain contract dated ＊＊, ＊＊, 2012 by and between the undersigned A and ＿B＿, a copy of which is annexed hereto.

"in and to a certain contract dated"就体现了时间的相继性，这表明从某一合同的日期到收到日期，应包括那一具体日期当天；如果忽略"in"，则在计算利益时可能就不包含当天。

参考译文：双方如数知悉，特此同意将本合同项下的标的物的所有权利、所有权及相关利益出售、转让到甲方名下，双方于2012年＊月＊日同意并签署协议，合同随后附件一份。

EG－1－4 Party A shall be unauthorized to accept any orders or to collect any account on and after September 20.

通过类聚词"on and after"明确表明了授权时间的截止日。该处强调的是甲方在当天与之后的时间不能接受订单。

参考译文：自9月20日起，甲方已无权接受任何订单或收据。

由此可见，类聚词在时间表述上具有否定词不可替代的排除作用。其常因数额、数值、数量及数序的不间断和顺序性而产生，如包括并从某一数值开始计算到某区域的数值就常常用"from and on/in/at"、"before and on/in /at"、"on/in /at or after"等来表示，一般由from/before/after与on/in/at根据具体情况选择性组合。

（2）因表达事物概念的本质、属性相同、相似而产生。如"undertake and agree"、"fit and proper"等。

不同民族的语言对于概念的本质、属性表述并不完全相同，在没有一一对应的概念表述时，就常用相同或相似甚至采取概念间内涵的增删等方式达到类似或近似。如"any dispute or controversy"、"disputes and discrepancies"等。

EG－1－5 The contractor shall always have the sole responsibility for the due and proper execution and performance of all of its rights and obligation under the contract.

"execution and performance"就属于通过相似词的类聚形成行话关键词，具有执行和履行的意思，实际翻译成"履行"或执行都是可以的，而不能根据原文所含词义逐词翻译。

参考译文：承包人已恰当地、负责任地履行完合同的所有义务并享有其权利。

EG－1－6 Nothing contained in this agreement shall be deemed to obligate Seller to permit Buyer to examine any patent application of Seller otherwise than upon a secret and confidential basis and upon the written request of Buyer.

"secret and confidential"就属于通过相似词的类聚形成行话关键

词，即"保守秘密"的意思。

　　参考译文：本合同中所包含的内容不应视为卖方允许买方去测试或检验卖方所拥有的专利，除非买方的书面要求才可对其揭密。

　　（3）因表达事物的可选择性而产生。

　　在事项或行为之中往往存在多种选择性，或某些概念不完全同质但同属，在这一选择性或因同属而异质中，虽相互排斥或矛盾但需要用"or"来建立"或"的逻辑关系，或因相互等同或互不排斥而需要用"and"来建立"和"的逻辑关系。

　　如发生争议，既可通过诉讼程序，也可通过仲裁，一般应遵循"或裁或诉"的原则，这样就可用类聚词表述"litigation or arbitration"这一法理原则。

　　EG－1－7 The constitution of a limitation fund for maritime claims liability shall not be restricted by an agreement between the parties on litigation jurisdiction or arbitration.

　　此即用"or"表明了"或裁或诉"的司法理念。

　　参考译文：设立海事赔偿责任限制基金，不受当事人之间关于诉讼管辖协议或者仲裁协议的约束。

　　EG－1－8 Where the party in a labor dispute consists of 10 workers or more, and they have a common request, they may choose one worker to represent them in mediation, arbitration or litigation.

　　显然，"mediation, arbitration or litigation"条款中各种解决争议的方式是互斥的，因此使用了"或"逻辑关系。

　　参考译文：发生劳动争议的劳动者一方在 10 人以上，并有共同请求的，可以推举代表参加调解、仲裁或者诉讼活动。

　　（4）因某一事物的类分而产生类聚。

　　事物不是独立的，总会形成与其他事物之间的关联，这一关联既可能是事项过程的连续性，也可能是行为方式的相续性，这就会出现类聚情形。

如合同的中止、解除与终止本身是合同处理的三种不同行为方式，因此常形成类聚词"suspend"、"expire"或"terminate"。

EG-1-9 This contract shall automatically terminate and expire upon the full performance or discharge of all the obligations of the Parties hereunder.

"terminate and expire"中的"terminate"和"expire"是合同法中导致合同失效的两种方式，如果用逻辑词"并"，则可直接译为"失效"；如果是"suspend"、"terminate"和"expire"，就要用逻辑词"或"（or）类聚在一起，则指双方当事人可任意选择中止、终止或撤销其中的一种方式解决纠纷。

参考译文：本合同自双方在合同项下所有义务全面履行或被解除之日起自动期满失效。

EG-1-10 During the lease term, because of force majeure cause or for urban planning and construction, cause both sides to terminate and cancel the contract, party a shall be refunded part not expire rent.

这里的"terminate and cancel"显然要表明的是双方要在某一情况出现"because of force majeure cause or for urban planning and construction"时约定解除合同，并不管是因为单方或双方的意愿终止还是请求司法机关来撤销，实质上是合同因出现某一情况而不能正常履行了。

上述使用"and"连接词，说明"terminate and cancel"可同时存在；但如改成"and/or"则更适当，因为合同的终止并不一定非要司法机关撤销才可以。

参考译文：在租赁期限内，因不可抗拒的原因或者因城市规划建设，致使双方解除和/或撤销合同，甲方应退还未到期部分租金。

（5）在某一大概念下通过对小概念的枚举而产生。

在涉外合同中，为了说明某一具体的事项或行为，常通过其子概念的枚举来达到大概念所要表达的中心意思，这就形成了类聚，该类聚词的方式、数量就看构成小概念的多少或起草人关注的程度和重点了。

如对因违约而产生损失的索赔方式或索赔内容："the indemnity，release，hold harmless，defend and protect obligations"、"income，costs and expenses，assets"等。

再如，"royalties，claims，damages and expenses involved"枚举出了可能减少的利益，可以预测的子项包括专利权使用费、索赔费、损害赔偿金及有关费用。其一般使用"and"连接词说明这些项目之间可能存在重叠，但并不影响表述；如果使用"or"连接词，则一般会排除相互的重叠。其在表述上可重叠，但在计算时应按照实际发生情况依照"最近原则"划分到某一具体的小类而不能重复计算。如果使用"or"就可能产生歧义，即只能主张索赔一种损失，而实际中上述子项都是有可能出现的，因此用"and"就不会产生索赔种类上的排斥。

（6）因行为理解方式上的多样性而产生。

涉外合同中的很多类聚词往往是因为人对事物或行为理解上的差异形成的，因此，可通过类聚词达成共识，同时防止出现歧义，并起到重点强调的作用。如各方签订合同的过程也可认为是对权利义务加以认可的过程。

EG－1－11 This agreement is made and entered into by and between party A and B.

"made and entered into by and between"显然是合同起草人为防止语意歧义或限定不清而有意通过相似词的排列而形成的类聚词，具有"由合同双方签订并达成"的意思。

参考译文：本合同由甲乙双方（共同）签订。

（7）因表述上的尽量模糊含混而形成。

涉外合同的表述并不都是十分精确的，有时可能因当时签订合同时一些条件并不成熟，有些事项并不一定能够完全估计到，双方为避免影响谈判进程而找到协商一致的突破口，这就可考虑使用一些含混或模糊的词来满足这一目的。如考虑某一事项时用"所有"表述，"所有"是一个概数，于是就会有人提出是否单个的就不行呢？这样人们就会形成联想或否定推理，为避免这种情况的产生，就出现了"所有和其中任何一个"这种表述，如"any and all"、"all of and part of"等。

EG－1－12 Marketing and public relations professionals work to earn new customers and keep existing customers through any and all forms of communication.

"any and all"可能是为了达到各种沟通方式的组合，也包括单一的沟通方式。此时，用"and"和逻辑连接较为合适，以避免产生歧义。

参考译文：市场营销和公共关系的专家都是致力于开发新客户以及通过某种或各种交流方式和现有客户保持联系。

EG－1－13 In the event of transfer of share of property in the partnership between the partners, whether in whole or in part, the other partners shall be notified.

"in whole or in part"表明无论是整体转让还是部分转让，这显然是为了避免出现单一整体转让不包括部分转让的情形。

参考译文：合伙人之间转让在合伙企业中的全部或者部分财产份额时，应当通知其他合伙人。

EG－1－14 In fact several of these steps might be performed in only particular situations and not for each and every use case.

虽然每一个案件都应是可数的，但就案件的性质所涉及的标的物而言，既可能被理解为可数，也可能被理解为不可数的，所以针对每一个的表述都应包含其中，以免形成不必要的歧义。

参考译文：实际上，其中的一部分也许只在某种特别情况下才被执行，而且并不是对每一个案例都适用。

3. 合同文本中类聚词之间的关系

类聚词之间并不都是等效的平行关系，一般有属种、群分与路径三种关系。

（1）属种关系：是指一个意义包含在另一个意义之中的关系。如"contract"与"agreement"之间。属种关系可能存在上下之间的父子关系，也可能存在平等的平行关系。也就是说，一定特定的类聚词中的词与词之间实施划分群分，存在父与子之间的上下关系和子与子之间的平行关系。如所有权分为占有权、使用权、收益权和处分权。所有权与占有权、使用权、收益权和处分权之间存在父子关系，占有权、使用权、收益权和处分权之间存在平行关系。

（2）群分关系：是指由于实施特定的分类原则而形成的各词之间的关系。群分并不一定存在某种属种关系，而只是人们的偏好而已，如植物与动物之分、动物之中的家畜与野畜的划分等。

（3）路径关系：是指一些类聚词中词与词之间并不存在上下、包含等关系，但在路径上具有相互依存的关系。如合同的签订、变更、中止、终止这四个类聚词是合同从签订到终止路径上的四个过程。路径关系往往存在时间上的先后、顺序上的次序、方位上的相对关系或程序上的序列关系等，但它们之间也不一定存在属种关系。

4. 类聚词的分类

根据上述分析，对类聚词不难作以下分类：

（1）根据所类聚的概念间是否同属、同质，可分为"同属、同质"类聚词与"同属、异质"类聚词两种。

所谓"同属、同质"，是指所要类聚的概念本属于同一个属概念，且各概念间具有相同或相似的本质特征。

所谓"同属、异质"，是指所要类聚的概念本属于同一个属概念，但各概念间不具有相同或相似的本质特征。

（2）根据所类聚的概念间是否因同一属内划分或归类，可分为划分类聚与归类类聚两种。

所谓划分类聚，是指同一属下的种概念间存在严格的划分标准，属下的种概念存在严格的边界甚至本质的差异。

所谓归类类聚，是指同一属下的各概念间并不存在严格的划分标准，属下的种概念也不存在严格的边界，各种概念间具有相同或相似的属性。

（3）根据所类聚的概念列举是逐一枚举还是典型枚举，可分为逐一枚举类聚与典型枚举类聚两种。

所谓逐一枚举类聚，是指所类聚的概念形成了一个完整的属，不存在其他没被枚举的种概念。

所谓典型枚举类聚，是指所类聚的概念没有形成一个完整的属，还存在其他没被枚举的种概念，所类聚的概念只是所有种概念中的一个典型代表。

（4）根据类聚所使用的连接词，可分为"和"（and）类聚、"与"（or）类聚和"复合"（and/or）类聚三种形式。

一般来讲，同属、同质的类聚与归类类聚可用"和"类聚形式。"和"类聚还具有强调整体性的目的。同属、异质的类聚与划分类聚可用"与"类聚，也可用"复合"类聚。"与"类聚具有强调可选择性和任意组合两个目的。

一般来讲，对于权利的要求，强势方力求使用"and"，以此强调权利的整体性；对于义务的履行，强势方力求使用"or"，以此强调义务的可分性。反之，对于弱势方来讲，由于受强势方的制约和谈判地位的不对等性等因素的影响，对于弱势方的权利主张，强势方往往力求使用"or"；对于弱势方的义务履行，强势方总要求使用"and"。这是弱势方值得关注的风险所在。

（5）根据类聚词是采用单一词素还是采用多个词素形成的词组之间所形成，类聚可分为词素类聚与意群类聚两种。

词素类聚为单一的词素之间形成类聚词。

意群类聚为多个词素形成的词组之间形成的类聚词。意群可进一步分为词组类聚与子句或结构类聚。

EG－1－15 This decision shall apply to the crimes committed against Article 9, Article 10 and Article 11 hereof by the staff and workers of enterprises other than limited liability companies and companies limited by shares.

"staff and workers" 属于"同属、同质"类聚词，用"and"连接词，如采用"or"连接就会产生歧义了。

参考译文：有限责任公司、股份有限公司以外的企业职工有本决定第9条、第10条、第11条规定的犯罪行为的，适用本决定。

EG-1-16 We hereby certify to the best of our knowledge that the foregoing statement is true and correct and all available information and data have been supplied herein, and that we agree to provide documentary proof upon your request.

"true and correct"、"information and data" 都是"同属、同质"类聚词，具有相同、相似的含义。

参考译文：特此证明，据我们所知，上述声明内容真实，正确无误，并提供了全部现有的资料和数据，我们同意，应贵方要求出具证明文件。

EG-1-17 The establishment of a limited liability company or a company limited by shares shall comply with the conditions and provisions of this Law. A company complying with the conditions and provisions hereof may be registered as a limited liability company or a company limited by shares. Provided that if a company fails to comply with the conditions and provisions hereof, the company in question shall not be registered as a limited liability company or a company limited by shares.

"a limited liability company or a company limited by shares" 属分类类聚词。"conditions and provisions" 属"同属、同质"类聚词，也属于归类类聚词。

参考译文：设立有限责任公司、股份有限公司，必须符合本法规定的条件。符合本法规定的条件的，登记为有限责任公司或者股份有限公司；不符合本法规定的条件的，不得登记为有限责任公司或股份有限公司。

EG－1－18 The parties to this agreement agree that either Party hereto shall, immediately and fully, notify the other Party hereto of any such matters comprising an improvement, modification, further invention or design as the party in question may discover, make or develop with respect to manufacture and assembly of the Licensed Products or components thereof.

"improvement, modification, further invention or design"和"discover, make or develop"有"of any such matters comprising"的限定，因此可判断为逐一枚举类聚词。

参考译文：本协议各方同意，一方对于有关生产及装配许可证产品或部件所作的改进、修正、更新发明或设计均应立即全部通知另一方。

EG－1－19 If, as a result of withdrawal or any other reasons, an arbitrator fails to perform his duties as an arbitrator, another arbitrator shall, in accordance with the provisions hereof, be selected or appointed.

"selected or appointed"属划分类聚词，只有熟悉仲裁员任命规则的人才明白仲裁员的产生有"当事人自由挑选"或"仲裁庭指定"两种形式，因此不能用"and"连接。

参考译文：仲裁员因回避或者其他原因不能履行职责的，应当依照本法规定重新选定或指定仲裁员。

EG－1－20 The Employer hereby covenants to pay the Contractor in consideration of the execution and completion of the works and the remedying of defects therein the contract price or such other sum as may become payable under the provisions of the contract at the time and in the manner prescribed by the contract.

"the execution and completion of the works and the remedying of defects"显然是合同执行中的三个不同阶段。这里使用"and"连接强调的是合同条款的整体性，即支付条款应综合考虑的整体事项，其中任何一项不符合都可能构成对支付条款的影响。

参考译文：业主特此立约保证在合同规定的期限内，按合同规定的方式向承包人支付合同价，或合同规定的其他应支付的款项，以作为本工程施工、竣工及修补工程中缺陷的报酬。

EG – 1 – 21 This contract is hereby made and concluded by and between ＊＊ Co.（hereinafter referred to as Party A）and ＊＊Co.（hereinafter referred to as Party B）on ＊＊（date），in ＊＊（place），China, on the principle of equality and mutual benefit and through amicable consultation.

"made and concluded"和"by and between"都是归类类聚词，并强调行为的完整性。

"equality and mutual benefit and through amicable consultation"为归类类聚，强调整体性适用，说明三个原则具有同等的作用，并要整体遵守，因而不能使用"or"连接，否则就可能存在歧义。

参考译文：本合同双方，＊＊公司（以下称甲方）与＊＊公司（以下称乙方），在平等互利基础上，通过友好协商，于＊＊年＊＊月＊＊日在中国＊＊（地点），特签订本合同。

EG – 1 – 22 If , in the opinion of the Buyer, any item of equipment provided by the Seller is not or is no longer suitable for the purpose intended, then the Seller shall at no additional cost to the Buyer and at the option of the Buyer, either make adequate repairs or arrange for immediate replacement.

"is not or is no longer"属划分类聚，"either make repairs or arrange for replacement"属"与"类聚，强调的是权利行使的可选择性。

参考译文：如果买方认为，卖方提供的设备不满足或不再满足合同欲实现的目的，卖方应按照买方选择进行维修或安排立即进行替换，并不得额外增加买方的费用。

EG – 1 – 23 The contract shall be interpreted and construed by law of peple's republic of china.

If a material change occurs to the contractor's economic benefits after the signature of the contract due to the promulgation of new laws, decrees, rules and regulations or any amendment to the applicable law, the parties shall consult promptly and make necessary revisions and adjustments to the relevant provisions of the contract in order to maintain the contractors normal economic benefits hereunder.

"laws, decrees, rules and regulations or any amendment" 类聚中的 "and" 强调 "归类"，"or" 强调 "制订" 与 "修正" 的划分作用，二者属于两个完全不同质的立法手段。

参考译文：本合同适用中华人民共和国法律。

在本合同签字后，如果由于中华人民共和国颁布了新的法律、法规、条例或政府令，或对适用的法律进行了修改，使合同者的经济利益发生了重要的变化，双方应及时协商，并对本合同的有关规定作必要的修改和调整，以在本合同项下保持合同各方的基本的经济利益。

二、意群阅读：加快涉外合同阅读与理解的有效方法

涉外合同由于句式复杂、长句较多，同时由于专业术语与法言法语较多，因此应注意意群阅读。

所谓意群，就是句子中根据语法结构和逻辑关系必须停顿的若干部分组成的一个具有特定意思表述的词组或句型结构。意群划分的正确与否直接影响到对句子结构的把握和对句子意义的理解。意群是语法结构和意义上较为紧密的一组词的类聚，这组词包括关键词与非关键词。在单一的句子中，关键词常为实词；在复合句中，关键词常为虚词。关键词提供关键信息，非关键词表达辅助信息。把意义与语法结构上有关联的几个词组合成较为完整的信息，联系起来理解，有助于快速而准确地理解合同条文的基本内容。

在涉外合同的阅读中，如果碰到 "if"、"but"、"however"、"nevertheless"、"nonetheless" 等条件句或转折性词汇时，就应当划分意群，

这样有助于理解前后的意思变化。

在研究条款之前，我们应对英文的句型表达方式有所掌握。

1. 涉外合同中静句与动句表述方式的意思差别

为了更好地理解静句与动句的表述方式，笔者先枚举出英语的六大基本句型：

（1）主系表：SVP；

（2）主谓（状）：SV；

（3）主谓宾：SVO；

（4）主谓宾宾：SVOi Od；

（5）主谓宾补：SVOC；

（6）There be 句型：There be ＋主语。

除此之外，句子中的同位评语、插入语、定语和状语都是对句中的主语、表语、谓语、宾语和补语等起修饰作用。

一般认为主系表（There be 句型可看做是特殊的主系表）结构属于静句，用来描述主体的性质或事物的状态；"（2）～（5）"句型结构属于动句，用来描述事物的动态事件。

所谓静态，就是思维者从静态角度反映出来的事物状态或具有的某些属性。在涉外合同中静句常是对事项性质或属性的描述，一般用"is to"、"refer to"、"have"或"means"等方式描述。

所谓动态，就是思维者从动态或事物运动角度反映出来的事物动态状态或处于变化的状态。同一事物状态和属性有差异只是思维者所站角度不同而对客观世界反映的结果。由于客观世界本身并无绝对的静止或绝对的运动，一切都是相对的，因此同一事物的描述既可用静句，也可用动句，这一切都是思维者情感类聚的结果。也就是说，用什么句型结构完全依赖思维者的情感因素，或者说只是其对事物的关注角度与关注重点不同而已。

静态性描述一般是对特定事项的描述，静态性描述的主语一般为非人称或单位，而是具体的需要强调的事项。

用谓语动词性的描述称为动态性描述。动态性描述的主语一般为人称或单位，而非具体的需要强调的事项。

在涉外合同中动句常用来描述主体的行为方式或权利义务的实施手段等，一般用主谓宾结构加补语句型描述。

在涉外合同的阅读与审核中，一定要注意用辩证的观点对涉外合同条款形成一个初步的直观认识：静句描述往往属于双方当事人对客观事物的认同；用动句描述是要赋予某方或各方某种权利和义务，或要求承担或免除某些责任，具有较大主观因素，往往是当事人的意思表达或是双方当事人协商一致的结果。因为合同中约定"你做什么，我做什么"都需要相对方的同意，这样动态描述就不能是一方的陈述，也少用一方的陈述形式来表达需要自己做什么或需要对方做什么事项。

人类思维反映客观现实，具有较大的主观能动性。人类思维因情感而类聚，也会对不同的类进行不同的分割和联系，从而形成各种不同的实体概念，包括具体的事物概念和抽象的事物概念。人会因情感类聚方式、方法不同而把实体、运动、属性、情态看做是静止的或动态的，也可把不同的事物当做整体为不可分的，也可把整体分成不同的子项，又因类聚而异或因异而表现本质与属性。

这样，在涉外合同的起草与审核中，我们可以把握以下规律：

第一，当合同条款用主系表结构表述的时候，思维是从静态角度来反映事物的，静态说明思维者的思维相对集中，也体现出需要描述事物的重要程度和客观真实性。其目的是要说明与合同有关的事项往往具有陈述性属性，一般要求双方遵循"the principle of good faith"（诚实信用原则）或不得违反"estoppels"（禁止反言原则）。

第二，当合同条款用主谓宾结构表述的时候，说明描述者的思维是从动态角度来反映现实的，既然是运动，就会有变化，而变化又具有不可确定性，因此，用动句描述相对于静句描述的风险较大，这样就会出现一些限制性条款，也就是说动句往往会嵌入很多从句或条件或假设一些不确定性因素对行为方式的限制等，使得主体执行某一动作时受到某些条件限制或有约在先，为其设置特定的约束事项。

第三，如果句中出现把本应用动句描述的事物特意描述为静句，那是对运动状态的强调，这就是所谓的运动的物化或者说运动的对象化，这是思维者关注的侧重点发生的变化。

EG－1－24 The Seller shall timely delivery of goods.

如转化为：The Seller's delivery is timely. 显然前一句强调的是交付，后一句强调的是交付的及时性。

参考译文：卖方应及时交付货物。

第四，如果本是对主语或宾语属性描述的定语、表语转化为主语、宾语，也就是所谓的"喧宾夺主"，这是思维者把具有某些性质的事物当做一个整体来看，这是属性的物化，也是强调事物的性质或者是强调事件的品质，这就是思维者情感的对象化。这是一种偏好，能否投其所好一定要正确评估风险所在，因为这种转化可能构成一种"陈述与担保"，要求真实可信，即使发生较大变化也不可提出变更，否则就可能构成"estoppels"。

EG－1－25 The Seller shall deliver new and never used goods to Buyer.

如转化为："The goods of delivered by the Seller to Buyer that are new, not used." 显然前一句强调的是交付，后一句强调的是交付的货物具有"新的和未使用过的"属性。两者之间的显著区别是：货物是新的和没用过的构成卖方的陈述，应是真实可信的，而不是一种交货的品质要求。如果是品质要求，可通过检验这一动作来实现，如果按照前一句，则属于质量品质达不到要求，可以通过换货、折价来弥补；如果按照后一句理解，就构成根本违约，根本违约是不可补救的，因为涉及卖方的诚信受到了质疑，买方可因此终止或撤销合同。

参考译文：卖方应交付新的、从没使用过的货物。

转化后则译为："卖方交付买方的货物应是新的、没使用过的。"

第五，本是动态性描述，如果改用静态，则说明思维者想要强调动作的重要性。

EG－1－26 The Contractor shall notify on force majeure to owners promptly.

The Contractor is promptly notice to owner on force majeure.

前者强调的是通知；后者同样强调的是通知这一行为，但后者属于系表结构，其强调性带有不可协商性。如果发生承包商没有及时将不可抗力事项通知业主的情况，则前一种情形构成一般性违约，可视为承包商的一时疏忽，可以延时通知弥补过错；而后一种情形则构成根本违约，因为这可认为是一种承包商对自己承诺的否认，或者说作了虚假陈述，一般来讲，在英美法系，合同一方如果在合同中作了虚假陈述，无责任一方是可无条件提出终止合同或撤销合同的，并可要求责任方承担赔偿责任。

参考译文：承包商应就不可抗力（事项）及时通知给业主。

承包商应及时就不可抗力（事项）通知给业主。

上述是涉外合同条款中常用的强调方式，同时也间接简述了单方"陈述"与双方"约定"在涉外合同条款中的显著差别，应引起阅读者或审核者的关注。

还需要说明的是，合同双方在就权利义务的协商过程中可能会出现对于相对运动的静态性描述，这就可能需要利用英语分词这种特殊的语法形式。

分词的本质在于它是由动词演变而来的，是对事物运动状态的静态性描述，以反映说明事物由于运动而具有的性质和状态。

分词一般是用来表示事物由于运动而产生的性质或状态，可以用做定语和表语，当在涉外合同中用分词做表语或状语时，往往是思维者想通过主系表结构或状语的强调形式等特有的静句形式来强调动作的严格或规范性。

EG-1-27 The Buyers may, within 15 days after arrival of the goods at the destination, lodge a claim against the Sellers for short-weight being supported by Inspection Certificate issued by a reputable public surveyor.

"being supported by Inspection Certificate issued by a reputable public surveyor" 为方式状语。

参考译文：货物抵达目的港15天内，买方可以凭有信誉的公共检验员出示的检验证明向卖方提出短重索赔。

EG – 1 – 28 Within 30 days after the signing and coming into effect of this contract, the Buyer shall proceed to pay the price for the goods to the Seller by opening an irrevocable L/C for the full amount of USD ＊＊ in favor of the Seller through a bank at export port.

"within 30 days after the signing and coming into effect of this contract" 为时间状语。

参考译文：在合同签订和生效后 30 天内，买方应在出口港银行以卖方为受益人开具金额为 ＊＊ 美元的不可撤销的信用证，以向卖方支付全额货款价格。

从语用的角度来看，商务合同中许多时间状语表示的是某一缔约方必须在何时何地承担某一义务和享有某一权利，即时效性。因此，整个句子的重心不是句子的动词，而是发生动作的时间。

译成中文时，为了突出行为的时效性，时间状语应尽量靠近表示义务责任的关键词"须"之后。上述条文中还含有一个较为复杂的方式状语 "by opening an irrevocable L/C...",其中含有三个介词短语作定语修饰 "an irrevocable L/C"。按照汉语的行文规范，方式状语一般应位于动词之前。

此外，若动词同时带有时间状语和方式状语时，英文的通常顺序是方式在前而时间在后；而汉语正好与之相反，为方式在后而时间在前。

EG – 1 – 29 The time for the performance of the Seller's obligations set forth in this contract shall be automatically extended for a period equal to the duration of any nonperformance arising directly or indirectly from Force Majeure events including but not limited to fire, flood, earthquake, typhoon, natural catastrophe, and all other contingencies and circumstances whatsoever beyond the Seller's reasonable control preventing, hindering or interfering with the performance thereof.

"preventing, hindering or interfering with the performance" 为定语从句。

参考译文：本合同规定卖方履行义务的时间应自动延长等同于由于直接或间接不可抗力事件导致的不能履行的期间。不可抗力事件包括但不限于火灾、洪水、地震、台风、自然灾害和卖方无论怎样也无法合理控制的阻止、妨碍、干扰本合同履行的其他风险和情形。

2. 意群分析

涉外合同在起草过程中总会受起草人母语、文化背景的影响，而合同语言本身要求严谨，同时又与起草人的思维、情感类聚行为及客观事项之间有着必然的关系。

这样，合同的语言描述就有两种形式：一是对客观事项真实、正确及客观的描述；二是对主观意思明确、具体及相互认同的描述。

在涉外合同中，对客观事项的描述常用一般现在时；对主观意思的表示常用一般现在时或将来时。这是因为对客观事项的描述基本都是对静态事物的描述，如主体属于某一类型，或具有某种性质或特征，或说明某一主体处于某种状态。而主观意思描述基本上都是对动态事物的描述，如主体进行某一动作、采取某一行为，或主体实施某一行为涉及某些客体。

所谓静态与动态之分也是相对的。用语言描述静态还是动态，主要是看描述主体在思维过程中所处的角度和关注的参照点不同。

这样，在阅读或审核涉外合同时就要先分析具体的条款是属于静句表述还是动句表述。

在英文合同中，静句表述一般用系表结构，静句的核心是表语。

EG – 1 – 30 Party A is a limited liability company duly incorporated and validly existing under the laws of its place of incorporation, and has all corporate power and authority to executed this agreement, exercise the rights and perform the obligations hereunder in accordance with the provisions of this agreement.

本条款的核心显然是 "a limited liability company" （有限责任公

司），后面的描述只能是围绕有限责任公司的行为能力。

"a limited liability company duly incorporated and validly existing" 采用动句形式描述，其核心是谓语动词。

参考译文：甲方为依照公司设立地法律依法设立并存续的有限责任公司，具备签署执行本协议、依照本协议规定行使本协议规定权利和履行本协议规定义务的所有法人权力。

EG－1－31 Party A has obtained all consents, approvals and authorizations necessary for the valid execution and delivery of this agreement and all of the contracts referred to herein to which it is a party; provided, however, that this agreement shall be subject to the approval of the Examination and Approval Authority before the same may become effective.

此条款用动句描述了 Party A 公司应履行的义务，即"has obtained all consents, approvals and authorizations"，关键词是"获得了"（"has obtained"）。

参考译文：甲方已经得到履行本协议所必需的同意、批准和授权，所有合同文件均已提交，本协议在审批部门批准后生效。

从静句与动句中关键词的位置来看，阅读人员应明确涉外合同句中各关键词在句中所处成分所表现的重点秩序如下：

表语—谓语—主语—宾语—补语—定语。

表语成分的强调作用是最强的，其次是谓语，定语的作用最弱。

如果除表语外的其他成分需要强调，则可将非系表或非谓语转化为"it is…"来强调句中的表语。

EG－1－32 It is a duly organized legal entity, validly existing and in good standing under the laws of the People's Republic of China.

该句用静句方式描述了公司的性质："organized legal entity, validly existing and in good standing"。

参考译文：本公司为依中华人民共和国法律合法组织存在、享有良好商誉之法律主体。

从涉外合同的结构来分析，涉外合同的以下条款一般适用于静句描述：

合同双方的基本情况，合同方属性描述及性质、资质、资格情况等；所提供货物的品质情况及服务标准。

因此，合同条款中的定义条款、双方陈述与保证条款、鉴于条款等也就一般使用静句来描述。

静句的最大特点是表示主体所具有的性质，相当于汉语中的"有"字结构，因此，从一定程度上讲，涉外合同中的"have"除充当助动功能外，还可用来表述主体的某些属性，具有系动词"be"的基本特征。

涉外合同的以下条款适用于动句描述：

动句适用于各方权利义务的约定、行使、履行。如纠纷的解决、违约责任的限定、其他需要双方依情况采取行动的特殊约定等。

由于动作也不可能持续下去，因此权利义务的行使、履行也会处于某种状态，其权利义务完毕的结果也是以某种状态存在，我们不能一味排除用静句描述权利义务的行使。权利义务处于中止、暂停或终止状态时，就可用静句描述。

合同条款采用何种方式描述的关键是思维者是以静态的观点看事物还是以动态的观点看事物，再就是思维者强调的是主观因素还是客观因素，就如同动名词描述一样，词尾不一样，表达的意思截然相反。

EG - 1 - 33 The Seller must deliver the goods, hand over any documents relating to them and transfer the property in the goods, as required by the contract and this convention.

该句的主旨句是首句，后句以"as"引导一个参照性事项，用以说明履行义务的依据。

主旨句采用了主谓宾 + （主）谓宾补和（主）谓宾补结构，强调的是货物交付与文件的交付。

参考译文：卖方必须依照合同和本公约的规定交付货物，移交一切与货物有关的单据，货物所有权（也随之）转移到（买方）。

EG – 1 – 34 The ownership of the goods is belong to the Buyer, upon the Seller has delivered the goods, and has handed over any documents relating to them as required by the contract and this convention.

主旨句采用了系表结构，显然强调的是货物所有权的归属。

参考译文：一旦卖方交付货物，并依照合同和公约的要求交付相关文件，则货物的所有权属买方。

3. 意群理解的关注要点

意群的存在可以让我们更容易理解或学习。其不仅体现了行业的专业性，还能更好地提高我们的阅读速度，加深对合同的综合理解。

对于涉外合同的阅读与理解中的意群观念，并不能像发音似地用"/"来划分句子的意群，而是要用专业的悟性来快速地形成行业用语，或者用专业习惯思考问题。也就是说，要通过意群较好地掌握法言法语与一些专业术语，并能够有效地通过意群达到对涉外合同语法结构、句式结构的理解。因为意群可以是一个词、一个词组或短语，也可以是并列句的一个分句或复合句的一个主句、从句等。

在涉外合同的理解中，对于意群的理解应从以下几个方面关注：

（1）类聚词。类聚词是由一个以上的相同、相似或相关联的词组成的一种具有特定意思的词组，其意群表达十分强烈，也就是说在翻译时要注意节省或精简，而不能逐字意译，应抽取其中的核心思想，用最简洁的语言表达其中的专业或行业意思。

（2）专业术语。专业术语是在社会实践中发展演化而来的，因此用专业的观点来理解就不会存在大的失误。也就是说，遇到特殊的词汇应结合合同所要表达的专业或结合相关的专业知识来理解与把握。对于一些法律、商务、金融等专业术语，要一一对应地理解。这类术语具有严格的单义性，只在相关语境下被使用。

（3）法言法语。

所谓的"法言法语"主要是指一些中古英语和外来词汇。法律界人士普遍认为这些中古另类语言的使用可以使法律语言更加高贵和庄重。

（4）句式结构。

对一个较为复杂的难句进行意群划分在知识上表现为语法的实践，所以，一般的思维多用语法知识去分析句子的结构，但是在快速阅读过程中是没有时间去检验语法知识的合理性的。快速阅读依靠的是悟性或语感而不是语法知识。因此，从感觉层面去感知句子的结构更能体现认知的基本过程。

对于语感较差的读者来说，一个句子在视觉上首先表现为一串词汇，而不是意群已经划分清楚的句子。语感问题是个感觉上是否习惯的问题。如果已经习惯了涉外合同的各种表达方式与句式搭配，就肯定能较快理解某一条款的设置目的，再通过关键词的抽取，就能够很快对主旨句所要表达的意思与相应的条件形成反射，从而更好地把握条款。

三、逻辑识别：有助于理解事项之间的关联性

在分类过程中，要掌握好类与类之间的逻辑关系。通过对逻辑关系的正确识别，可以较好地掌握意群。

能够帮助意群理解的逻辑关系词通常有以下七种逻辑关系。

1. 并列关系

并列关系就是用来表达语言组织与结构之间具有并列关系的逻辑词。如"and"、"furthermore"、"more than that –"、"also"、"likewise"、"moreover"、"in addition"、"what is more"、"for instance"、"for example"等。

EG – 1 – 35 In further consideration of employment, the Employee shall not engage in a business in any manner similar to, or in competition with, the Company's or the Company's affiliated businesses during the term of his or her employment. Furthermore, the Employee shall not engage in a business in any manner similar to or in competition with the Company's business for a period of years from the date of termination of his or her employment with the Company in the geographical area within ＊＊ mile radius of any present or future office opened by the Company during the term of employment and the geographical area within ＊＊ mile radius of the Employee's home address.

"Furthermore" 意为此外，将两个 "the Employee shall not engage" 开头的句子并列起来。

2. 转折关系

转折关系就是用来表达语言组织、结构之间具有转折意思的逻辑词。如 "although"、"however"、"on the contrary"、"but"、"in spite of"、"nevertheless"、"yet"、"otherwise"、"despite" 等。

EG-1-36 In case party A takes back the leasing items before prescribed time and party A shall pay 12 times as much as the rent then and there as compensation . On the contrary, in case party B quit the contract and move out of the leasing items before the prescribed time, he shall also pay 12 times as much as the rent then and there as compensation.

"On the contrary" 将两个具有反对关系的事项连接起来。该条款的风险主要是对于租金的计算要弄清是按照月计算还是按照年计算，双方都应根据其他条款约定好，否则一旦出现一方退租就可能造成纠纷。

参考译文：一旦甲方在合同约定时间前退租，甲方应支付不少于 12 倍的租金，以此作为补偿。相反，一旦乙方在约定租期前解除合同并腾空租赁物，同样应支付相当于 12 倍的租金，以此作为补偿。

3. 顺序关系

顺序关系就是用来表达语言组织、结构之间的相对顺序的逻辑词。如 "first"、"second"、"third"、"and so on"、"then"、"after"、"before"、"next" 等。

EG-1-37 Should the Contractor not attend, or neglect or omit to send such representative, then the measurement made by the Engineer or approved by him shall be taken to be the correct measurement of such part of the works.

"be taken to" 为实意性关键词，意为 "被当做" 或 "被视为"。

"Should"为倒装型假设条件句,是业主不希望发生的事项。"then"表明一种顺序关系,前者为先,后者采取的行为在后。

参考译文:如果承包商不参加,或疏忽或遗忘而未派这样的代表参加,则由工程师进行的或由他批准的测量应被视为对工程该部分的正确测量。

4. 依存关系

依存关系就是描述两事项之间相互依存的状况或相互以何种形式依存。

EG-1-38 Where there are reasonable interest payments incurred from loans in connection with production and business operation, the enterprises shall submit the proof documents in respect of the loans and interest payments. The interest payments in question shall, after the examination and verification and approval by the local tax authorities, be permitted to be itemized.

"in connection with"意为"相关",表明"借款利息与生产、经营状况相依存"。

参考译文:企业发生与生产、经营有关的合理的借款利息,应当提供借款付息的证明文件。经当地税务机关审核同意后,准予列支。

EG-1-39 All activities of the cooperative venture company shall be governed by the laws, decrees and pertinent rules and regulations of the People's Republic of China.

"pertinent"(有关的,相关的)出现在涉外合同中似乎较"relevant"更为正式。

参考译文:合作经营企业的一切活动均应受中华人民共和国的法律、法令及有关规定和规章制约。

EG-1-40 In accordance with the Law of the People's Republic of China on Chinese-Foreign Cooperative Joint Ventures and other relevant

Chinese laws and regulations, ABC Company and XYZ Company, in accordance with the principle of equality and mutual benefit and through friendly consultations, agree to jointly set up a Cooperative venture in Beijing, the People's Republic of China.

"relevant" 意为"相关"。

参考译文：根据《中华人民共和国中外合作企业法》及有关法律、法规，ABC 公司与 XYZ 公司，本着平等互利的原则，经过友好协商，同意共同在中华人民共和国北京设立合作企业。

EG - 1 - 41 In respect of the computation of depreciation of fixed assets, the salvage value shall first be estimated and deducted from the original cost of the assets. The salvage value shall not be less than 10% of the original value. Provided that if any retaining a lower salvage value or no salvage value is requested, the matter in question shall be approved by the local tax authorities.

"In respect of" 意为"关于"，表明了固定资产折旧与残值的关联。

参考译文：对于固定资产的折旧计算，应当估价残值，从固定资产原价中减除。残值应当不低于原价的 10%；需要少留或者不留残值的，须经当地税务机关批准。

EG - 1 - 42 This agreement shall be executed in the languages of Chinese and English. In case of any dispute as to the interpretation, the Chinese version shall prevail.

"as to" 意为"有关的"。

参考译文：本协议以中文和英文签署，如果两种语言出现解释异议，以中文为准。

5. 因果关系

因果关系主要是表述两事项或行为之间的因果关系的逻辑词。如

"as a result"、"for"、"thus"、"because"、"for this reason"、"so"、"therefore"、"as since"、"consequently"、"hence" 等。

需要说明的是，在因果关系的描述中，一般不能像汉语那样"因为……所以……"可以连用，在英文描述中，表达因或果的词只能选其中之一，具体忽略哪一个要通过判断或选词偏好确定。

EG - 1 - 43 Should the Buyer be unable to arrange insurance in time owing to the Seller's failure to give the above - mentioned advice of shipment by cable or telex, the Seller shall be held responsible for any and all damages and/or losses attributable to such failure.

该条款在条件句中嵌入了一个因果从句，"owing to" 意为"因为"。

参考译文：如果因为卖方未能以电报或电传形式发出上述装运通知，买方不能及时安排保险，则卖方应对此产生的损失和/或损害赔偿承担责任。

EG - 1 - 44 Now, therefore, in consideration of the mutual premises and covenants herein contained, it is hereby agreed.

"in consideration of" 表示"以……为约因/报酬"。

约因是英美法系的合同有效成立要件之一，没有则合同不能依法强制履行。大陆法系的合同则无此规定。

参考译文：兹以上述各点和契约所载条款为约因，订约双方协议如下。

EG - 1 - 45 A party may suspend the performance of his obligation if, after the conclusion of the contract, it becomes apparent that the other party will not perform a substantial part of his obligations as a result of : (a) a serious deficiency in his ability to perform or in his creditworthiness; or (b) his conduct in preparing to perform or in performing the contract.

"as a result of" 意为"由于……原因"。

参考译文：如果订立合同后另一方当事人由于下列原因显然将不

履行其大部分重要义务，一方当事人可以中止履行义务：（a）他履行义务的能力或他的信用有严重缺陷；（b）他在准备履行合同或正在履行合同中的行为。

6. 说明目的

英语和汉语的目的状语表述方式不完全一样，英文商务合同中的目的状语通常由"in order to"和"so as to"或"so（such）that"引导。前者引导的目的状语既可以位于句首，也可以位于句末；后者引导的目的状语只能位于句末。

EG - 1 - 46 Notice of particulars of shipment shall be Buyer at such time and by such means that the said notice shall be received by Buyer within 7 days after shipment.

句中"at such time and by such means"为非具体化的时间状语和方式状语，译成中文时也相应地采用比较含糊的词语。

参考译文：卖方须及时以适当的方式将装运详情通知买方，以便买方在装运后 7 天内收到该装船通知。

EG - 1 - 47 The equipment and material shall be carefully and properly packed in the best and stable condition according to the figures and characteristics of the equipment and materials so as to withstand long distance sea and inland transportation and numerous handing.

"so as to"引导目的。

参考译文：设备和原料须依据其形状和特点以完善而牢固的方式精心妥当地包装。包装须适合于长途海、陆运输，能经受多次装卸。

7. 归纳总结

归纳总结就是用来表述"因此；于是；相应的"或"简而言之，一句话"等概括性小结的用词，它可体现为对上述的概括或总结。如"as a result"、"finally"、"therefore"、"accordingly"、"in shout"、"thus"、"consequently"、"in conclusion"、"so"、"in brief"、"in a word"等。

EG - 1 - 48 The Engineer shall, after due consultation with the Employer and the Contractor, determine such amount of the costs in respect of the above - mentioned additional works as shall be added to the contract price, and shall notify the Contractor of the matter in question accordingly, with a copy to the Employer.

"accordingly"在这里意为"相应地"。

参考译文：工程师应在与业主和承包人适当协商后，确定上述额外工程费用的数额，并加到合同总价中去，同时通知承包人，并将一份副本呈交业主。

第2章

关键词抽取：涉外合同起草、
阅读与审核的利器

对于涉外合同而言，可能更难的是在语言的转换方面，一方面它要求法务人员具备一定的法律理论功底；另一方面又要求其有较高的英语语言表达能力，并在深刻理解法律含义的基础上将其转化成比较通俗的语言。笔者在实际的涉外合同的起草、谈判与审核中深深感受到了涉外合同业务的难度，通过几年的经验积累，认为掌握好法律关键词是克服涉外合同起草、谈判与审核难度的捷径，深深体会到关键词的正确把握能很好地表达法务人员的法律语言，也能很好地与不同语种的同行实施有效的沟通。

一、关键词应用的实质意义

法务人员在合同起草、谈判和审核中要善于应用关键词，并以此引导自己的思维，这具有较为现实的实用意义。

1. 关键词有助于法务人员从复杂的语言中抓到条款设置的目的

英美法系施行判例法，大陆法系施行成文法，成文法相对于判例法的重大不同点就是比较稳定，合同的很多内容在已成文法律中都有直接规定，双方无须在合同中再作详细约定。也就是说，按照成文法是"合同未约定依法条"；而按照英美法系推行的判例法是"合同有约定先依合同"，成文法大多只作为参考而不具有强制性，因此合同双方在涉外合同的订立过程中都力求使合同结构完整、语言精确，大量使用定语从句、状语从句，避免使用省略句，也尽量不使用有可能引起指代不明的代词。涉外合同还有一个特点就是篇幅冗长、惯用复杂长句和法言法语，且逻辑严密并极具规律性，这一特点是由英美法系国家与大陆法系国家不同法律特点所决定的。这直接导致了涉外合同中充斥着复杂的语法结构，大句套小句，小句套分句，有时一句话就长达数百字符。这就要求参与涉外合同起草、谈判与审核的法务人员必须尽最大努力把各种可能性都考虑在内，将语言所能起到的明确表述对象的功能发挥到极致。但在实际的合同起草、谈判与审核过程中，为节省时间，尽快减少双方的分歧，需要法务人员能够从其中一两个字词中及时捕捉到每一条款的中心思想，分析其是否满足了商务要求，是否达到了条款设置的目的。

EG－2－1 The Seller shall indemnify the Purchaser (in addition to any other remedies to which it may be entitled under this agreement) against all Loss which the Purchaser or the group may incur or suffer arising out of any liability or penalties imposed or to be imposed by a Governmental Authority in relation to [Target Company's] having no [* * * permit] as disclosed in the disclosure letter.

显然，上述条款的关键词是"indemnify"，这属于买卖双方达成的"specific indemnity"条款，指针对目标资产存在的具体瑕疵和/或潜在风险明确由卖方承担相应责任。这一关键词当然是资产收购方法务人员所特别关注的，也能让法务人员很快理解该条款设置的目的。

参考译文：被收购方应赔偿（除本合同已明确的补偿外）所有收购方或其公司发生或可能发生的因政府权威部门就目前公司应予披露而没有披露的各项债务或罚款等。

2. 关键词能够让法务人员达到事半功倍的效果

涉外合同的另一重要特点是其严密的逻辑性和显著的规律性。这符合英美法系判例法的特点，因为绝大多数涉外合同会选择遵循先例，尽量采用先前行业所认同的语言和逻辑结构，于是合同专业词汇和逻辑结构经过千百年的积累逐渐固定下来，形成了很强的规律性。

这里的规律性包括合同结构及其模块的稳定性，如一份完整的涉外合同通常由四个模块组成，即标题（Title）、序言（Recitals）、主文条款（Terms and Conditions）和结尾（Conclusion）。主文条款又由若干个子模块组成，而每一模块就可用一个关键词来分析、理解，并通过谈判来传达各自希望表达的商务思想。

另外，合同的用词也有很强的稳定性，这就形成了涉外合同的特有语言。这一特有的语言规律和稳定性其实就是法务人员在合同起草、谈判与审核过程中所应高度关注的法律关键词，正确提取关键词就可达到事半功倍的作用。由此可见，在涉外合同的起草、谈判与审核中，对于法律关键词的熟练掌握对职业法务人员来说是何等的重要。

EG - 2 - 2 Each of S and ＊＊＊（company）shall use its best endeavors to obtain the consent of M to the issue of the Replacement Guarantees by ＊＊＊ Parent in accordance with Clause ＊＊＊（a）and the giving of the New S Guarantees by S in accordance with Clause ＊＊＊（b）by the Replacement Date（provided that the obligation under Clause ＊＊ and this Clause ＊＊ on ＊＊＊ Parent and ＊＊＊（company）respectively to use their best endeavors shall include without limitation（i）full and prompt compliance by ＊＊＊（company）and ＊＊＊ Parent and each of their Affiliates with any and all reasonable requests by M,（ii）the payment by ＊＊＊（company）or ＊＊＊ Parent of reasonable cash settlements requested by M and（iii）the taking of all steps by ＊＊＊（company）and ＊＊＊ Parent to procure that, as an alternative to a guarantee issued by ＊＊＊ Parent or an Affiliate, a credit institution with a financial strength equivalent to the Credit Ratings issues a financial instrument acceptable to

M in relation to the Participating Interest Share of all amounts, obligations or liabilities of ＊＊＊ and ＊＊＊ and any of their Affiliates under the Charter, the Purchase Option and the O&M Contract).

显然，"best endeavors"是该条文的关键词。合同审核人员考虑如果不加任何限制地规定合同一方应实现某种目标时，债务方很容易违约。债务方通常只愿意承诺"努力"来实现该目标，而非一定实现目标，从而降低违约的风险；权利方也希望债务方能够尽最大努力以达到目标。作为审核人员，应从风险防范角度分析是否开口，进而考虑可承担责任的兜底条款的设置。

Notwithstanding the foregoing, the maximum aggregate amount to be paid by ＊＊＊ and ＊＊＊ Corporation as a cash settlement pursuant to Clauses ＊＊＊ or to a credit institution pursuant to Clauses ＊＊＊ , shall not exceed USMYM ＊＊＊ .

参考译文：尽管有上述约定，＊＊＊公司或其集团公司根据＊＊
＊条款或＊＊＊信用证条款，以现金解决的最大支付累计额不应超过
＊＊＊美元。

3. 关键词能够帮助较好地识别隐含的法律风险

在合同的起草、谈判或审核过程中，法务人员无时不关注风险的存在，无时不希望将法律风险降至可接受的程度，而关键词的应用能够帮助法务人员较好地识别隐含的法律风险。如很多时候，"例外"、"条件"和"权利义务"部分在整个句子中的位置会因各个法务人员的习惯不同或为了强调某个部分而存在较大的差异。如《联合国国际货物销售合同公约》第39条的规定。

EG - 2 - 3 In any event, the Buyer loses the right to rely on a lack of conformity of the goods if he does not give the Seller notice thereof at the latest within a period of two years from the date on which the goods were actually handed over to the Buyer, unless this time limit is inconsistent with a contractual period of guarantee.

参考译文：无论如何，如果买方在实际收到货物之日起两年内不

将货物不符合合同情形通知卖方，他将丧失声称货物不符合合同的权利，但这一时限与合同规定的保证期限不符的除外。

本条结构采取了"权利义务"、"条件"和"例外"的结构，"if"引导"条件"，"unless"引导"例外"。该条款的"条件"部分显得比较复杂，因为在这个条件状语从句中又嵌入了一个定语从句："on which the goods were actually handed over to the Buyer"修饰限定"the date"。另外，也并非每个条款都同时具备这三个要素，有的可能就只有单纯的权利或者单纯的义务；而有的则附加了"条件"，但没有"例外"；还有的则只有"例外"，但没有"条件"。正是由于"例外"、"条件"和"权利义务"并非在每个条款中都出现，并且其在不同条款中的位置也并非一成不变，这无形中加大了风险识别的难度，也就隐含了相应的法律风险；但由于引导"例外"和"条件"的英文词汇比较固定，法务人员在审核合同时也能比较迅速准确地识别出来。因此，应常从关键词出发来思考与引发审核思维线索。

如引导"例外"的英文词汇主要包括"save（that）"、"save as"、"except（that）"、"except as"、"unless"、"subject to"等；引导"条件"的关键词主要有"if"、"in the event that"、"provided（that）"、"suppose（that）"等。

在合同审核中，一旦看到这些关键词，就要引起极大的关注，根据某一关键词，将"例外"和"条件"的言外之意识别出来。也就是说，如果法务人员抓住了"例外"、"条件"这样的关键词，就可通过专业的理解，很快地识别其中隐含的法律风险。

二、关键词在涉外合同的起草、阅读与审核中的作用

不难分析，法律关键词在涉外合同的起草、阅读与审核过程中的作用非凡。这主要可以从以下几点来理解。

1. 关键词是合同审核人员适用法律分类的标识

在合同审核过程中，法务人员应当想到如何适用法律、适用什么国家的法律、适用什么类型的法律，还可具体到适用哪一部法律以及

与之相关的司法解释。而关键词就成了法务人员适用法律的分类标识，某一关键词往往是一看便可明了，通过其可以看出法务人员所审核的合同应当适用什么样的法律才能对当事人最有利。如何选择，既要看法律的层次，又要由法务人员根据不同的合同，靠业务水平的直觉或悟性去感觉最能让当事人的利益最大化的选择。例如，在涉外合同中，不可抗力条款是不可或缺的。不可抗力条款通常包括不可抗力的定义；遭遇不可抗力的通知义务；不可抗力的影响程度，如延期履行等；发生不可抗力后的补救措施，如尽力减小不可抗力的影响、终止合同等；不可抗力结束后的恢复履行等。法务人员在审核合同时见到不可抗力条款（force majeure），就要职业性地意识到《中华人民共和国合同法》（以下简称《合同法》）第117条规定以及《联合国国际货物销售合同公约》对不可抗力规定的差异性；同时，要联想到不可抗力事件所引起的法律后果，进而思考对于不可抗力的因素的概括或枚举形式是否能够完全认同；再思考两种可供选择的处理方式：一是双方协商延长履行合同的期限，二是双方协商决定是否解除合同。例如，按照不可抗力对履行合同影响的程度，由双方协商决定是否解除合同，或者部分免除履行合同的责任，或者延期履行合同。

通过具体合同的不同表述，法务人员就能意识到适用于哪一具体的法律、法规了。如果双方产生分歧，就可直接指出引用哪一国家的法律或法规的准确性。这样，关键词就成了引导法务人员检索法律、法规的标识。

2. 关键词是法务人员在合同谈判中形成思维线索的联结点

在合同的谈判过程中，由于谈判需要解决的问题很多，而双方接触的时间往往有限，一般都在十分仓促的时间里搞定一些法律问题，这就要求法务人员能够以关键词作为联结点，形成自己的思维线索，以此简洁明了地说明争议、风险、责任等，把握合同条款的性质，让商务人员理解、接受自己的修改意见。在合同谈判、审核过程中，要反复研究关键词中所隐含的风险，分析条款设置是否达到了风险保留、转移或化解的目的。例如，在合同起草、谈判、审核中，法务人员都要注重鉴于条款的设置，该条款无论在标的确定、双方权利义务确定、违约责任确定等方面都可相互链接引发思维，从而分析出所设条款是否违背了合同的目的。因为"whereas clause"（鉴于条款）常在涉外合同的开头部分，通常是合同双方谈判的开场白，也可能是某一方对合同谈判目的的简介，用以介绍合同签约方的基本情况、签约背景、签约目的等内容。实质上，"whereas clause"（鉴于条款）的主要内容和作用就是解释合同签署的背景和目的。

　　中国的《合同法》没有将鉴于条款作为合同的必备条款，但其揭示了签约方之所以签约所基于的一些既定事实。既然是事实，签约方就不得在事后对这些事实进行否认，并不得以此为由提起诉讼，否则就构成违约，这就是英美法中一项重要的法律原则——"estoppels"（禁止反言原则）或"estoppels by representation"（意思表示禁止反言），亦即一方在合同中即使进行了不真实的陈述，对方信赖其所述并据之采取行动，则不真实阐述方应当对自己的误导行为负责，不得以己方所述不实为由主张客观真实的情况。

　　因此，"whereas clause"（鉴于条款）常出现于涉外合同和重大资产收购、专利许可、合作开发、特种设备买卖等合同中，以防止双方因文化等差异形成对合同标的的理解上的不同。根据"presumption against tautology"（避免赘言推定原则）可知，法律文件中没有一个多余的词句，合同中的每一句甚至每一个词都会对当事人的利益产生影响。因此，就起草和谋划合同而言，策略显然要比用词更为重要。对于关系到对方的事宜，要让对方陈述得尽量详细，己方的陈述则尽量简化。法务人员应善于选择"whereas clause"（鉴于条款）作为关键词的起草、谈判、审核的思维线索，这样才能抛弃那些大而无用的空话、套话，让该条款与其他条款相适应，并达到相互支撑的目的。如笔者在审核"whereas clause"（鉴于条款）时，常与"representation and warrants"（陈述与保证条款）、合同标的描述条款、双方权利义务条款相联系，以确保合同属双方真实的意思表示而能够形成一致，即合意。

　　"陈述与保证条款"（representation and warrants）通常是由签约一方所掌握的对另一方非常重要但无从知晓或者将耗费超过合理范围内

的精力去了解的内容。如公司组建设立情况、签约代表是否取得合同一方的授权、合同一方是否存在其他债权人或有正在进行的诉讼仲裁等，再如专利转让许可方对专利技术的关键描述、是否存在对第三方侵权、是否存在权利瑕疵等。这些信息对于合同另一方来说是很难通过其他渠道获取的，这对于决策是否希望通过对价获得标的物十分重要。因此，陈述和保证条款要求合同一方和双方对彼此关心的问题作出陈述并就这些陈述的真实性或有效性作出保证是十分重要的。如果一方违反了其在该条款中所陈述或保证的内容，则同样可能被认定为"estoppels"（禁止反言）并将承担相应责任；合同另一方则可以采取包括终止合同在内的相关救济措施，从而最大限度地保护己方利益。

这样，通过关键词"whereas clause"（鉴于条款）与"陈述与保证条款"（representation and warrants）作为思维引发点，以此来分析双方的权利义务及违约责任等就具有十分重要的作用。

3. 关键词是法务人员向对方陈述观点中简单明了的专业术语

无论是合同谈判还是合同审核，还是与相关人员的沟通，法务人员都要善于用最简单明了的专业术语来向对方陈述条款设置的目的，尤其是用法律术语，让对方一听到法务人员所陈述的术语就能把握合同条款的性质，并能够进一步以此明白双方在合同谈判中的争议焦点，法务人员也可以此来引导合同条款的修改，从而寻找缩小分歧的突破口。而法务人员所选择的专业术语就是合同起草、谈判与审核中的关键词。即使合同已签订完成，法务人员也要利用一切机会与合同执行人员来说明合同条款中的关键词，让合同执行人员完全明白每一条款的设置目的，从而有利于合同执行风险的防范。

成文法相对于判例法的最大不同点就是比较稳定，合同的很多内容在法律中都有直接规定，双方无须在合同中再作约定。但英美法系推行判例法，提倡高度的私法自治，成文法大多只作为参考而不具有强制性，法官不得轻易否决当事人的意愿。由于合同所载的文字是法官解释合同、探求当事人意愿的唯一依据，因此合同方在订立合同过程中都力求使合同结构完整、语言精确，从而大量使用定语从句、状语从句，避免使用省略句，也尽量不使用有可能引起指代不明的代词。

　　涉外合同的另一重要特点是其严密的逻辑性和显著的规律性。这是根据英美法系判例法的特点，绝大多数涉外合同会选择遵循先例，尽量采用先前法官所认可的语言和逻辑结构，于是合同专业词汇和逻辑结构经过千百年的积累逐渐固定下来，形成了很强的规律性。

　　涉外合同的语言体现了与普通英语非常特殊的风格与特点，"法言法语"在涉外合同中体现得非常充分。这些所谓的"法言法语"主要是指一些中古英语和外来词汇，比如常见的"herein"（于此）、"hereof"（于此）、"whereby"（借以）、"inter alia"（其他的事物）等。之所以形成这样独特的"语言群"，一方面与英国语言的历史发展有关，另一方面是因为法律界人士普遍认为这些中古另类语言的使用可以使法律语言更加高贵和庄重。因此，法务人员应在谈判中善于应用关键词向对方陈述观点，善于应用简单明了的专业术语或法言法语来说明某一专业问题。这能够很快让对方接受自己的观点，也容易让双方的差距缩小。

4. 关键词的使用能够加深对合同意群的理解

　　意群主要应用于阅读理解，是意思相同或相似的一组句子的组合。在阅读中，如果碰到"but"、"however"、"nevertheless"、"nonetheless"等转折性词汇，就应当划分意群，这样有助于理解前后的意思变化。听力是阅读理解的一种，只不过不用眼睛而用耳朵；而阅读更多的是使用眼力，因此意群尤其重要，把握意群有助于阅读者把握阅读内容的核心意思。英文"sense group"（意群）就是指句子中按意思和结构划分出的各个成分，每一个成分即称为一个意群。同一意群中的词与词之间紧密相关、密不可分，否则就会引起误解。"意群"是由一个稍长的句子分成的具有一定意义的若干个短语；"停顿"是在意群之间进行的，它是根据语意、语速的需要而自然产生的一种语音停顿现象，在中文中也就是我们通常说的对于句子所划分的具有相对完整性的成分。意群其实就是概念的组合。概念并不是无序的组合，而是根据一定的关系组合在一起的。所以，和单个概念相比，意群包含了很多稳定的关系。在人们头脑里，其实活跃的不仅仅是一个个独立的概念，还有其间的稳定的关系。意群更注重与关系的结合，所以其中必然有明示的或隐含的联系，而这一联系的熟练就在于关键词的抽取。在涉外合同的阅读与审核中，必然存在几个相邻的表示同类意思的词，而阅读意群就是要把这几个词一眼看出来，并很快根据其稳定的联系形成初步的核心意思，从而成倍地提高阅读速度。

5. 关键词的巧妙利用能够有效地打破谈判的僵局

谈判进入实际的磋商阶段以后，谈判各方往往由于某种原因而相持不下，陷入进退两难的境地。我们把这种谈判搁浅的情况称为"谈判的僵局"。来自国内不同企业以及其他不同国家或地区的谈判者，怀着对各自利益的期望或对某一问题的立场和观点，一时难以达成共识，双方又不愿互作让步，就很容易形成僵局。僵局形成后必须进行迅速的处理，否则就会对谈判的顺利进行产生影响。妥善处理僵局，必须对僵局的性质、产生的原因等问题进行透彻的了解和分析，并加以正确的判断，采取相应的策略和技巧，选择有效的方案，使谈判得以继续。商务谈判伴随整个合作过程，而项目合作过程分为合同协议期和合同执行期，谈判僵局也就有了协议期的谈判僵局和执行期的谈判僵局两大类。前者是双方在磋商合作条件过程中意见产生矛盾而形成的僵持局面；后者是指在执行项目合同过程中双方对合同条款理解不同而产生分歧，或出现双方始料未及的情况而把责任推向对方，抑或一方未能严格履行协议而引起另一方的严重不满等，由此引起对责任分担的争议。按照狭义的理解，僵局可以发生在谈判的初期、中期或是后期等不同的阶段。因此，谈判初期僵局一般不会发生，因为双方对谈判都充满了期待，除非由于误解或是双方对谈判的准备不够充分，抑或一方感情受到很大伤害时，才有可能导致谈判草草收场。

众所周知，法律英语作为一种专业性极强的工具语言，其严谨和缜密使其难度要远远大于普通英语。所以说，单纯一个法律功底深厚的法学家或是一个经验丰富的英语老师都不可能成为一名优秀的法律英语翻译，而具备这种能力只是成为一名优秀涉外律师的前提条件和基本素质。如果遇到难懂的专业问题，法务人员可寻求专业人员的帮助，通过关键词定义条款（definition）来解决很多难以解决的问题。

所以，在合同谈判中，双方会用很长时间来分析合同的定义条款，而定义的目的也是一个关键词抽取、提炼的过程，从而让合同谈判双方的观点很快接近一致。

所以，在合同谈判中遇到僵局时，法务人员要及时想到是否能够对容易产生分歧的问题进行简化，通过定义来引导双方的思维相互接近。也就是说，通过定义合理地抽取关键词或者巧妙利用关键词是能够有效地打破谈判僵局的。

三、涉外合同中关键词的具体分类

笔者按照关键词在合同条款中所表达的意思或所起的作用及本身的属性将之具体分为五大类，即术语性关键词、法意性关键词、实意性关键词、协意性关键词和群意性关键词，具体划分如下。

（一）根据关键词在合同条款中所起的作用可分为实意性关键词与群意性关键词

实意性关键词在合同中具有较强的语义特征，即与其所表达的概念之间存在某种相互联系的关系特征。一般来讲，实意就是有实际的、明确的意思表达，即合同要求合同主体明确、责任明确。实意性关键词的研究重点是处于主旨句谓语及表语位置的实意性关键词。

1. 实意性关键词的特征

实意性关键词一般由实词构成，如名词、代词、动词等，是在合同条款中具有实际的意思表达，能够明确描述主体、事物属性或主体行为属性的词语。

实意性关键词的语义特征主要有单义性、类聚性和对义性。

（1）单义性是指一个术语只能表达一种概念，而且这种概念只有唯一性的解释，因此，在合同文本中要求实意性关键词语义精密、明确、固定，同时避免使用同义词或近义词。为避免歧义，对于容易产生歧义的实意词可在定义中专门进行定义，以达到消歧的目的。

合同文本中常用的单义词如：

consideration——对价

sufficient——资格

adequate ——胜任

fairness——公正

assign——转让

transfer——转让

convey ——财产转让

domicile——住所

residence——居所

deposit ——定金

subscription——订金

（2）类聚性。类聚词是指词类相同且语义上有着某种联系的一组词，这些词在合同中常通过"and"或"or"等连接在一起，出现在句子的同一位置，用来表示类似但不同的含义。这类词由于常有很强的主观性，实质上是一种类聚现象，因此也可把这种现象构成的词组叫类聚词。

（3）对义性。对义词是指在合同文本中词语的意义相互矛盾、相互对立，即词语所表达的概念在逻辑上具有一种矛盾或对立的关系的词。其实质上是指合同中的一对用词的概念在逻辑上具有意义相互矛盾、相互对立的关系。

对义是由合同文本的性质及法律术语的要求决定的，具有一一对应的关系（relational opposites）。一般来讲，由于合同本身涉及合同各方的利益关系，当事人所处立场各不相同且存在对义性，如一方权利往往是另一方的义务，这就决定了合同文本中存在着大量的对义词。

根据合同文本中对义词在合同中内容的意指不同，一般可分为主体性对义词和责任性对义词两种。

① 主体性对义词：

the first party – the second party – the third party

either party – neither party

the contract letting party – party issuing contract

EG – 2 – 4 A construction project contract refers to a contract whereby the Contractor undertakes the construction of the project and the contract letting party pays the cost and remuneration.

"the Contractor" 为承包人，"the contract letting party" 为合同发包人。

参考译文：建设工程合同是承包人进行工程建设，发包人支付价款的合同。

EG－2－5 A contract for supply and use of electricity refers to a contract whereby the supplier of electricity supplies electricity to the user of electricity, and the user of electricity pays the electric fee.

首先要弄清合同主体的对义性："the supplier of electricity"（供电人）——"the user of electricity"（用电人）。明确了具有对义性的主体，权利义务就好分配了，也就能明白谁向谁输送电力、谁向谁支付电费了。

参考译文：一个供电合同就是供电方与用电人之间就电力供应与电费支付达成的协议。

② 责任性对义词：

明确了合同主体的对义性后，在权利义务的安排中就能很好地理解责任的对义性了，即一方的权利是另一方的义务，或者说一方的义务是另一方的权利。

如："权利"与"义务"就是一对对义词；交付与接收也是一对对义词。

以下为常用的涉外合同中的对义词：

rights － obligations

rights － duties

delivery － receiving

bidding － tendering

rent － tenant

collection － acceptance

offer － acceptance

（4）要用心注意合同中相关语词的对义性，以防权利义务倒置或错位。权利义务的倒置或错位是法务人员的大忌，一定要慎之又慎，通过多次核查以确保各方当事人的权利义务适当。

合同条款的对义性审核主要从合同主体（Party A – Party B）之间与各方权利义务（right – obligation）之间的对义性加以关注。

2. 群意性关键词的特征

群意性关键词也称为结构性关键词，在涉外合同中主要起连接实意性关键词或独立语句或分句的作用，使合同条款具有较好的结构性、完整性，好似房屋的构架，能够让人感觉到一层或一层以上的意思表达，起着意群集合的作用。

群意性关键词的基本特征是一般处在句首、句中或句尾，起句子之间的连接作用，常由介词、连词等虚词构成。

群意性关键词又可细分为条件型、依据型、结果型、原因型、方式型、并列型、除外型、让步型等。

EG – 2 – 6 In case of force majeure, the Seller shall not be held responsible for late delivery or non – delivery of goods.

上述"In case of"为条件型，"for"为结果型，均属于群意性关键词，"force majeure"、"the Seller"、"be held responsible"、"late delivery or non – delivery of goods"等属于实意性关键词。

参考译文：在人力不可抗拒的情况下，卖方对迟交或不交货物概不负责。

EG – 2 – 7 If a party fails to perform a contract owing to force majeure, it shall inform the other party promptly, so as to reduce the possible damages inflicted on the other party, and shall also provide a certificate of non – performance owing to force majeure within a reasonable time.

本条款以条件型关键词"if"引导"a party fails to perform a contract"的原因。"owing to"属于原因型关键词，"so as to"属于结果型关键词。实意性关键词"inform"加上一个并列型关键词"and also"引导关键词"provide"。其中，条件型关键词、原因型关键词、结果型关键词及并列型关键词都属群意性关键词。

参考译文：当事人一方因不可抗力不能履行合同的，应当及时通知对方，以减轻可能给对方造成的损失，并应当在合理期限内提供证明。（摘自《合同法》第 118 条）

再如，不可抗力事件所引起的法律后果一般有两种：一是双方协商延长履行合同的期限；二是双方协商决定是否解除合同。

EG - 2 - 8 Both Parties shall, through consultations, decide whether to terminate the contract or to exempt the part of obligations for implementation of the contract or whether to delay the execution of the contract according to the effects of the events of force majeure on the performance of the contract.

首先要找到主旨句中的实意性关键词。涉外合同条款中的主旨句一般是在主语前无群意性关键词引导的句子。该条款主旨句中的实意性关键词有"Both Parties"、"decide whether to"。

上述条款中有两个群意性关键词："through"属方式型，"according to"属依据型。

参考译文：按照不可抗力对履行合同影响的程度，由双方协商决定是否解除合同，或者部分免除履行合同的责任，或者延期履行合同。

（二）根据关键词在合同条款中的定性与定量作用可分为定性关键词与定量关键词

定性关键词在合同条款中对主体、事物或行为的描述具有定性的作用，定性关键词又有精确与模糊之分。

定量关键词在合同条款中对主体、事物或行为的描述具有定量的作用。

EG - 2 - 9 It is requested that the two orders be shipped in one lot.

"two orders"、"one lot"作了定量性描述，虽是两次订货，限定的交货次数却是一次性的，权利义务十分明确。

参考译文：要求两次订单一次装运。

EG – 2 – 10 As requested, the Buyer is sending by the Seller herewith commercial invoice in duplicate.

这里用"in duplicate"（一式两份）作了定量描述，要求商业发票是一式两份。

参考译文：按照要求，卖方应随同送达给买方商业发票一式两份。

EG – 2 – 11 The draft will fall due on May 20.

The steamer is due at 20：00.

上述两例"due"都意为"到期时间"，属对时间精确性的定量描述，到具体的日或时点。

参考译文：汇票将在 5 月 20 日到期。

轮船到达时间为 20 点整。

（三）根据描述事物或行为是否精准分为精确性关键词和模糊性关键词

精确性关键词在合同条款中对主体、事物或行为的描述十分精准。

模糊性关键词在合同条款中对主体、事物或行为的描述十分含混。

1. **精确性关键词**

EG – 2 – 12 The next shareholders meeting will convene on the coming Sunday of the same place.

显然，上句用"next"、"coming"、"same"引导的三个精确性关键词准确地限定了开会的时间（Sunday）、地点（the same place）及事项（shareholders meeting）。

参考译文：下一次的股东会定于本周（以周日为一周开始日的，应译为下周）的星期日在本次会议地点召开。

EG – 2 – 13 Seller shall, prior to the closing, enter into an employment agreement with aaa satisfactory to Buyer.

"prior to closing" 是插入语，属于精确性关键词，对时间进行了限定。

参考译文：为满足买方的要求，卖方提前结束与 aaa 签订了聘用协议。

EG – 2 – 14 All of the terms, conditions, provisions and covenants contained in the license are made a part of this agreement.

显然，"contained" 在此作 "包括" 讲，对合同条款内容作了精确限定。也就是说，无论如何表述都属于本合同的条款，不能排除。

参考译文：许可证中所包含的条款属于本协议的组成部分。

EG – 2 – 15 Notice may be waived by the unanimous consent of all directors.

显然，"unanimous" 对 "consent" 作了精确的限定，要求必须是同意，且同意的内容是一致的，不得有异议。

参考译文：通知是所有经董事一致同意的弃权。

EG – 2 – 16 Purchase order shall be approved by the owner before a commitment is made.

显然，"before" 在此起到了精确限定时间的效果。

参考译文：在承诺作出之前，采购订单应经业主批准。

EG – 2 – 17 It is agreed that if the licensee shall breach any of the terms contained in the now existing license between the licensor and the licensee, then this agreement shall immediately become null and void in all respects.

显然，"in all respects" 精确限定了合同当事方，即各方都将合同视为无效，而不是哪一方。

参考译文：双方同意：如果被许可方违反了许可方与被许可方就

已有的授权所含的任何条款，则本合同立即在双方失效。

EG－2－18 This Guarantee shall be valid up to the date of the provisional acceptance of the plant at which date this Guarantee will be nullified.

显然，"up to the date"、"at which date"属于精确性关键词，对保证书的有效日期作了限定，也就是保证书只限于在验收日之前有效。

参考译文：本担保将至本装置临时接受日一直有效，装置临时接受当日失效。

EG－2－19 The import license requires the goods to arrive on/before September 15.

显然，"on/before"对达到时间作了精确的限定，否则就要承担不能按期交货的风险。

参考译文：进口许可证要求的货物在 9 月 15 日前（含当日）到达。

EG－2－20 As the question is an important one, it requires careful thinking over/it requires being careful thought over.

这里显然用"one"作了精确界定，重复指代"the question"，以引起对方的关注。

参考译文：重要的问题是要求细致思考。

2. 模糊性关键词

在实际的商务活动中，由于客观事物本身的不确定性或由于受某些条件限制而难以用确定性词语表达时，有时用模糊语言来表达反而显得合同内容更准确、更灵活，更能达到合作效果，因此，涉外合同中并不完全排除模糊限制语的使用。

在英美合同法中，模糊用语可分为两大类：模糊词语——词义和表达形式本身就是模糊的词；模糊附加词——附加在意义本来明确的表达形式之前的词或者短语，使表达模糊。如"within"、"about"、"more or less"等。

模糊词的一个显著特点就是用于表达有关时间、空间、程度、范围、估量或其他类似词语时，其内涵和外延都难以定量或准确地确定。主要特征是其修饰的程度、范围具有不稳定性或外延的不明确性。

EG – 2 – 21 Transactions concluded between governmental bodies of Party A and Party B shall not be restricted by the terms and conditions of this agreement, nor shall the amount of such transactions be counted as part of the turnover stipulated in Article ∗.

"not be restricted"和"part of"两个范围虽可准确地表达出双方达成交易的条件，但并不能确切地说出其具体的数额，也就是没有作出准确的表达。

参考译文：由甲乙双方管理团队之间达成的交易不应该受到本合同条款的限制，也不得将该第 ∗ 条失误的部分视为交易量。

EG – 2 – 22 Should the effect of the force majeure cases last for more than 120 days, both parties shall settle the problem of further execution of the contract through friendly consultation as soon as possible.

"more than"、"friendly"、"as soon as possible"三个模糊性关键词给协议双方提供了可操作性，比较准确地表达了协商的方式。虽然"120 天以上"好似明确的数字，但具体是哪一天则没有明确。

参考译文：当不可抗力持续超过 120 天以上时，双方应尽快通过友好协商解决合同的进一步执行问题。

3. 涉外合同中使用模糊语应遵循的基本原则

在涉外合同条款中确需使用模糊词语时，应遵循以下原则：

（1）整体原则。在使用模糊语时，首先应保证模糊语的使用不影响合同或协议预期的目的，不得因使用模糊语和模糊概念而导致条款缺乏基本要素。其次，在运用模糊语时应将其与具体语境相结合，特别是当同一法规、约定中出现同类、同性质或同义的词语时，应遵循整体原则，避免出现同样的词语在使用和解释时所表示的意思差异过大的情形。有一些词语虽然概念清晰却存在一定的模糊意思，使用此类模糊语时务必要从整体出发，综合考虑语境和实际情况。对于合同或协议中表意不清的模糊词句一般采取三种方式解决：依商业习惯解释；依当事人在先前交易中就此词的适用；依合同自身约定的解决方法。

（2）善意原则。英美合同法属民法，案例大都涉及当事人的财产等物质利益纠纷。善意原则用以限制行为人使用模糊语，通过玩文字游戏的方法钻法律漏洞。首先，在订立合同时必须限制双方恶意利用各种模糊语设置语言陷阱，查清双方是否有故意隐瞒或模糊重要信息之嫌。其次，当合同内容确有疏漏之处时，合同行为以意思表示为核心，它包括内心意思和表示行为两个要件。在解释合同时，既要根据解释的目的探求当事人的内心意思，也要通过合同及表示行为探求当事人的内心意思，以衡量各方当事人利益，作出双方当事人均可接受的解释。

在英美案例中，法官一般会根据以往的判例以及英美合同法中的合理预期等原则作出裁决。法官所作的判决应保护善意方的合法利益，合同的争议部分应该按照通常解释和不利于恶意滥用模糊语一方的意思表示进行解释。

（3）最小解释原则。基于合同意思自治原则及司法的被动性和中立性原则，在英美案例中，法院一般尽可能以超然的姿态面对当事人的争议，合同解释的对象仅限于争议的内容，对于不违反法律、法规强制性规定的合同，即使存在用语模糊、词不达意，也会尽可能地选择尊重当事人的合意，对其中不清楚或难以执行的地方进行变更，尽可能说服当事人维持合同的效力。

EG - 2 - 23 The contractor shall forthwith notify the owner of such fact.

The parties acknowledge and agree that joint venture company shall be formed forthwith upon satisfaction of the conditions.

上述"forthwith"属于模糊性关键词，意为"立刻"、"随即"。

参考译文：承包商应随即将这一事项通知业主。

双方当事人同意合资公司在条件成熟时应立刻成立。

EG – 2 – 24 The distributor shall no use or employ any colorable imitations of the trademarks or anything similar thereto.

显然，"anything similar"属于模糊性关键词，意为"其他类似的"，而不能理解为"任何类似的"。

参考译文：分销商不得使用仿制或类似商标。

EG – 2 – 25 Under no circumstance, shall be Buyer be required to register with the securities and exchange commission.

"Under no circumstance"意为"绝不"，具有无条件答应对方所设定的条件的意思。

与之具有相同意思的短语关键词还有"in no case"、"at no time"、"by no means"、"in no sense"、"on no account"等，都可作"绝不"理解。这些否定短语常放在句首，且句子要倒装。

该种条款一般是强者对弱者的限制。

参考译文：买方绝不要求进行担保登记和兑换佣金。

EG – 2 – 26 The quality and prices of the commodities to be exchanged between the ex – importers in the two countries shall be acceptable to both sides.

显然，"be acceptable"作了模糊处理，至于到什么程度可接受并没有说。

参考译文：货物的质量和价格必须使进出口双方都能接受。

（四）根据关键词在合同条款中的特定意思表述可分为术语性关键词、法意性关键词和协意性关键词三种

术语性关键词主要是根据合同内容所涵盖的专业需要而引用的一些专业词汇，其词汇由于历史、社会和人文的原因已约定俗成，形成一种表达特定意思的习惯性表述的词汇。

法意性关键词主要是根据合同内容所涉及的法律领域或法域或法系而具有特定意思表达的词汇。

协意性关键词主要是根据合同双方当事人通过约定或定义形成的一些具有特定意思表达的词汇。

四、节点抽取：学会找到合同条款组织与思维的逻辑规律

涉外合同有其自身的结构特征，也有其固有的思维节点，因此，要想提高阅读涉外合同的速度，在关键词抽取的过程中还要把握节点抽取，从而找到合同条款组织与思维的逻辑规律。

1. 审阅者的立场不同，所关注的侧重点也不同

对于合同的审阅，持不同立场的人具有不同的情感因素，会关注不同的重点，对不同的关键词有不同的理解，对合同条款风险的评估、理解也会存在较大差异。

EG - 2 - 27 Notwithstanding any other provision of this contract, including a shipment term such as CIP, ownership of the contract commodities, including title and risk of loss or damage, will pass from Seller to Buyer at the point in time immediately after the contract commodities leave the territorial waters of the country of origin or leave the territorial airspace of the country of origin.

上述条款是一宗化工原材料的采购合同，卖方是美国 B 公司，买方是中国 A 公司，双方商定按照 CIP 条款交货，但卖方坚持风险及货物所有权从货物离开美国国界起转移，而买方认为应从交运港之时起转移。实质上该条款对双方都不利：买方委托卖方投保，是从启运地到目的港，一旦在美国海域内出险，由于买方在合同约定中没有约定出险货物所有权的转移，因此，保险方往往会以买方不具有投保利益而拒赔；卖方由于没有以自己为受益人投保，也不能获得理赔，这样买方就会从风险控制角度要求卖方自付费用来额外投保装运港到美国国界内的保险。该条款确实存在于某一中美两企业的化工原材料的采购合同中，由于该化工原材料是涉及与两企业先前达成的工艺包技术转让合同而配套适用的。笔者认为该合同条款是在中国没加入 WTO

前适用的，因为那时美国对中国的一些关键技术是限制出口到中国，所以才会出现上述所谓"空域（领海）的货物追及扣押权"。

在实际的外贸谈判中，就合同文本而言，因各方所持立场不同而容易形成的争点主要有以下几点值得关注：

（1）货物的原产地；原产地确定后，其交易条件就基本可明确，这样价格条件也可随之确定。

（2）货物交付的适用标准。货物交付条件会涉及各方的具体权利与义务，一般应在合同中明确约定适用《国际贸易术语解释通则》（International Rules for the Interpretation of Trade Terms, INCOTERMS）。该通则是国际商会为统一各种贸易术语的不同解释于 1936 年制定的，目前最新适用的版本为《INCOTERMS 2010》，以后如无明确说明，本书所选用术语皆以此版本内容为准。

（3）支付条款及相关保函的适用。重点关注保函内容与支付条款及明示担保或默示担保之间是否有矛盾或者存在不一致的地方。如相互引用的文本编号是否一致、金额数量是否一致（包括单位、币种）等。

（4）违约金的约定。违约金的约定应注意可定量性，同时避免与合同价款形成联动。

（5）兜底责任及免责情形。重点关注兜底、免责与明示担保及默示担保之间是否会形成矛盾，以及一旦形成矛盾哪一约定优先适用的问题。

（6）合同文本语言及适用法律。文本语言的选择应尽量与所适用法律国家的官方语言保持一致，否则就可能被司法机关判定为合同文本无效。笔者曾经手一宗涉外合同案件，合同文本为英文，而适用法律为中国，且双方当事人为中国登记的公司，因一方提出是另一方强制要求使用的英文文本，最终导致了合同文本的无效。

（7）纠纷处置约定。纠纷处置的重点是确定纠纷处置方式及司法机构管辖权选择。

2. 搞清涉外合同的性质

在涉外合同阅读或起草之前恐怕先要搞清合同的性质，只有确定了合同的性质，才能把握好合同的重点和风险所在。

更好地理解合同的性质应从以下几点把握：

（1）通过相关当事人了解合同签订的背景与需求，询问当事人希望通过合同得到什么，并了解他最担心的是什么。

（2）明确合同当事人（个人、组织）的登记国及所处法域，重点关注合同的涉外因素，如是至少一方当事人涉外，还是合同标的涉外，还是合同价款支付涉外等。

（3）明确双方约定的法律适用。明确合同文本约定采用单一文本还是双语文本；如果是双语文本，应规定其中某一文本优先适用，或各文本具有同等效力。如约定各文本具有同等效力时，应注意有良好的协商解决争议的机制或争议解决条款。

（4）弄清自己处于合同阅读者或审核者所处的阅读与审核立场。笔者认为"立场决定用语"，"立场决定对未来不确定的初步判断"，"立场决定合同的实质性内容对己方当事人是否有利"。

3. 判断好各方当事人所持基本立场

涉外合同涉及不同的国家和不同的文化背景，双方经常会对合同条款产生不同的理解。在阅读和审核涉外合同时，法务人员应判断所持立场方所处的地位是否有利，一般来讲，应注意以下几点：

（1）谁起草合同往往对谁有利。相反，根据各国法律对格式条款限制解释规则，发生纠纷时其合同条款的解释不利于起草方而对非起草方有利。

（2）谁比较熟悉合同标的物所涉及的行业，合同就会对谁有利。

（3）注意国内条款对涉外合同条款的影响。特别是要防止用国内法的习惯、思维方式来处理涉外合同的相关事项。

（4）在合同条款中，要特别注意时间、地点、方式与手段四要素对商务中约定权利与义务的影响，同时要考虑双方维持商务关系平衡的差距。

（5）为便于合同的执行，强势的一方应尽量规避不公平的优势。签订合同的目的是为了更好地执行，各方当事人更好地履行义务。

（6）用己方的文化、法律背景草拟出反映对方文化背景的条款，便于双方理解。以此表现出起草者对对方文化背景的理解，更重要的是能够找到有哪些与己方所处的立场不同，以确保双方的意思表达一致。

（7）在翻译成对方国家适用的语言时，更要注意对方术语、行话与合同本体语言的一一对应，体现翻译者对对方国家法律、社会、文化和历史背景的了解水平。如果意思不能充分表达，就可能造成纠纷或执行上的困难。特别是在不同文化背景下更要注意这一点。

（8）合同条款是否能够满足对方的商务需求，是否能够规避风险。所谓风险就是未来支出的不确定性。这一不确定性可能使企业陷入纠纷或债务危机，甚至引发经营危机，严重时更可能导致企业不得不申请破产。在争议发生之前要预料如何去解决，这是涉外合同最首要的原则，也是最后的原则。在发生纠纷时，合同中应约定双方可接受的处理方法，如果合同签订前没有预料到，那就是法务人员的水平不到位。

（9）注意合同条款描述的方式、方法。如静句与动句的选择、群意性关键词的选择等。

4. 理清合同阅读与审核的思维顺序

在涉外合同的阅读与审核中应遵循以下思维顺序去寻找思维节点，并结合对关键词的理解，达到读懂、弄清的目的。

（1）先了解双方的基本情况，是否属同一法系。了解法系的目的在于理解一些法理系关键词，并能够结合一些术语对双方认为有歧义的词进行定义，从而减少纠纷。

（2）了解合同优先适用的语言。不同语言的描述方式是有差异的，了解了合同优先适用的语言，就可知道合同条款关注的重点或可能产生歧义的地方。

（3）了解合同所适用国家的法律。不同国家的法律有不同的法律术语，因此，在涉外合同的关键词选择中要重点关注合同约定适用国家的法律，这就要重点关注所在国家普遍适用的法律专业术语，并按照该国家法律的惯常解释理解相关法律术语，特别是不要用本国的且在合同中没约定优先适用所在国的法律术语，那样容易形成理解上的歧义，甚至影响合同对价的形成。

（4）了解双方当事人是否有权优先解释适用的顺序。在较重要的合同中，一般会设定多文件组成合同的内容的解释适用顺序，这样就要关注优先适用的关键词是否是自己所理解的意思表达，是否也能够表达对方具有相同的意思。

（5）在了解合同主要条款的基础上熟悉定义与附件部分。对于与法言法语或通俗理解有歧义的定义要重点了解。

（6）在理解一般条款的基础上重点了解特殊约定条款。特殊约定条款在设置过程中往往会设置很多优先适用或保留适用的条件，如对于假设、除外、但书等结构性关键词一定要多加留意。

（7）对于嵌入式引导条款要重点理解。对于嵌入式引导条款句一定要结合合同条款作综合理解，防止方向性的错误。

（8）在了解违约责任的基础上重点理解免责条款。

（9）在了解权利义务的基础上重点理解担保条款。

5. 重点关注权利义务条款的描述

在涉外合同中使用条件句，其目的都是为了确保所描述权利义务的内容与当事人意思表达的一致。任何合同条款都是从权利义务的安排出发，发现权利义务的外延过大，就通过除外条款来削减；发现所描述权利义务的外延过小，就通过附加条件来增加。为了实现与其他条款权利义务的均衡、互不妨碍，就出现了隔离条件句、独立性条件句等，这些值得引起重视。其目的就是为了实现双方意思表达上的一致、翻译上的一致。

涉外合同条款的组织无不是围绕相关事项或行为所产生的权利义务而设置的，但在设置的过程中会与其他条款的事项或行为产生冲突或矛盾，从而也就会产生所谓的句法歧义，即无法确定哪一条款优先适用的问题，这样就要实施条件前置，将已达成的条款或双方已有共识的事项或行为排除在外，或以但书形式作出特别申明，以消除无法判断谁优先适用的句法歧义。

在组织权利义务描述的过程中要思考以下几个问题或情形：

（1）选择何种句型来描述双方当事人所关注的权利义务，同时考虑是否需要强调或排他性问题。

（2）用较为直观的方式指出设置权利义务的依据，并同时考虑权利义务设置的时空价值观，即行使权利或履行义务的时间、地点、方式、手段、原因或需要达到的效果。

（3）指出权利义务适用的条件，这一条件既可能是业已存在的，也可能是对未来不确定性因素的合理假设。

（4）新设置的权利义务产生所涉及的事项或行为可能与业已存在的事项或行为相冲突或矛盾而产生不知哪一事项或行为具有优先适用的问题，这需要就此指出或权衡取舍。

（5）新设置的权利义务所出现的事项或行为与业已存在或预期将要发生的事项或行为虽不矛盾，但可能存在并行或选择性问题，这一选择虽互不影响，但可能会让人产生联想、类推或否定上的歧义，包括是否选择某一权利就排除其他权利、接受某一履行义务方式是否意味可不按照其他方式履行，即使存在可能的选择，还存在谁应优先、谁可被忽视的问题。

（6）在设置权利义务时，可能会因未来不确定性因素的不可预测性而存在新权利义务的设置是否可能导致对一方当事人的额外负担甚至不可接受的风险，这就要考虑如何规避与排除这一风险，以让双方当事人能够接受。

（7）在设置权利义务时，可能会超出合同之债的范畴，因此要在其他条款中作出一些特别约定，以消除歧义。

（8）在设置权利义务时，可能会在双方当事人之间形成超过合同范围的其他关系，而这一关系的形成又可能导致一方当事人处于不利地位，因此要求通过特殊的条款来排除这些关系的形成。

为便于读者对合同条款的理解，笔者通过类聚思想对一些关键词进行了分类，并绘制了涉外合同条款关键词导读图，以便更好地掌握涉外合同的思维节点。

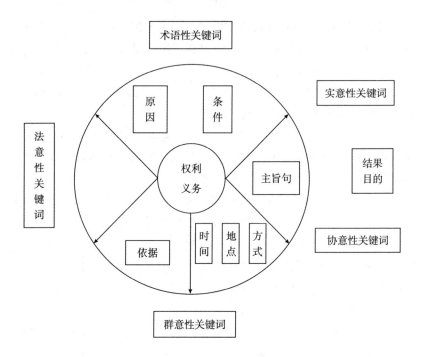

第3章

术语性关键词：熟练阅读
涉外合同的良好开端

　　合同文件是合同双方签订并必须遵守的法律文件，因此合同中的语言应体现其严谨、明确和权威。涉外合同用语的显著特点就表现在用词方面尽量准确无误，力争达到双方对合同中使用的词义的无可争议。这也就使得合同文本在商务活动的发展中行成了自己的行业术语或行文习俗或标准制式或法律行话。这些术语的应用可极大减少双方的分歧，缩减谈判的时间。

一、路径分析：涉外合同术语形成的历史渊源

　　通过对合同文本术语关键词的分析，涉外合同文件中的术语在漫长的成俗过程中主要源于以下几个路径而得以形成。

1. 习文落俗

　　涉外合同的语言体现出与普通英语非常特殊的风格与特点，"法言法语"在涉外合同中体现得非常充分。这些所谓的"法言法语"主要是指一些中古英语和外来词汇。其之所以形成了一些独特的"语言群"，一方面是与各国

语言的历史发展有关；另一方面是因为法律界人士普遍认为这些中古另类语言的使用可以使法律语言更加高贵和庄重。就如现在的美国青年一代喜欢学说正宗的英式英语一样。法律英语词汇在词源上大量吸收了拉丁语、法语、德语和西班牙语中的法律词汇，虽不能考察是否因"酷"而形成，但确实严谨、精准。如"ad hoc"（特别、临时）、"lex situs"（物所在地法）、"vice versa"（反之亦然），还有一些中古英语，如"aforesaid"（如前所述）、"hereinafter"（在下文中）等。

即使不是这些中古英语和外来词汇，涉外合同中一些看似很平常的英语词汇也具有不同于普通英语的含义。如"重大违约"或"严重违约"用"a material breach"表示，而不用"serious breach"；"合同终止"用"terminate"表示，而不用"finish"或"end"；"开始"用"commerce"表示，而不用或少用"start"或"begin"。

值得一提的是，古英语词汇在现代英语中所剩不多，但在法律英语中常常出现，法学家们对之也是情有独钟。这主要是因为古词语可以使法律公文更加简练、庄重，给法律英语增加了很强的文体特色；但其也不可避免地在一定程度上脱离了大众，为此以美国英语为代表的法律英语倾向于运用简单明了的常用词汇来表达法律意思，用简单易懂的词替代难词或法律行话。

习文落俗还有一点就是源于合同起草人在合同起草过程中通过应用以前合同模板，从而将一些简洁的前人经常使用的词沿袭下来，保留至今。它们在长期的使用过程中已形成了为人们所公认的特定含义，具有古旧词汇的特点，有的书中称之为制式词汇，如"whereby"、"hereby"、"hereto"、"herein"等。

EG - 3 - 1 The Employer hereby covenants to pay the Contractor in consideration of the execution and completion of the works and the remedying of defects therein the contract price or such other sum as may become payable under the provisions of the contract at the time and in the manner prescribed by the contract.

这里使用了"hereby"，相当于中文"特此"的意思，十分贴切，也能够简明表达行文者的意思。

参考译文：业主特此立约保证在合同规定的期限内，按合同规定的方式向承包人支付合同价，或合同规定的其他应支付的款项，以作为本工程施工、竣工及修补工程中缺陷的报酬。

EG - 3 - 2 Whether the custom of the port is contrary to this clause or not, the owner of the goods shall, without interruption, by day and night, including Sundays and holidays (if required by the carrier), supply and take delivery of the goods. Provided that the owner of the goods shall be liable for all losses or damages including demurrage incurred in default on the provisions hereof.

这里使用了"hereof"（本合同），显得十分庄重、典雅。

参考译文：不论港口习惯是否与本款规定相反，供货方都应昼夜地，包括星期日和假日（如承运人需要），无间断地提供和提取货物。供货方对违反本款规定所引起的所有损失或损坏包括滞期应负担赔偿责任。

因习以成俗，逐渐成为制式词汇，在英文合同中这些制式词汇主要由"here"、"there"、"where"分别加上"by"、"of"、"after"、"to"、"in"、"for"、"under"等介词组成。"here"强调的是"this"，"there"强调的是"that"。

2. 判例成俗

由于英美法属判例法国家，法院的判决具有相对的法律效力或普遍约束力。因此，在合同起草过程中会出现一些经法院判决认可的行为，从而成为专业术语。还有一些术语主要来源于拉丁语和法语词汇，具有特定的历史渊源。这主要与本土受外来民族入侵、占有的历史有关，反映了本国曾经遭受外来民族殖民统治的历史、文化演变的痕迹。在受殖民统治的一段时期内，本国法院在判决书中会按照统治者强加的意志使用统治国的语言，而一些涉外合同的起草人就会在合同文本中采用具有法律约束力的判决用语，从而沿用成俗。如"ex-post facto"（追溯）、"versus"（对抗）、"in rem"（对物）、"ad hoc"

（专门的）、"debt"（债务）、"voir dire"（照实陈述）等。

在涉外合同中，拉丁词仍然很常见，如"比例税率"用"pro rate tax rate"要比"proportional tax rate"更普遍，"contract"、"force majeure"也属拉丁语。

再如"estoppels"（禁止反言，the essentials of traditional version of estoppels were stated by lord Birkenhead in maclaine v gatty［1921］），该判决后，"estoppels"成为对价的补充规则。法务人员在合同起草过程中发展出了"whereas clause"（鉴于条款）、"representation and warrants"（陈述与保证条款）等，从而更有效地保护了善意当事人的合法权益。

3. 消歧通俗

法律人士或商务专业人员在合同起草过程中，为消除词语的歧义，采用了一些技术的处理或权威性推荐使用，从而达到消歧的目的，这样沿用下来，一些消歧方式也就越来越被行里人接受。如类聚词的使用、专业术语的固化等。

"may"、"shall"、"must"、"may not（shall not）"对于学过英语的人是再熟悉不过了，但在合同中用这些词时要极其谨慎。权利义务的约定部分构成了合同的主体。这几个词如选用不当，就可能会引起纠纷。

"shall"约定当事人的义务（应当做什么），"may"旨在约定当事人的权利（可以做什么），"must"用于强制性义务（必须做什么），"may not（shall not）"用于禁止性义务（不得做什么）。"may do"不能说成"can do"；"shall do"不能说成"should do"或"ought to do"；"may not do"在美国一些法律文件中可以用"shall not"，但绝不能用"can not do"或"must not"。例如，在约定解决争议的途径时可以说：

EG－3－3 The parties hereto shall, first of all, settle any dispute arising from or in connection with the contract by friendly negotiations.

Should such negotiations fail, such dispute may be referred to the People's Court having jurisdiction on such dispute for settlement in the absence of any arbitration clause in the disputed contract or in default of agreement reached after such dispute occurs.

本句中的"shall"和"may"表达准确。出现争议后应当先行协商，所以采用了义务性约定；如果协商解决不了，作为当事人的权利，用选择性约定"may"也很妥当。如果"may"和"shall"调换位置，后半句的"may"换用"shall"后就变成了应当诉讼解决，而诉讼是双方当事人的自由选择权，同时解决纠纷也不一定非得通过诉讼不可，还可调解、提起仲裁等。

参考译文：双方首先应通过友好协商，解决因合同而发生的或与合同有关的争议。如无仲裁条款约定或争议发生后未就仲裁达成一致的，可将争议提交有管辖权的人民法院解决。

4. 专业为俗

不同的专业有不同的术语，不同的国家有不同的语言特色，很多术语在两种语言的转换过程中，通过权威人士或国家立法部门的使用，逐渐演变成了不同的行业专业术语。如定金与订金、担保与保证、质押与抵押等。

合同文本中的专业术语主要有以下几种。

（1）商务专业术语。

商务合同英语文体中使用了大量表意清楚的商务专业术语。如"policy"（保险单）、"negotiable"（可转让的）、"liability"（责任、义务）、"right of recourse"（追索权）、"factoring（保理）"等。

再如，在商务活动中为简洁、明了而大量使用的缩略词也成了一些专业术语。缩略词（主要为首字母缩略词和截短词）以其规范、简明、省时的特点而被广泛运用在商务合同中：价格、支付及保险方式、货币、度量衡、常见的重要机构或组织、公司和国家等多以缩略词形式出现。例如"T/T"（Telegraphic Transfer，电汇）、"FOB"（Free onboard，船上交货）、"WA"（With Average，水渍险）、"a/r"（all risks，全险）、"AS"（after sight，见票即付）、"ACN"（air consignment，航空托运单）、"ICC"（International Chamber of Commerce，国际商会）等。这些用语的解释在国际上已形成惯例，所以其意义单一、含义准确，适用于商务合同这一特定文体。因此，熟知缩略词全称、领会其含义也就成为起草、翻译经贸合同所应具备的基本条件。

（2）法律专业术语。

法律专业术语的形成主要有以下几种原因：

a. 不同法系国家之间对同一事项的表述，通过翻译人员的习惯使用而成为专业术语。如"imputed negligence"（转嫁的过失责任）、"action"（诉讼）、"party"（当事人）、"financial responsibility"（经济责任）。违约责任具体可指"赔偿损失"、"支付违约金"和"支付迟延支付金额的利息"。如果对这类词语把握不准确，则很容易导致翻译和理解中的模糊性，因此要格外留意。如"The contract is concluded in case of acceptance of the offer."这句很容易被译为："提议一旦接受，合同随即订立。"而实际上，"acceptance"与"offer"是合同法中两个重要的法律术语，其规范的译文分别为"承诺"、"要约"，前者是指受要约人对要约内容表示同意，而后者则指一方希望与另一方订立合同。

b. 由于法务人员在工作中的习惯使用而形成的专业术语，如复杂介词短语的合理应用。

英语合同的专业性还体现在倾向使用较复杂的介词短语来代替非正式语体中常见的简单介词与连词。例如，用"with regard to"和"prior to"分别代替"about"和"before"。又如，All disputes in connection with this contract or the execution thereof shall be settled by way of amicable negotiation. 在此句中，用"in connection with"就比用"of"显得更为正式。

c. 为准确严谨而选词。

合同英语的用词极其考究，具有特定性，要求选词专业化（professional）、正式（formal）、准确（accurate）。

二、意思真实：术语性审核是合同审核的重中之重

术语性审核就是要对合同的专用术语或特殊语词定义进行审核，

分析是否是当事人的真实意思表示，同时分析对于专业术语的定义是否会产生歧义，是否与实质性条款相矛盾。

合同的术语性审核主要包括以下几点要求：

（1）合同的术语性审核首先要明确术语是否能够被正常人所理解，不能用已被正常人接受或法律有明确定义的术语进行另类解释，否则会适得其反。

（2）术语定义应简洁、明了，符合英文的词句搭配规范，不能违背英语的基本解释意义。

（3）术语一般具有专业性，对其解释尽量符合专业解释的原意，不能与专业技术解释明显矛盾或不一致。

（4）术语尽量要集中在合同文本的开始，切忌分散定义，也不要安排在合同尾部。

（5）经过定义的术语在合同其他地方出现时，不要另有解释或过多的限定词，避免出现理解上的差异或前后不一致的理解。

（6）术语解释要依法合规，不能有违背法律实质精神的意思表示。

第*4*章

基本理念：从法意性关键词入手

英美法学的基本架构源于自古以来发生的一个个案例。所谓的"case law"就是指在这种背景下产生的，与我们所熟悉的大陆法系的"statutory law"以及立法机构立法法的文化、传统相差很大。虽然现在很多英美法系的国家也开始进行了许多法律编纂工作，但是其规模仍然不及大陆法系国家，并且许多成文法法规仅限于公示或参考的性质或是对案例的整理，不具有完全的约束力。因为案例引用的一个显著特点是案件评审中持反对意见的观点也可能被后来的法官所采用或认同，而这不同于成文法，只是对法律规定的正面引用。例如，美国 American Law Institution 所编撰的 Restatement 虽然越来越常被法官引用，但是仍没有完全的法律拘束力。

在涉外合同的阅读与审核过程中，在考虑上述背景的情况下，法务人员的思维里还要有一种特定的语言环境、语言背景、文化背景、社会背景与法律背景作支撑，这样就会自觉与不自觉地利用法理思考合同中语词的意思表示。为便于理解，这里将之简单地表述为法意性关键词，也就是指在合同中具有一定法域意义的特定词或词组。如

"合同"一词在不同的法系或法域就有不同的定义，而对于不同的定义就有不同的解释。

下面所讲的语词，除另有说明外，均从英美法系合同方面进行理解，通过法意性关键词的简述，以有助于对本书其他关键词的正确理解。

一、几个常用的法意性关键词理解

（一）contract—agreement（合同—协议）

1. 概念理解

"contract"的定义：Steven H. Gifts 编著的《Law Dictionary》中将"contract"定义为："Contract is a promise, or a set of promises, for breach of which the law gives remedy, or the performance of the which the law in some way recognize as a duty." 根据这一定义，合同是一种承诺，违反承诺可以得到法律的救助，从某种意义上将法律体系视为履行该承诺的一种补偿机制。

L. B Curzon 在其编撰的字典《A Dictionary of Law》对"contract"的定义是："Contract is a legally binding agreement." 根据这一定义，合同就是有法律约束力的协议。也就是说，合同之所以称为协议，是因为有国家强制力作为合同能够得到履行并具有法律约束力保障的基础。

根据这些定义，协议是对已经做或准备做的相关事宜，经过谈判、协商后取得一致意见，以口头或书面形式作出的约定，该约定以供当事人日后遵守或作为行动指南。

显然，从上述定义来分析，两者之间的逻辑关系是："agreement"是广义概念，是种概念；"contract"是狭义概念，是属概念。从内涵的角度看，"contract"中双方的权利义务的约定比"agreement"更明确、更具体。

无论如何理解"contract"与"agreement"及其相互的关系，合同的成立必须具备几个主要因素，即由（要约和承诺构成的）协议、约因、设立法律关系的愿望和缔约能力四大部分组成。

从上面的分析不难看出，属于成文法的合同法对条款的规定更明确具体，英美法对合同的理解更注重法理，而实质上对法理的理解也是通过法官在具体判案时的理解与应用，因此判例对其他法官同样具有约束力。

2. 涉外合同的分类

合同无外乎是对双方未来合作事项有关人、事、物、方、时、地的事先约定，根据合同的具体内容、形式及确定性，主要将涉外合同从以下几个方面进行分类：

（1）按照合同内容完整性可分为："契约性合同"（contract of deed）；"框架式协议"（framework agreement）；"意向性协议"（Letter of Intent）；"函件式合约"（agreement of Letter）。

契约性合同（contract of deed）直接标明"contract"或"agreement"，且该文件通常是约束双方权利义务的主要合约内容。

框架式协议（framework agreement）是指合同的基本内容已经确定，由于采购信息不明朗，合同需求量或具体规格还需要以后明确的协议。框架式协议还有一个显著特点就是合同的价格为暂估价，一般依日后成交的数量或服务的范围及市场的因素来确定。该确定实质上是需双方的另行认定，或订单或补充协议或其他确认书等。

意向性协议（Letter of Intent）是指合同的主要内容并不明确，双方只是形成了以后在某一领域或某一方面合作的意向，一般来讲合作意向对双方不具有完全的约束力。文件名称一般会标明为"Letter of Intent"、"Memorandum of Understanding"或直接称为"Memorandum"。意愿书往往是双方日后行动的安排或初步的打算，一般不具有排他性，也不具有法律的约束力。

函件式合约（agreement of Letter）主要是一方以函件形式发起某一商务行为，另一方收到函件后，通过回复的形式予以确认或认同，如果是单一承诺性，另一方也可不予回复。

简短英文合约常用"Letter"（函）、"Waiver"（弃权书）、"Guaranty"（保证书）、"Power of Attorney"、"letter of authorization"（授权委托书）等简单明确的单字作为合约的名称，由于此类合约的外表行式通常很像一封英文信函，此外还有"General Agreement"（总约定书)、"Credit Letter"或"Facility Letter"(授信书)、"Letter of Comfort"(安慰函)等。

(2) 按照合同标的的具体内容可分为：国际贸易物资买卖合同；国际工程总承包合同；涉外服务类合同；涉外知识产权转让、许可等合同；国际劳务输出合同；涉外融资、保险合同；国际技术转让合同等。国际技术转让合同又可分为以下几种：国际许可证合同，或称国际技术许可证协议(International Licensing Agreement)；国际技术咨询服务合同(International Consulting Service Contract)；国际合作生产合同(International Cooperative Production Contract)；国际工程承包合同或协议(International Contracting Agreement)。

(3) 按照合同之间的关系可分为："母子式合同"(Mother and child type contract)；"夫妻式合同"(Husband and wife type contract)；"兄弟式合同"(Brother type contract)。

所谓"母子式合同"，就是一份合同与其他几份合同形成母子关系，母合同约定总的权利义务，可约定标的额，也可无标的额(如经济责任状形式)；子合同是对母合同中权利义务的具体拆分或复合，子合同之间可形成夫妻合同，也可形成兄弟合同，依具体情况而定。

所谓"夫妻式合同"，就是两份合同的标的指向一致，各合同的权利义务不能完全区别划分，如同婚姻法对夫妻共同财产的权利义务约定一样。夫妻合同往往要确定其中一个合同为主合同，另一个为辅合同，主合同上一般要描述对辅合同承担连带保证责任。如涉外附带专有设备的专利技术转让合同可将设计、文件成果提供、安装服务等约定在与软件有关的主合同中，将设备、备品备件约定在硬件辅合同中，这样就构成了一个完整的夫妻式合同。

所谓"兄弟式合同"，就是两份合同的标的可以独立出来，各自的履行不影响另一合同权利义务的履行。如同兄弟过日子一样，各是各家的事。如同一集团各子公司分别与同一需求方签订的供货合同等。有的为了保证整体工作进度，也可要求两份合同互负连带责任。特别是基于对标段的划分而形成的兄弟合同，可能会要求在其中一个合同中约定对总体协调承担连带责任。

（二）meeting of minds（合意）

在判例法国家，对于合同法中"contract"（合同）的理解意味着允诺的互换（exchange of promise），即一方以将来为一定给付的允诺换取对方为给付的允诺。这也就是我们所理解的一种债，也正是因为相互答应为对方做什么，或者说还欠对方某一承诺没有实现，因而形成了一种合同之债。合意即意思相合，指双方当事人订立合同的意思表示相一致。如果双方发生纠纷，若无事实证明双方之间形成了合意，则双方不受合同的约束，或者说一方可诉诸法院撤销合同。

笔者曾经办一宗涉外案件，甲乙双方约定：甲方同意从乙方购买青油 500 吨，每吨价格 5000 元，标准桶装，每桶 170 千克，采购从加拿大某港发货，价格条件为 CIF（厦门港），乙方同意采取 L/C 方式支付货款。后来，乙方货物准备好后，通知甲方到发运码头验货，并要求开出 30 日内有效的即期信用证。当甲方安排人员验货时，发现此青油非彼青油。原来，甲方认为的所谓青油是一种化工物品，也就是所谓的光亮油；而乙方认为的青油是一种优质的菜籽油。双方因此而诉至法院，法院经合议，准备判决撤销合同。法院的理由是双方没有形成合意，对于无合意的合同，则双方不受合同约定。双方得知法律的判决主旨后，经协议由原告撤诉，双方另行达成补充协议，要求原告按照被告的要求组织新的货源。

对于合意的认定有两个标准：一是主观判断；二是客观判断。现代适用案例法的国家奉行客观判断主义，认为决定合同是否成立的关键因素在于客观意图，而不在于主观意图。主观的实质是双方是否形成重大误解，而客观上是否构成显失公平，或者说合同的实际履行与其签订合同时的情形是否会形成较大的差异。合同赋予的义务首先建立于当事人客观上表现出来的意思。客观判断强调的重点是当事人的声明或行为与客观存在的事实表现意思相一致（manifestation of mutual assent），这就构成了合意。当然，客观判断也有例外，那就是法律履行对弱者保护的道德底线，如格式合同，一方在欺诈、胁迫、乘人之危、重大误解等情形下所签订的合同，即使符合合意的形式，法院也会因一方的主张而裁决合同无效或撤销合同。

合意也可理解为意思表示真实，真实既反映于合同主体的内心真实，也反映于客观物体与合同描述内容的真实。为充分表现合意，在涉外合同中一般通过开头语或在鉴于条款中说明某一具体合同的目的及双方的意思表达。

涉外合同常用开头语来表明合意的思想。以下是常见的描述方式。

EG-4-1　The contract is made by and between the Buyer and the Seller, whereby the Buyer agrees to buy and the Seller agrees to sell the under-mentioned commodity according to the terms and conditions stipulated below.

参考译文：买方同意购买，卖方同意出售下述商品，并按下列条款签订合同。

EG-4-2　In consideration of the payments to be made by the Purchaser to the Supplier as hereinafter mentioned, the Supplier hereby covenants with the Purchaser to provide the goods and services and to remedy defects therein in conformity in all respects with the provisions of the contract.

The Purchaser hereby covenants to pay the Supplier in consideration of the provision of the goods and services and the remedying of defects therein, the contract price or such other sum as may become payable under the provisions of the contract at the times and in the manner prescribed by the contract.

参考译文：考虑到买方将按照合同向卖方支付，卖方在此保证全部按照合同的规定向买方提供货物和服务，并修补缺陷。

考虑到卖方提供的货物和服务并修补缺陷，买方在此保证按照合同规定的时间和方式向卖方支付合同价或其他按合同规定应支付的金额。

（三）consideration（对价）

对价（consideration）是英美合同法中的重要概念，其内涵是一方为换取另一方做某事的承诺而向另一方支付的金钱代价或得到该种承诺的承诺。其本意是为换取另一个人做某事的允诺，某人付出的不一定是金钱的代价，也许是购买某种允诺的代价。对价从法律上看是一种等价有偿的允诺关系；而从经济学的角度说，对价就是利益冲突的双方处于各自利益最优状况的要约通过承诺来实现或保证，而当互不被对方接受时，通过两个或两个以上平等主体之间的妥协关系来解决这一冲突。这也是冲突双方处于帕累托最优状况时实现帕累托改进的条件。换句话说，在两个以上平等主体之间由于经济利益调整而导致法律关系冲突时，矛盾各方作出让步才会真正形成对价，而没有让步是不可能形成对价的。这种让步也可以理解为双方从强调自身利益出发而给对方造成的损失的一种补偿。或者说，没有让步的交易实质是没有实现帕累托的改进，始终强势的一方迟早也会被市场所淘汰，因此，为适应市场，强势的一方也不得不作出让步，以充分形成对价。

不难理解，对价是指一方得到权利、权益、益处或是另一方换取对方的某种承诺，或所作的或所承诺的损失，或所担负的责任或是牺牲。后来，随着经济的不断发展，对价的使用范围扩展到合同的履行、纠纷的解决等其他方面。1875年的居里诉米沙案判例将其定义为："一方得到权利、利益、利润或好处，或者另一方抑制一定行为，承受损害、损失或责任。"但需要补充的是，两者都必须是对履行义务当事人的回报。此外，接受义务履行的当事人诚实地放弃了某项请求权（不论该请求是否能成功）也被视为有效的对价。

对价的实质是判例法国家法院遵循道德准则的一道底线。也就是说，对价必须具有道德责任的真实价值，即必须是为促使对方履行合同义务所付出的真实代价或损失。如果法官认为某一项允诺的作出没有获得相应的对价或获得对待履行，那么道德义务在法律上不具有约束力，当事人只能通过良心或善意地回归本性去解决问题，也就是说，如果双方的争议是因为没有形成对价，一般不会得到法官的认同，除非当事人自愿。如超过诉讼时效的追索权问题，只要对方自愿履行义务，法院也不会判决该履行无效，因为履行超过诉讼时效的行为可以用道德来评判，而不能再上升到法律层面。

目前，中国合同法律体系中还没有明确的"对价"概念或相关规定。但在司法实践中，根据当事人取得的权利有无代价（对价），往往将合同分为有偿合同和无偿合同。有偿合同是交易关系，是双方财产的交换，是对价的交换；无偿合同不存在对价，不是财产的交换，是一方直接付出财产或劳务。最典型的无对价合同可能就是捐赠合同了，但捐赠如果是在特定的场所（如救灾晚会现场），也可能通过对捐赠人的社会人格产生重新评价或社会的影响而被法院认定产生了对价，这是更深层次的法理问题，不再赘述。

对价又称约因（consideration），它是盖印合同以外各类合同有效成立的必备要素。英美各国法律认为："没有对价的许诺只是一件礼物（或单方的捐赠）；而为对价所作出的许诺则已构成一项合同。"

不难理解，对价是现实的允诺互换或对未来的一种预期或可接受的利益或服务和相当价值的互换。需要说明的是，对价并不是价值的等同，而是一种价值的相当或者价值的类似，而价值的差异是双方可接受的。

对价是涉外合同有效成立的必备要素；但为了提供有效对价，又必须遵循一定的规则。根据判例法国的相关法律，一项有效的对价必须符合相应的一般规则。

（四）estoppels（允诺禁止反悔）

作为对价原则的一个补充原则，出现了允诺禁止反悔制度，该制度源于衡平法的禁止反言制度。允诺禁止反悔制度被视为对价原则的替代物而与对价原则互为补充，两者相互照应。

根据允诺禁止反悔原则，一项允诺无对价，但是如果该允诺有意地使对方产生依赖或信赖并使对方因此相信从而遭受实质性的损害，那么基于公平正义的理念，不能允许作出该允诺的人对自己的允诺反悔，这是实现法律正义的唯一选择，也就是所谓"君子一言，驷马难追"或者说"君无戏言"吧。

在《法律的训诫》中，丹宁法官将允诺反悔原则定性为："当一个人的言论或行为已经使另一个人相信按照他的言论或行为办事安全，而且的确是按照他的言论或行为办了事的时候，就不能允许这个人对他说的话或所作的行为反悔，即使这样做对他是不公平的，也应如此。"其实质是指即使一项允许无对价，但是如果该允许有意地使对方产生信赖并使对方因此信赖而遭受实质性损害，那么从公平正义的理念出发，不能允许作出该允许的人对自己的允许反悔。这是实现法律正义的唯一选择。

当然，该原则也有其应有的限定性，主要适用于下列类型的合同纠纷：

（1）家庭成员间的赠与性允许（interfamilial promise）；

（2）公益性的允诺（charitable subscriptions）；

（3）给付退休金的允诺（promise of retirement benefits）；

（4）订立保险合同的允诺（promise to insure）；

（5）缔约阶段的允诺（preliminary and incomplete negotiation）；

等等。

实质上，上述原则的限定在中国合同法中都可以看到其借鉴的痕迹，如《合同法》第42条规定："当事人在订立合同过程中有下列情形之一，给对方造成损失的，应当承担损害赔偿责任：（一）假借订立合同，恶意进行磋商；（二）故意隐瞒与订立合同有关的重要事实或者提供虚假情况；（三）有其他违背诚实信用原则的行为。"《合同法》第186条规定："赠与人在赠与财产的权利转移之前可以撤销赠与。具有救灾、扶贫等社会公益、道德义务性质的赠与合同或者经过公证的赠与合同，不适用前款规定。"

一般来讲，英美各国的判例也不是完全遵循"必须严格限制于允诺人因信赖而使其合同地位产生实质性的转变的情形"这一原则，也就是说该原则具有灵活性，允诺人仅仅对其预见到或可预见的信赖承担责任，而且强制执行该允诺必须是出于避免不公正现象的要求。因此，法官要综合考虑：①允诺人产生依赖的合理性；②损害的确定性；③损害的实质性；④允诺作出的形式；⑤商事交易的证据性；

⑥是否保持了合理的谨慎性；⑦形式要件是否足以依赖；⑧是否能合理地判断允诺人预见到受允诺人会对此允诺产生依赖；⑨受允诺人必须确实信赖了该允诺，依据允诺行事；⑩只有强制执行允诺才是公正的；⑪该原则的适用以实现法律正义为限度。

不难得出结论，"允诺禁止反悔"在一定程度上是对"对价原则"的补充，在商务合同的发展过程中也促进了英美合同中当事人对于"鉴于条款"、"陈述与保证条款"及"定义条款"的重视。

"definition clause"（定义条款）是涉外合同主文条款部分以"定义"开始的相关术语解释，即为防止不必要的争执或理解上的歧义，双方提前对合同中需要明确的词汇在此加以明确或限定性的解释。其最根本的原因是，在国际贸易中，双方当事人所处国家的文化背景不同，对相同法律或技术用语的理解也可能存在差异，而定义条款可以使双方对某些关键用语在理解上达成共识，减少争议的概率。还有一点就是根据英美法的契约自由原则，当事人可以根据自己的实际情况来订立一份个性化十足的合同，因此就必须在合同中注明某些用语在合同中的特殊含义。另外，定义条款的价值主要体现在双方对合同的理解发生争议时，如果定义条款中没有相关的条款可以提供判断标准，或者定义条款本身的界定也存在含混之处，则定义条款既未能防患于未然，又不能解决争议于事后，只能算是失败的条款。了解了这一点，就不难理解律师为何总是试图在定义条款中将语言的精确性提升到最高而不留任何想象与发挥的空间了。实质上，定义条款也可看做是双方达成的共识，属于特别的约定，一旦形成纠纷，法院在解决纠纷时就可依照双方的定义来确认，当事人一般也不得反悔。

（五）impressed warranties（默示担保）

在判例法系国家，根据担保责任产生的不同方式，对于货物、技术、服务的提供方的担保分为"明示担保"与"默示担保"。

"明示担保"主要是指货物、技术、服务的提供方以明确的意思表示向接受方承诺其提供的产品或服务质量。提供方的明确承诺使接受方对货物、技术、服务的品质、质量产生合理的充分依赖或合理的期待，提供方必须按照其承诺向接受方提供货物、技术或服务，否则构成违约。这样，提供方就要对自己提供的货物、技术、服务进行详细的陈述或描述，该陈述或描述必须与提供的标的相关，且该陈述或描述构成标的物将交付、转移的基础。而法院判决是否构成交易的基础，主要看提供方是否在陈述与描述上构成了本意上有诱使对方决定接受依赖提供方的陈述或描述而存在的标的物的意思表述。

与明示担保不同，默示担保不是基于当事人口头或书面的承诺产生，而是基于法律直接规定而产生的。所以，默示担保具有法定性。它根据法律的规定而成为双方当事人当然的选择或内心的服从，除非当事人明确将其排除适用。

一般来讲，在合同中如果约定了提供方的明示担保，即使双方在合同中约定了对于明示担保的免责，法院一般不会支持提供方的排除理由或者说一般不会接受提供方排除责任的内心意愿。而默示担保不同，双方是可以通过约定选择性地对提供方进行免责的，除非该免责严重违反了合同的基本原则或法律的正义原则，如格式合同的适用、过于强加于人等。

（六）risk of loss（损失的风险）

从合同角度来看，所谓风险，实质上就是合同履行过程中的不确定性给当事人带来的非正常损失，而这种不确定性的因素既可归因于合同一方或双方当事人的事由所导致的损失，又包括不可归责于合同双方当事人的事由所导致的损失。一般来讲，不可归责于合同双方当事人的事由所导致的损失通常是指不能预见、不能避免并不能克服的客观情况。该客观情况不是双方当事人可以控制和预防的，因此可在合同中通过不可抗力专门描述。

这里所说的风险实质上是指可归因于一方或双方当事人事由的风险。一般来讲，合同的风险主要体现在以下几方面。

一是合同目的不可实现，如采购合同中，因各种原因卖方不能按照合同规定交付货物，或者交付的货物不符合合同的约定。

二是导致无法预见的损失，或者说因合同条款约定不当而使一方或双方造成额外的损失，如合同标的物形成对第三方的侵权、使一方涉诉而造成额外的费用支付等。

三是因合同履行或不履行而形成新的法律关系，给一方或双方造成额外的负担。

为有效化解合同风险，合同中就出现了有关分担、隔离、转移与责任限定的条款。

标的物的风险损失直接影响到当事人的经济利益，所以，当事人在如何承担买卖合同风险责任的问题上易起纠纷。一般要在合同中约定风险的转移时点，如买受人拒绝接受标的物或者解除合同的，标的物毁损、灭失的风险由出卖人承担。风险应被限定为标的物因法定免责事由毁损、灭失的不利状态。

在合同中，对于风险的描述一般可参照以下条款实施。

EG – 4 – 3 The Seller must deliver goods which are free from any right or claim of a third party, unless the Buyer agreed to take the goods subject to that right or claim. However, if such right or claim is based on industrial property or other intellectual property, the Seller's obligation is governed by article 42.

参考译文：卖方所交付的货物，必须是第三方不能提出任何权利或要求的货物，除非买方同意在这种权利或要求的条件下收取货物。但是，如果这种权利或要求是以工业产权或其他知识产权为基础的，卖方的义务应依照第 42 条的规定。

EG – 4 – 4 If the contract of sale involves carriage of the goods and the Seller is not bound to hand them over at a particular place, the risk passes to the Buyer when the goods are handed over to the first carrier for transmission to the Buyer in accordance with the contract of sale. If the Seller is bound to hand the goods over to a carrier at a particular place, the risk does not pass to the Buyer until the goods are handed over to the carrier at that place. The fact that the Seller is authorized to retain documents controlling the disposition of the goods does not affect the passage of the risk.

参考译文：如果销售合同涉及货物的运输，但卖方没有义务在某一特定地点交付货物，自货物按照销售合同交付给第一承运人以转交给买方时起，风险就转移到买方承担。如果卖方有义务在某一特定地点把货物交付给承运人，在货物于该地点交付给承运人以前，风险不得转移到买方承担。卖方受权保留控制货物处置权的单据，并不影响风险的转移。

EG – 4 – 5 Nevertheless, the risk does not pass to the Buyer until the goods are clearly identified to the contract, whether by markings on the goods, by shipping documents, by notice given to the Buyer or otherwise.

参考译文：但是，在货物以货物上加标记，或以装运单据，或向买方发出通知或其他方式清楚地注明有关合同以前，风险不得转移到买方承担。

二、两个基于法理的重要涉外合同条款

在涉外合同中有两个条款是基于禁止反言原则、对价原则及合同目的性原则发展而来的，属于合同成立的条件，其重要性可想而知。

这两个基于法理而形成的重要条款就是"whereas clause"（鉴于条款）和"representation and warrants"（陈述与保证条款），下面对之重点详述。

（一）鉴于条款：明确当事人所表达的意思真实

任何一份合同的签订都有其目的性。因此，在合同的开始就应明确签订某一特定合同应达到的目的。目的的描述可开宗明义，用简洁的语言说明签订合同的宗旨；对于较复杂或特殊的涉外合同，应通过"whereas clause"的设计指出合同签订的目的。

为了确保理解合同签订的目的性，对于比较重要的合同，在阅读、审核之前，法务人员应事先通过电话、电子邮件，最好是面谈的形式或直接参与谈判，与各方人员进行有效沟通，从而大致判断、分析出双方签订合同的目的，必要时可以要求商务人员提供满足商务条件的采购需求、合同计划等规范性文件或上司的审批指令，从而准确把握拟定合同的目的。当然，对于法务人员来讲，更重要的是通过对

现有资料的核查和通过与双方业务人员的沟通来了解双方当事人签订合同的动机。特别是要注意合同对方是否企图以合法形式掩盖非法目的。如果感觉到有一方当事人签订合同的动机与合同所描述的标的所折射的动机存在差异，就要引起足够的重视，重点分析在未来合同履行中的法律风险所在，必要时要及时与其上级主管领导进行汇报、沟通，弄清合同签订的真实目的，并假设按照不良动机履约会给本公司造成的可能经济损失，同时要通过但书、违约、结算与支付等条款的设计，拟定含有风险防范、补救措施的保护性条款。必要时，可要求动机不良一方提供相应的安慰函、保函等书面承诺来消除其纠结所在。

法务人员通过对合同的目的性审核，要达到以下几个目的：

（1）明确了合同的目的才能搞清各方的真实意思。

（2）明确了合同的目的才能确定合同的性质，才能对合同名称的准确性进行判断，才能以此进行合同类别的划分。

（3）明确了合同的目的才能正确审核合同双方的权利、义务及违约责任是否恰当、对等和完备。

（4）明确了合同的目的才能确保合同条款的依法合规，并能够对效力性作出适当判断。

鉴于条款的设计除基于禁止反言原则外，还有一点需要明确的就是满足合同目的。如果违反了合同目的，可视为违反了合同条件，即违反了合同的默示保证，因此，守约方可要求终止合同、拒绝付款、拒收标的物以及采取补救措施。除非违约方能够举证说明守约方知晓其合同目的与需求目的存在显著差异。

当然，针对合同的目的性审核要有的放矢，确保合同签订的主旨不发生偏离。

描述合同签订的目的性条款要简洁明了，不得含糊其辞。同时，每一份合同的签订目的尽量单一，如果审核中发现多目的性，应尽量对合同进行拆分，以确保合同目的的单一。

一般来讲，涉外合同的鉴于条款从以下几个角度来描述或组织语言：

（1）通过鉴于条款说明合同签订的背景。

（2）通过鉴于条款说明双方签订合同的意思表示。

（3）参考鉴于条款说明合同当事人希望达到的目的。

（4）参考鉴于条款说明当事人的合同成立的对价。

（5）通过鉴于条款说明双方签订合同应遵循的原则与适用的法律。

（6）通过鉴于条款明确一方的承诺。

（7）通过鉴于条款说明上述综合情况。

鉴于条款还可以综合上述六条及其他情况，形成一段较为全面、综合的鉴于条款。

（二）承诺性条款（representation and warrants）：确保合同的有效性

对于涉外合同，无论是合同起草者还是合同阅读者或执行人，都应明确合同条款中哪些属于合同成就的条件，哪些属于合同双方的事先约定。合同成就的条款往往属于某一方或双方的保证与陈述（定义条款一般可认定为双方的共同陈述），这是不可改变的合同成立或合同有效的基础。如果合同成就的条件不真实或发生了实质性的改变，就会导致一方主张合同无效或申请司法机关撤销合同。对于事先经双方约定的事项，在执行过程中如果出现了偏差一般是可以补救的，或通过变更，或重新协议签订补充协议予以完善。

审核一份合同的真实性，主要是通过资料的核对、合同目的性分析，并结合合同的合法依规性研究，综合判断合同条款是否为双方当事人的真实意思表示。

审查合同是否为当事人的真实意思表示，应从以下几点进行关注：

（1）重点审核陈述与保证条款。陈述与保证是当事人最真实的意思表示。对于涉外合同来讲，如果出现事后的基本事实达不到其陈述时的情形时，陈述与保证者就不得以有违公平原则为由而主张合同无效或可撤销。法院会依照"禁止反言"（estoppels）原则判断当事人是否存在"反言"行为，即使合同存在不公平事项，如果陈述与保证者不依约履行合同义务，照样会被法院判决承担违约责任。这样，若一方当事人担心对方虚假陈述会导致自己作出错误判断时，应要求对方作陈述与保证，以确保合同权益得到维护。

（2）注意判断合同条款是否存在欺诈性。存在欺诈将直接影响交易的安全，当事人的合法权益也难以保障。为此，要分析双方当事人达成的意见是否存在误解或误导，是否存在符合法律规定的变更、撤销、中止情形，是否会发生误解或者对当事人产生不利的误导。

（3）审核是否存在虚假或错误陈述。通常情况下，在合同谈判过程中，总有一方处于相对强势地位，合同的实际谈判往往会因强势方的先入为主而使得另一方的真实意思难以表达；如果弱势一方急于签约或者为了拿到订单而违心地接受一些不利于己的条款，那么这种不利于也可能就是基于当事人一方在不情愿的情况下在谈判过程中对事实的陈述与事实不相符合或者不真实，从而构成错误陈述，或称为虚假陈述。错误陈述具有欺诈性，很有可能成为该合同无效的条件。

（4）判断合同客体是否真实。通过双方提供的证明性文件，审核一方的需求与满足另一方的需求是否完全一致。

（5）判断合同内容是否真实。通过双方的陈述和合同谈判记录及相关法律、法规的引用，审核双方的权利义务是否能够实质履行，以及是否为双方的真实意思表示。对于合同内容的分析，关键是要掌握当事人的要约与承诺是否相一致，对于涉外合同还要分析双方的意思表示是否形成对价。

（6）判断合同的标的是否存在对价（consideration）。对价的实质是各方的相互许诺。英美合同十分重视对价的存在。对价也是分析判断合同客体与内容是否真实的有效方法，是合同签订的直接动因所在——确保对价的实现。

陈述与保证是指合同双方当事人的一种声明。这是关于与合同有关的各种事实与问题的情况声明。例如，在设备购买合同中，卖方对设备的品质与性能进行一般的、非技术性的保证，在供货后如发现并非如其所述，则可以获得救济或赔偿，如退货并取回货款等。

陈述与保证条款通常包括两方面内容：第一是关系到合同本身是

否成立的有关信息，如签约一方是否为合法有效的公司、是否有权签署本协议中的陈述与保证条款内容，包括签约一方公司的组建设立情况、签约代表是否已获得本方真实有效的授权等内容。第二是关系到合同目的是否达到的有关信息，即依据合同性质和合同标的需要一方或双方所作出的特别保证内容，如一方对其所交付的货物是否拥有完全的所有权、签约方现在是否还有其他债权人或者正在进行债权纠纷等。合同一方很难从另外的渠道获得这些信息或者获取这些信息将耗费较大成本。因此，在合同中一方可通过该条款要求另一方对这些信息作出陈述与保证。

一般来讲，涉外合同的陈述与保证条款可从以下几个角度来描述或组织语言：

（1）通过承诺条款说明其所有权、相关批文的有效性等；

（2）通过承诺条款说明其提供货物或服务的质量状况，以此安慰对方；

（3）通过承诺说明主体经营资格的合法依规；

（4）通过承诺说明授权的有效性；

（5）对是否存在债务纠纷或者是否存在对履行合同的能力产生障碍的陈述与保证；

（6）通过承诺说明相关转让的合法所有权不存在瑕疵，也不存在对第三方的侵权；

（7）通过承诺，确保不存在未了结的诉讼等或有债务；

（8）对承诺所述事实真实性的保证；

（9）通过陈述与保证条款说明上述综合情况。

陈述与保证条款还可以综合上述八条及其他情况，形成一段较为全面、综合的陈述与保证条款。

第5章

关注群意：突破涉外合同复合句的捷径

在涉外合同中，复合句的出现频率较高，句子结构复杂，逻辑性强，这无疑给阅读增添了许多困难，但是，无论多长的句子、多么复杂的结构，都是由一些基本的成分组成的。只要弄清了合同原文的句法结构，找出整个句子的中心内容及各层意思，然后分析各层意思之间的逻辑关系，再按汉语的特点和表达方式组织译文，就可以保证合同阅读与理解的准确性。

一、思路清楚：看懂涉外合同复合句的关键所在

对于复杂的涉外合同条款，一定要注意思维清晰、层次明了。

1. 涉外合同中表述条件关键词的分类

在涉外合同中，除了必要的文头、格式、形式条款外，各类条款的设置都是围绕各方权利义务的设定而构思的，也就是说，任何一条条款的设置都是为某一方或双方设置应享有的权利或应承担的义务。

在权利义务的设置过程中，双方往往要经过较为激烈的谈判，权利义务的落实不是仅符合对价原则就可达到

的，有时还需要附条件才能成就，否则双方就可能很难达成一致意见。也就是说，可能因为某一方提出的条件过于苛刻而难以满足双方的意思表示，因此就需要围绕权利义务设置相应的条件，这样一来，权利义务的设置与条件的设置恰当与否就十分相关了。

条件有积极的条件，有利于权利的享有、义务的承担；还有可能设置消极的条件，不利于权利的享有或义务的承担。由于文化背景与语言习惯的差异性，对于条件的表述在用词、用意上精彩纷呈，有时让人眼花缭乱。为便于理解，笔者特以关键词为线索进行了分类。

从涉外合同中条件关键词与该条款中权利义务的关系角度可分为必要性条件关键词、非必要性条件关键词、关联性关键词与消解关联性关键词四种。

根据涉外合同中英文习惯用法可将条件关键词主要分为假设性关键词、但书性关键词、除外性关键词与让步性关键词四种。

在涉外合同中，常见的条件关键词主要有以下三种：

（1）由"if"、"should"、"in case"、"in the event of"等连接词引导的表示假设条件的状语。此类状语从语用的角度来看，通常表示的是在某一假设条件下合约的某一方须承担的义务和责任或享有的权益，因此句子的语义重心在主句部分。

（2）由"provide（that）"所引导的表示某种先决条件的状语。从语用角度来看，其所表示的是只有在出现或具备了某种条件的情况下合约的某一方才有义务承担某一责任或享有某一权益，或者才有可能采取某一行动，因此，句子的语义重心在从句上，或者至少说状语从句表示的信息相对而言为比较重要的新信息。

（3）由"expect"、"with the exception of that"、"in the absence of"和"unless"等引导的表示除外情况的状语从句。从语用的角度来看，它们表示合约某一方在某种特殊情况下可以例外地不受某一合约条款制约的特殊条件，通常用来作为某一合约条款的补充说明。

（4）由"notwithstanding"等引导的表示让步情况的状语从句。从权利义务设置的角度来分析，其往往是为了避免不必要的争论，提出一些相关问题与条款设置的权利义务不相关联，迫使某一方作出适当让步，从而使双方的意见尽量达成一致。

2. 涉外合同基本意群结构

在英文合同的阅读与理解中，应按照以下思维节点弄清其基本的意群结构：

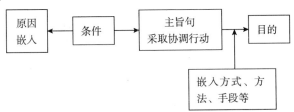

分析阅读涉外合同复合句时，粗略地应从以下几点加以把握：

第一，找到主旨句，弄清其需要协调或说明解释的基本权利义务。要知道，除基本的格式形式条款外，绝大多数合同条款是围绕一定的权利义务展开描述的。

第二，通过主旨句，分析权利义务得以实现的条件，通过该条件分析嵌入的原因。

第三，通过原因或条件说明权利义务实现的目的。

第四，分析为实现目的需要采取的手段、方式及其中的关联关系。

从精细方面来看，应从以下几点加以把握：

第一，阅读者要找出全句的实意性关键词，如权利义务的承担者、通过条款应赋予的权利义务、以什么方式履行合同的权利义务等。实意性关键词通常充当句首不含介词或介词结构的句子中的主语、谓语和宾语成分，即某一具体条款中主句中的主干结构。

第二，找到句首没有群意性关键词的主旨句，重点分析主旨句的描述方式，从而确定权利义务所处的状态方式。

第三，找出所阅读条款中含有的其他关键词，特别是涉及当事人权利义务的关键词。

第四，找出为履行权利义务而约定的依据、假设或限定的条款以及不适用的情况，重点关注介词短语和从句的引导词的导向。

第五，分析条文中是否存在履行权利义务要求达到的目的或设定的理由或具体的要求。

第六，分析条文中是否有履行权利义务对时间、地点与方式的限定。

第七，分析句子中是否有固定搭配、插入语等其他成分。

EG - 5 - 1 In the event of a conflict between the clauses and the schedules, the parties shall endeavor, in the first instance, to resolve the conflict by reading this agreement as a whole and the provision that is most specific to the subject matter shall govern, if, notwithstanding the parties * good faith efforts to resolve the conflict as provided in the preceding sentence, the conflict persists, the provision in the clauses shall govern.

本条款的主旨句是 "the parties shall endeavor... to resolve the conflict by reading this agreement as a whole and the provision that is most specific to the subject matter shall govern"，为主旨句嵌入的行为方式。

"In the event of a conflict between the clauses and the schedules" 为前提条件，"if, notwithstanding the parties * good faith efforts to resolve the conflict as provided in the preceding sentence, the conflict persists , the provision in the clauses shall govern" 为让步条件句。

参考译文：如果合同条款和附件的意思发生冲突，各方应首先尽力将整个协议作为一个整体阅读理解，对协议主题最为明显的条款应优先考虑；如果各方本着信用的原则努力按照前句话规定解决冲突，但冲突依然存在，则协议条款优先。

EG - 5 - 2 If the contract of sale involves carriage of the goods and the Seller is not bound to hand them over at a particular place, the risk passes to the Buyer when the goods are handed over to the first carrier for transmission to the Buyer in accordance with the contract of sale. If the Seller is bound to hand the goods over to a carrier at a particular place, the risk does not pass to the Buyer until the goods are handed over to the carrier at that place. The fact that the Seller is authorized to retain documents controlling the disposition of the goods does not affect the passage of the risk.

该条款的主旨句是 "the risk passes to the Buyer", "the risk does not pass to the Buyer", "The fact does not affect the passage of the risk"。

第一个主旨句前的条件句嵌入了一个但书条款，后接一个时间要求和履约依据；第二个主旨句前为一个条件句，后接一个时间、地点要求；第三个主旨句嵌入了一个定语从句。

参考译文：如果销售合同涉及货物的运输，但卖方没有义务在某一特定地点交付货物，自货物按照销售合同交付给第一承运人以转交给买方时起，风险就转移到买方承担。如果卖方有义务在某一特定地点把货物交付给承运人，在货物于该地点交付给承运人以前，风险不转移到买方承担。卖方受权保留控制货物处置权的单据并不影响风险的转移。

EG – 5 – 3 If a Party breaches any of the representations or warranties given by it in Articles 18. 1 or repeated in 18. 2, then in addition to any other remedies available to the other party under this contract or under Applicable Laws, it shall indemnify and keep indemnified the other Party and the company against any losses, damages, costs, expenses, liabilities and claims that such Party or the Company may suffer as a result of such breach.

阅读与理解：

第一步：找到实意性关键词：主体，合同主体：a party – the other party。

赋予的权利义务："indemnify and keep indemnified"。显然这是一条有关合同救济与索赔的约定。

第二步：找到主旨句。

第三步：其他关键词："breaches any of"、"remedies available" "suffer as"。

第四步：

A. 找到依据："in Articles 18. 1 or repeated in 18. 2, under this contract or under Applicable Laws"。

B. "If a Party breaches any of the representations or warranties given by it" 是条件限定。

C. "against…suffer as a result of such breach" 导出了具体的索赔要求: "any losses, damages, costs, expenses, liabilities and claims"。

第五步: 固定搭配词 "in addition to" 引导的是增补成分, 其关键词 "remedies" 跟了后置定语 "available to the other Party under this contract or under Applicable laws"。

由此不难理解本条款的意思为: "如果一方违反任何其根据第 18.1 条或 18.2 条所作的陈述及担保或重述, 则另一方除根据本合同或相关法律寻求任何可能的救济之外, 违约方应当赔偿另一方或合营公司因此种违反而招致的任何损失、损害、费用、开支、责任或索赔。"

EG – 5 – 4 Contracts referred to in this Law are agreements between equal natural persons, legal persons and other organizations for the purpose of establishing, altering and terminating mutual civil rights and obligations.

第一步: 实意性关键词 "Contracts"、 "agreements" 都可理解为合同。

在定义中如果出现表示相同词义的两个不同的词, 则一般来讲, 一个是广义的, 一个是狭义的。在这里, "Contracts" 是狭义的, "agreements" 是广义的。因此, 对于实质性内容确定的合同一般用 "Contracts"; 对于实质性内容不确定的合同, 如固定单价的框架协议、较长期限的保护伞协议等一般用 "agreements"。

"referred to" 是一个定义性实意关键词, 一般译为 "是"。

第二步:

A. "in this Law" 是依据性限定, 在此可理解为 "本法所指", 一般可省略。

B. "for the purpose of establishing, altering and terminating mutual civil rights and obligations" 是目的性。

C. "between" 是关系性关键词, 一般理解为 " * * * 之间的 *

＊＊关系"。

由此不难理解本款的意思为："（本法所指）合同是平等主体的自然人、法人、其他组织之间设立、变更、终止民事权利义务关系的协议。"

EG-5-5 If any event of the force majeure occurs which causes damage to the project or the infrastructure project, then C or New Company shall not be obliged to reinstate the same, or, as the case may be, complete the same, until the parties hereto have agreed upon the terms for such reinstatement or completion.

第一步：主体是"C or New Company, the parties"；权利义务的履行方式是"not be obliged have agreed"。

第二步：其他关键词是"occurs"、"reinstate"、"complete"。

第三步："If"引导条件；"until"表示"但书"或"例外"事项。

显然，该句的组织连接是条件先发生，权利义务承担后发生，但书事项次后发生。也就是说，但书发生后即意味着权利义务不可再履行了。

这样就可阅读和理解为："如不可抗力的发生损坏了工程或基础设施，C或新公司没有义务重新恢复之，或完成其修建，但双方就这种恢复或完成的条件达成一致意见则例外。"

二、条件支撑：合同权利义务保障的有效方法

涉外合同主要约定合同各方应享有的权利和应履行的义务，但由于这种权利的行使和义务的履行均附有各种条件，所以在英语合同中，引导条件句的关系词极其丰富，条件句的大量使用成为商务合同的一个特点。条件句多由下列连接词引导："if"、"in the event of"、"in case（of）"、"should"、"provided（that）"、"subject to"、"unless otherwise"等。

一般来说，条件句均置于主句之前，英译汉时译成"如果"或"若"即可。而当条件句置于主句之后时，在翻译这些引导条件句的

连词或短语时，可按动态等值理论视具体情况而定，切勿生搬硬套。

但有些看似条件的句子，实质上是通过条件句这种形式嵌入了支撑条件的方式、方法或手段，或弄清前因后果，或明确目的所在，或弄清方式、手段，或理清复杂的关系。

1. 弄清前因后果

在涉外合同中常用 "attributable to"、"due to"、"owing to"、"by virtue of"、"in view of"、"because of"、"on account of"、"considering"、"in consideration of" 等引导原因。

2. 弄清目的所在

从语用的角度来分析，涉外合同中含有目的状语的条款通常表示为了实现某一目标缔约方须采取的行动或承担的义务，所以目的通常是次要信息，行文时以位于句末为主。在通常情况下，目的状语译成中文时可以用 "以便" 译出，保持英文原文的顺序。

3. 弄清日期设定

在条件的设定中往往要附加时间限制，这样才能进一步明确条件的具体事项。

"prior to"、"on or before"、"no（not）later than"、"on or after" 常用在涉外合同中限定日期。"prior to" 表示 "某日之前，提前多少日"。"on or before"、"no（not）later than" 表示 "不迟于"，"on or after" 表示 "从某日起"。

4. 弄清实现方式

从形式上来看，涉外合同中的方式状语通常位于它们修饰的动词之前或之后，由副词或介词短语充当，结构上有的比较简短，有的相当冗长。从语用特征的角度来看，它们通常都是规定性的，其作用是规定合约方履行某项义务必须采取的方式或手段，在合同的语言环境下，即使有关合约方履行了合同规定的义务，但若其履行义务的方式与合同规定的方式不符，则仍构成违约。因此，方式状语有时尽管结构简单，但在句中的作用通常都是比较重要的。按照汉语的行文规范，方式状语一般应位于动词之前。此外，若动词同时带有时间状语和方式状语时，英文的通常顺序是方式在前而时间在后，而汉语正好与之相反，为方式在后而时间在前。

5. 理清相互关系

为了说明条件，有时也可能出现一些理清相互关系的关联词，关系明确了，权利义务自然清晰了。

三、平行结构：简单明了的合同条款描述方式

在涉外合同中，为便于对条款的理解，常使用平行结构进行条款描述。这既可以提高合同描述的语域，又能做到简洁明了，使权利义务的设置清晰，便于理解。

（一）平行结构的理解

所谓平行结构（parallelism），就是将一个词、词组或句子在逻辑上应属于同一句法成分的并列事物用相同的结构来表达。

1. 平行结构的特点与要求

平行结构指的就是内容相似、结构相同、无先后顺序、无因果关系的并列词、词组或并列句。

平行结构中总有其成分表现出一致 。它具有以下四个特点：

（1）形式上互补。

（2）结构上平行。

（3）内容上相互对应。

（4）术语用词上对等。

2. 使用平行结构的目的

平行结构应用在合同条款中主要为达到以下目的：

（1）防止歧义。

（2）相互照应。

（3）层次清晰。

（4）责任明晰。

平行结构主要由以下几种方式来连接形成：

（1）以词为主进行连接。

（2）以词组为主进行连接。

（3）以分句为主进行连接。

EG – 5 – 6 Whether, under the contract, the engineer is required to exercise his direction by:

①Giving his decision, opinion or consent, or

②Expressing his satisfaction or approval, or

③Determining value, or

④Otherwise taking action which may affect the rights and obligations of the employer or the contractor, he shall exercise such discretion impartially within the terns of the contract.

上述①、②、③、④以分句形式通过"or"（或）逻辑构成平行结构。

参考译文：凡按商务合同规定，要求工程师根据自己的判断，自行：

① 作出决定，表示意见或同意，或

② 表示满意或批准，或

③ 确定价值，或

④ 采取可能影响雇主或承包商权利和义务的行为时，他应当在商务合同条款规定的范围内，作出公正的处理。

前两种一般构成类聚词，后一种形成意群结构。

（二）平行结构的外部特征

为使句子前后保持平衡和协调，句中的并列成分应在结构上保持一致。这是平行结构最显著的外部特征。其一般常用"or"、"either...or"、"neither...nor"、"not only ...but also"等连接的名词或代词做主语，需要注意的是谓语动词形式要同最近的主语保持一致。

合同中有两种平行结构，一种是通过"and"或"by"连接句子；另一种是将短语逐个列出。但从外部特征来看，其主要有以下形式：

（1）所连接的主语形式必须一致。

① 具有相同的主语。

② 主语间互为对义词。

（2）所连接的谓语形式必须一致。

① 行为内容具有互补性。

② 行为内容具有反对关系。

③ 通过否定并列。

④ 所连接的词或短语形式必须一致。

⑤ 连接的非谓语动词的形式必须一致。

⑥ 所连接的介词短语或宾语补语一致。

⑦ 所连接的定语一致。

⑧ 所连接的句子结构必须一致。

第6章

依照性关键词：权利义务
条款约定的依据所在

"根据"、"依据"、"按照"的表达在涉外合同中使用得非常频繁，特别是有关重要的责任义务条款和相关当事人如何行使权利、如何履行合同的规定，总会设置一定标准或规范，以便当事人更好地执行。一般来说，依照性关键词所引出的内容要么依据法律、法规，要么依据本合同其他条款的相应规定或者依据双方当事人协商而进行。为便于对合同整体的分析与理解，此类表述必须非常明确、清晰，不可含糊，否则就可能存在较大风险。

一、依照性关键词的常用形式

能够在涉外合同中表达"根据"、"依照"等的英文关键词主要有"in accordance with"、"under"、"subject to"、"on the basis of"等10多个。这里统称为依照性关键词，详细分析如下。

1. any of the following

EG – 6 – 1 This agreement, and all rights vested in the

second party, shall forthwith become null and void, if the second party shall violate, or omit to perform, any of the following terms and conditions.

"any of the following" 就属于依照性关键词，意指前文所说的 "violate, or omit to perform" 要根据随后所附的条款作为对照或依据。其一般可引出较为具体、详细的约定。

"following" 意为 "下述"，"any" 意为 "下述的事项"，为 "or" 连接形式。

参考译文：本合同和所有授予乙方的权利，应立即生效，如果乙方违反或怠于行使下述条款。

2. by

EG‐6‐2 The contract shall observe and abide by all applicable laws, rules and regulations in connection with the work.

该条款中 "by" 就属于依照性关键词，为 "observe and abide"（遵守）提供了依据。其一般可引出相应的法律或具体的行为。

参考译文：合同应严格遵守所有与工程项目相适用的法律、法规和规章。

3. comply with

EG‐6‐3 All the activities of a joint venture shall comply with the provision of laws , decree and pertinent regulations of the people's republic of china.

"comply with" 属于依照性关键词，为 "all the activities" 提供了依据。其一般可引出相应的法律、法规。

参考译文：合资公司的所有活动应遵守中华人民共和国的法律、法规和相关规章的规定。

4. according to

EG‐6‐4 A tender price offered by a tender shall remain unchanged during the performance of the contract, and shall not be modified because of any reasons. According to clause 24 of the notice, tender documents contai-ning any adjustable prices will be rejected as non – responsive tenders.

"according to" 属于依照性关键词，为 "adjustable prices" 提供了参考。这样，"the tender" 就要认真研究 "documents containing any adjustable prices"，否则就可能被作为非响应性投标而予以拒绝。其一般可引出具体的条款。

参考译文：通过投标人的投标报价应在履行合同期间维持不变，不得因任何原因而被修改，不遵守通知的第 24 条规定，投标文件含有任何调价因素的，将被作为对招标没有响应而被拒绝。

5. subject as, subject to

EG – 6 – 5 Subject to article *. * hereof, the grant of rights to the distributor under article * shall be exclusive and the supplier agrees not to directly or indirectly sell the products to any party other than the distributor in the territory.

在涉外合同中 "subject to" 常用于限定性表达语言，意为 "以……为条件"、"受……限制" 等，即必须优先满足 "subject to" 引导的条件才可以行使主旨句中的权利或从事主旨句中的行为。

参考译文：以本协议第 *. * 条的约定为条件，根据第 * 条授予经销商的权利是独占性的，供货商同意不直接或间接地将商品出售给指定地域内除经销商以外的任何其他地方。

6. under

"under" 在普通英文中表示 "在……下"，但在涉外合同中通常用来表示 "根据……"，并且这种用法在涉外合同中极为常见。《联合国国际货物销售合同公约》中一共有 47 处用了 "under"，其中有 43 处用法皆表示 "根据……"、"依据……"。FIDIC 银皮书共 208 处用了 "under"，而红皮书则有 210 处，大部分也都是后一种用法。因此，"under this contract" 表示 "根据/依据本协议"；"under the laws of PRC" 表示 "根据/依据中华人民共和国法律"；"under article 5" 表

示 "根据/依据第5条"。"根据本公约" 可以用 "under this convention" 表示，而 "根据前款规定" 则可用 "under the preceding paragraph" 表示。

例如，《联合国国际货物销售合同公约》第42条（1）规定如下。

EG－6－6 The Seller must deliver goods which are free from any right or claim of a third party based on industrial property or other intellectual property, of which at the time of the conclusion of the contract the Seller knew or could not have been unaware, provided that the right or claim is based on industrial property or other intellectual property：(a) under the law of the State where the goods will be resold or otherwise used, if it was contemplated by the parties at the time of the conclusion of the contract that the goods would be resold or otherwise used in that State.

参考译文：卖方所交付的货物，必须是第三方不能根据工业产权或其他知识产权主张任何权利或要求的货物，但以卖方在订立合同时已知道或不可能不知道的权利或要求为限，而且这种权利或要求根据以下国家的法律规定是以工业产权或其他知识产权为基础的：

（a）如果双方当事人在订立合同时预期货物将在某一国境内转售或作其他使用，则根据货物将在其境内转售或作其他使用的国家的法律。

7. set forth in

EG－6－7 The contract price set forth in this contract shall not include any withholding tariff and any charges imposed on the contractor by the government in (countries).

分析：显然，"set forth in" 属于依照性关键词，限定了合同价格是本合同价格，而不能参考其他因素来决定，如市场、国家定价等。

参考译文：根据本合同规定，本合同价格将不包括代扣代缴任何国家机关对承包商征收的税款和费用。

EG－6－8 Nothing contained in exhibit shall supersede or annul the terms and provisions aforesaid.

显然，"aforesaid"属于依照性关键词，意指"上述"，也就是说不应延伸至以后的条款，是否适用根据具体情况具体分析。

参考译文：有所展示中含有的内容不应取代、废除前述合同条款。

8. such extent as

EG – 6 – 9 The architect may withhold or nullify the whole or a part any certificate to such extent as may be necessary in his reasonable opinion to protect the owner from loss.

显然，"such extent as"属于依照性关键词，意指"根据"。

参考译文：建筑工程师依据他合理的判断为保护业主免受损失，可以在必要时撤销或取消整个或部分证书。

9. as stipulated

EG – 6 – 10 Under FOB terms, the Seller shall undertake to load the contracted goods on board the vessel nominated by the Buyer on any date notified by the Buyer, within the time of shipment as stipulated in Clause 8 of this Contract.

上述"under"、第二个"by"和"as stipulated"都属于依照性关键词。"as stipulated"一般用来引出具体的合同条款。

参考译文：根据离岸价格术语，卖方应保证根据在本合同第8条规定的时限内，按买方通知的日期，装运货物至买方指定的船只。

10. on the basis of

EG – 6 – 11 The Contract is performed on the basis of equality.

关键词"on the basis of"引出了一个适用的合同法原则，一般译为"基于"、"依照"等。

参考译文：（双方当事人）基于平等原则履行合同。

11. in accordance with

EG - 6 - 12 In accordance with the Law of the People's Republic of China on Chinese - Foreign Cooperative Joint Ventures and other relevant Chinese laws and regulations,　__A__　Company and　__B__　Company, in accordance with the principle of equality and mutual benefit and through friendly consultations, agree to jointly set up a cooperative venture in ＊＊ the People's Republic China.

上述使用了两个依照性条款"in accordance with"，一个引出适用的法律、法规，另一个引出合同的基本原则。"in accordance with"所引导的两组介词词组紧凑在一起，为避免重复，可分别译为"根据"和"本着"。

参考译文：依照《中华人民共和国中外合作投资法》和其他相关中国法律、法规的规定，甲乙两公司基于平等、互惠和友好协商原则，同意在中华人民共和国＊＊地点联合设立合资企业。

12. adhering to

EG - 6 - 13 Whereas Party A and Party B, adhering to the principle of equality and mutual benefit and through friendly consultation, agree to jointly invest to establish a new joint venture company in China (hereinafter referred as "Joint Venture"). The Contract hereunder is made and concluded.

"adhering to" 意为"遵循"。

参考译文：鉴于甲乙双方遵循平等、互惠和友好协商原则，同意联合投资在中国设立一家合资公司（以下称合资企业），达成以下合同内容。

二、依照性关键词引导的内容

应用依照性关键词的目的就是为合同双方提供履行合同的标准或规范，保障所订立的合同能实际履行，或者说有依据可参照。一般来讲，通过依照性关键词可引出以下可供参照的标准或规范。

1. 引出合同规定或国际商务惯例

EG－6－14 Where the Supplier is required under the contract to deliver the goods CIF or CIF, transport of the goods to the port of destination or such other named place of destination, as shall be specified in the contract, shall be arranged and paid for by the Supplier, and the cost thereof shall be included in the contract price.

本条款以"under"引出依照标准为"CIF or CIF: under the Contract to deliver the Goods CIF or CIF"。

本条款以"as"引出依照标准为合同规定，即"other named place of destination, as shall be specified in the contract"。

对于卖方来讲，可能存在其他目的地不明确的问题，卖方因此要有承担这一风险的准备。

参考译文：当供货商不依照合同 CIF 或 CIF 条款规定移交货物，并将货物运输到指点目的港或依照合同约定指定的目的地时，供货商应自付费用，安排运输，且该项费用包括在合同价款中。

EG－6－15 The terms CFR, or CIF shall be subject to the International Rules for the Interpretation of Trade Terms (INCOTERMS 2010) provided by the International Chamber of Commerce unless otherwise stipulated herein.

"subject to"引出具体的通则规定。

参考译文：除非另有规定，"CFR"和"CIF"均应依据国际商会制定的《2000 年国际贸易术语解释通则》(INCOTERMS 2010) 办理。

2. 引出招标文件的相关规定

EG－6－16 The successful Bidder's bid security will be discharged upon the Bidder signing the contract, pursuant to ITB Clause 34, and furnishing the performance security, pursuant to ITB Clause 35, and payment of Tendering service fee, pursuant to ITB Clause 36.

本条款用了三个相同的依照性关键词："pursuant to"，以提示投标人中标后保证金的退回条件：一是按照须知第 34 条规定签订了合同；二是按照须知第 35 条交纳了履约保证金；三是按照须知第 36 条规定交纳了招标服务费。三个依照缺一不可，投标人应重点关注。

风险：如果招标人没有按照其中之一的依照性条款履行责任，就有可能被没收投标保证金。通过下面条款的描述就更清楚本条款的目的了。

参考译文：中标人的投标保证金，在中标人按本须知第 34 条规定签订了合同，按本须知第 35 条规定交纳了履约保证金，并按本须知第 36 条规定交纳了招标服务费后予以退还。

EG – 6 – 17 The bid security is required to protect the Tendering Agent and the Tenderer against the risk of Bidder's conduct which would warrant the security's forfeiture, pursuant to ITB Clause 15. 7.

"pursuant to" 引导具体的依据标准。结合招标文件前后条款的规定，本条中所谓的行为受到损害，其参照标准就是前述条款的三个依照。

参考译文：投标保证金是为了保护招标机构和招标人免于因投标人的行为而蒙受损失。招标机构和招标人在因投标人的行为受到损害时可根据本须知第 15.7 条的规定没收投标人的投标保证金。

3. 引出一方当事人的同意

EG – 6 – 18 Agency shall not commence work on any project pursuant to this agreement without first estimating costs for preparation, including copy, service layout, art, engraving, typography, processing, paste up and production. After determining the estimated cost, completion of the work shall be subject to Advertiser's prior approval.

本合同条款使用了两个关键词：一是 "pursuant to"；二是 "subject to"。广告商的预先批准显然对于代理商来讲存在风险，应假想如果到时广告商不批准如何处理的问题。

参考译文：根据此协议，代理商不可以不进行任何费用评估就开始针对任何项目的工作，包括复印、服务设计、版画、版面设计、加工、粘贴和生产。在决定预计费用后，工作的完成应由广告商预先批准。

4. 引出相关法律规定

EG - 6 - 19 This agreement shall be construed and enforced in accordance with the laws of the state of China.

本条款以"in accordance with"引出应根据相关法律来理解和实施。这涉及本合同所有条款的适用，因此也排除了其他国家法律的适用。

参考译文：本协议应根据中国的法律来理解和实施。

5. 引出具体情况确定

EG - 6 - 20 In accordance with the specific circumstances of the project for which bids are invited, the bid inviting party may organize an on - the - spot survey of the project for the potential bidders.

本条款用"in accordance with"引导了"依具体情况而确定"。

参考译文：招标人根据招标项目的具体情况，可以组织潜在投标人踏勘项目现场。

EG - 6 - 21 On the FOB basis, the Buyer shall book shipping space in accordance with the date of shipment specified in the contract.

上述两条款都选用了"in accordance with"关键词，前者指依据招标项目的具体情况，显得十分含混，招标人可能组织踏勘项目现场，也可能不组织。因此，招标人对此应十分明确，注意保持与招标联系人的联系。后者指依据合同规定的装运日期，这就十分精确。这就要求买方与卖方在合同中约定精确的装运日期，否则该条款就可能无法履行了。

参考译文：按照 FOB 条件，由买方负责根据合同规定的装运日期洽定舱位。

EG－6－22 Advertiser shall not be obligated to reimburse agency for any travel or other out－of－pocket expenses incurred in the performance of services pursuant to this agreement unless expressly agreed by Advertiser in advance.

本条款使用关键词"pursuant to"引出了广告商支付的免责内容，也就是说其免责的依据是该部分内容，可能包含在价格中了。对于代理商来讲，其就要进一步审核合同价格中是否包含有相关的描述。

再者，"unless"属于除外条款，该例外是对于包含在合同价款中的"合同旅行费用或其他实付费用"可由广告商明确同意后额外支付还是除"合同旅行费用或其他实付费用"之外的其他额外费用支付也需要广告商明确同意表述得不是十分清楚，这显然对代理商不利。

参考译文：广告商将没有责任支付根据此项协议任何在执行此服务中所产生的任何旅行费用或其他实付费用，除非提前由广告商明确同意。

EG－6－23 Party B shall provide economic assurance according to Party A's requirement. The warrantor should be national enterprises or other companies that has complete compensational abilities.

本条款用"according to"引出了甲方有权要求乙方提供经济担保，但判断标准完全在甲方，因此乙方应对此高度关注。一是其实际资信情况是否能够满足甲方的要求在合同签订前就应明确核实，不能等合同签订后再去核实；如果难以核实，就要考虑第二个问题，即是否有具备资格的经济担保人，对此，国有企业好确认，但其他经济组织就难以判断了，到时只能完全由甲方认定。该条款显然对乙方十分不利。

参考译文：甲方根据乙方的资信情况，有权要求乙方提供经济担保。经济担保人必须是具有代为履行或代偿能力的国有企业或其他经济组织。

EG - 6 - 24 In the event of any dispute between areas arising as to whether a particular vessel shall be considered for commission, Manufacturer shall be the sole arbitrator to give final judgment according to the situation.

本条款以"according to"引出引起的任何争议的情况。这显然对分销商不利。

参考译文：假如在地区之间出现了对一种特别船只是否应被考虑收取佣金产生分歧，生产商应是根据此情况给出最终裁决的唯一仲裁者。

6. 引出同一合同约定的条款

EG - 6 - 25 If, in accordance with the provisions of the preceding paragraph, a shareholder fails to pay its subscribed capital contribution, the shareholder in question shall bear the responsibility of default to the other shareholders who have fully paid their capital contributions.

"in accordance with"引导出同一合同的具体规定。

参考译文：假如股东不按照前款规定缴纳所认缴的出资，应当向已足额缴纳出资的股东承担违约责任。

7. 引出一方遵守某一政策

EG - 6 - 26 The Company acknowledges that the consultant is an employee of Texas A & M University and is subject to the UT's policies, including policies concerning consulting, conflicts of interest, and intellectual property.

本条款用"subject to"引出咨询方要遵守的政策，实质上是咨询方是否违约的依据。由于后随"including"关键词，这样咨询方就要重点熟悉所包括的相关方面的政策。否则就可能违反一个雇员应承担的责任。

参考译文：咨询公司承认服务方是得克萨斯大学的一个雇员，并且遵守 UT 的政策，包括咨询、利益冲突和知识产权方面。

EG – 6 – 27 The State shall, in accordance with the industrial policies, guide the orientation of foreign investment and encourage the establishment of such enterprises with foreign investment as adopt advanced technology and equipment and as export all or most of their products.

"in accordance with" 引导产业政策。至于是什么产业政策需要进一步查找、落实。

参考译文：国家按照产业政策，引导外商投资方向，鼓励举办采用先进技术、设备、产品全部或者大部分出口的外商投资企业。

EG – 6 – 28 If a bidder, on the basis of the actual circumstances of the project as specified in the bid invitation documents, intends to subcontract out some of the non – principal, non – key parts of the work after its bid is accepted, it shall specify the same in the bid documents.

If a bidder, on the basis of the actual circumstances of the project as specified in the bid invitation documents, intends to subcontract out some of the non – principal, non – key parts of the work after its bid is accepted, it shall specify the same in the bid documents.

上述两个条款应用 "on the basis of"、"as specified in" 两个关键词引出了项目的实际情况，判断分析是否能够分包的责任显然在投标人。作为一个有经验的投标人，对此应足够重视：一是要弄清项目的实际情况是什么；二是哪些应在招标文件中分包载明；还要考虑分包人也应当具备相应的资格条件，并不得再次分包，否则就有可能承担违约责任。

参考译文：投标人根据招标文件载明的项目实际情况，拟在中标后将中标项目的部分非主体、非关键性工作进行分包的，应当在投标文件中载明。

中标人按照合同约定或者经招标人同意，可以将中标项目的部分非主体、非关键性工作分包给他人完成。接受分包的人应当具备相应的资格条件，并不得再次分包。

8. 引出合同或当事人的同意

EG – 6 – 29 Subject to the provisions of the contract or the consent of the bid inviting party, the winning bidder may subcontract out the completion of some of the non – principal, non – key parts of the work for the project which it has won. The delivering of the goods be performed in accordance with the ＊＊ provisions of the contract.

该条款应用了"subject to"，意在引出依照合同条款或邀标方的同意。

"in accordance with"意在引出合同的具体条款，属于依照性关键词，意指交付货物的行为依照＊＊条规定。该关键词在合同文书中比较常用，比"according to"要正式。

参考译文：依据合同条款或投标邀请人的同意，中标人可以将中标工程项目的非主体、非关键性部分分包出去，根据合同条款第＊＊条规定履行货物的交付义务。

9. 引导参照市场价格

EG – 6 – 30 In respect of incomes obtained by enterprises in the form of non – monetary assets or rights and interests, the incomes in question shall be computed or appraised at prevailing market prices.

"at prevailing market prices"意为"参照当时的市场价格"。

参考译文：企业取得的收入为非货币资产或者权益的，其收入额应当参照当时的市场价格计算或者估定。

第 7 章

假设性关键词：合同约定不确定性因素的合理评估

在涉外合同中，由于不确定性因素的存在，谈判中的条件会随着时间的推移发生变化，因此要事先作出假设，对条件变化的情况进行合理评估，从而有效化解风险。对于英文合同来讲，英语从句中条件状语的位置十分灵活，可以位于句首、句中或句末，根据行文的需要以上下文的连贯性为依据任意摆布；汉语占主导地位的行文方式则通常将表示假设条件的状语从句放在句首。同时，由于汉语的句式结构以偏正结构为主，即通常是复句的主句在后、从句在前。所以，在一般的情况下，我们在翻译涉外合同中含有表示假设条件的状语的疑难长句时，可以首先考虑将状语的位置移到句首，从而突出句子的核心部位，而且简化其结构。此外，涉外合同中含有假设条件的条款通常又含有自己的时间状语和原因状语来界定该假设条件发生的时效性以及原因，对于此类条件状语中所含有的时间状语和原因状语，我们一般都可以按照前文所述置于所修饰的动词之前。

一、假设性条款的常用关键词

表达"如果"、"假如"、"只要"的条件关键词主要有"if and whenever"、"in the event of /that"、"in case"、"where"和"should"等。"should"和"where"从句假设的条件一般是在违背当事人意志的不利情况时采用，多属当事人不愿意发生的事项，且多用在条文开头并倒装。

此外，"provided（that）/providing（that）"、"on condition that"也可表示实现某结果的前提条件，一般用于句末，结合除外条件关键词，一般可译为"但是"，归入但书性关键词。

1. if

EG –7 –1 If under the contract the Buyer is to specify the form, the measurement or other features of the goods and he fails to make such specification either on the date agreed upon or within a reasonable time after the receipt of a request from the Seller, the Seller may, without prejudice to any other rights he may have, make the specification himself in accordance with the requirements of the Buyer that may be known to him.

本条款除了用"if"作引导外，还包含一个方式状语"without prejudice to any other rights he may have"，考虑到它在句中所起的补充说明的作用，翻译时转换成并列句处理。

条件状语从句用以表示"在某种条件下，会……"，常用"if"、"in case"，"on condition"等词来引导。"if"引导的条件句有真实条件句和非真实条件句两种：由于合同中约定的条款事项一般是将来与现在存在的事实或行为，因此合同条款一般不用过去时态或现在进行时态。合同条款都是真实条件，很少用非真实条件句，也就是说很少用虚拟语气。只是合同草拟方担心不可能发生的事项时，常用"Should"置于句首，以提醒己方合同执行人关注。

有时，存在"if"与其他副词或连词连用的情形，如"if and whenever"。

参考译文：若按本合同之规定应由买方决定货物的形状、尺寸或其他特征，但买方在双方议定的时间内，或在收到卖方的要求后的合理期限内，未能作出上述规定的，则卖方有权根据买方的已知要求自行规定。此情况不损害买方享有的任何其他权利。

2. in the event that

EG – 7 – 2 In the event that either party hereto fails to comply with the terms or conditions of this agreement, and, within 90 days after the written notice is issued by the other Party hereto, fails to remedy such failure, the Party giving notice may, forthwith, notify the other Party of the matter in question and terminate this agreement.

"in the event that" 引导具体的条件。"in the event that" 比 "when" 正式，在此条款中，其引导合同终止的条件。

参考译文：当任何一方当事人不执行本合同条款规定的，且在合同另一方当事人签发的书面通知 90 天后仍不修补这一缺陷的，给予书面通知的当事人可以就相关事项立即通知另一方，并终止本合同。

EG – 7 – 3 Either Party hereto may terminate this agreement in the event of the bankruptcy or insolvency of the other party.

"in the event that" 后可接从句，也可接名词性短语。

参考译文：当一方当事人处于破产或清算时，另一方当事人可以终止合同。

3. where

EG – 7 – 4 Where the contract provides for payment in whole or in part to be made to the contractor in foreign currency or currencies, such payment shall not be subject to variations in the rate or rates of exchange between such specified foreign currency or currencies and the currency of the country in which the works are to be executed.

"where" 在此处作 "如果" 讲。

参考译文：如果合同规定将全部或部分款额以一种或几种外币支

付给承包商，则此项支付不应受上述的一种或几种外币与施工所在国货币之间的汇率变化的影响。

4. should

EG – 7 – 5 Should for certain reasons the Buyers not be able to inform the Seller of the foregoing details 10 days prior to the arrival of the vessel at the port of loading or should the carrying vessel be advanced or delayed, the Buyer or their chartering agent shall advise the Sellers immediately and make necessary arrangements.

句中出现两个条件从句：第一个条件状语中又包含了一个原因状语和一个时间状语，译成中文时应保持原文的顺序。原因状语和时间状语位于所修饰的动词之前，通常的顺序是原因在前、时间在后。"should"引导的从句属于非真实条件句，即虚拟语气，表示该条件发生的可能性很小，是当事人不希望出现的不利情况。而"on condition that"引导的条件从句往往表示只要某情况出现就如何如何。

参考译文：若买方由于某种原因不能于装运轮抵达装运港10天前将上述详细情况通知卖方，或装运轮提前或推迟抵达，买方或其运输代理人须立即通知卖方并作出必要的安排。

5. on condition that

EG – 7 – 6 The Lessee was granted the lease on condition that they paid the legal costs.

"on condition that"虽可译为"基于某一条件"，但其更具有假设的成分。根据此条款，显然支付在先而获得租赁权在后，且获得租赁权前法定费用必没有支付。如果已经支付，就不是条件句而为依据性关键词了。

参考译文：在支付法定费用的条件下他们可获得租赁权。

6. in case

EG – 7 – 7 In case the quality, quantity, weight of the goods are not in conformity with the provisions of the contract after arrival of the goods at the port of destination, the Buyer may, under survey report issued by an inspection organization agreed by the parties thereto, lodge claim with the Seller, with the exception, however, of those claims for which the insurance company and/or the shipping company shall be responsible.

"in case" 意为 "假设"、"一旦"，一般位于句首，常与 "however"（但是）配合使用。

参考译文：在货物运抵目的港后，一旦发现货物质量、数量或重量与合同的规定不符，买方可以根据双方同意的检验组织所出具的检验证书向卖方索赔，但是应由保险公司或航运公司负责的损失除外。

7. in the case of

EG – 7 – 8 In the case of carriage by sea or by more than one mode of transport including carriage by sea, banks will refuse a transport document stating that the goods are or will be loaded on deck, unless specifically authorized in the credit.

"in the case of" 意为 "如果"，一般位于句首。

参考译文：如属海运或多种类型运输中包括海运，除非信用证特别授权，银行将拒收注明货装舱面或将装舱面的运输单据。

8. in so far as

EG – 7 – 9 Notwithstanding the completion of the sale and purchase of the ordinary shares in the company, the terms and conditions of this agreement shall remain in full force and effect as between the parties hereto in so far as the same are not fulfilled.

"in so far as" 意为 "只要"，一般位于句中。

参考译文：即使买卖公司普通股已经结束，只要该行为尚未履行完毕，本协议条款对双方仍然完全有效。

9. subject to

EG – 7 – 10 Subject to the conditions hereinafter set forth, Party B will protect…

"subject to"具有假设满足某些条件的意思，但更多地是为合同履行方提供依据，因此，本书将其列入依据性关键词中，具体详见前章相关条款。

参考译文：在下列情况下，乙方将保证……

10. suppose that

EG – 7 – 11 As an example, suppose that Stamps. com has a partnership agreement with a company called "Internet Marketing". In this example, "Partner Name" would be "Internet Marketing".

"suppose that"意为"假设"。

参考译文：试举一例，如果 Stamps. com 公司与一家名叫 Internet Marketing 的公司有一合伙协议。本例中，该"合伙名称"就是"Internet Marketing"。

11. provided that if

EG – 7 – 12 In respect of the computation of depreciation of fixed assets, the salvage value shall first be estimated and deducted from the original cost of the assets. The salvage value shall not be less than 10% of the original value. Provided that if any retaining a lower salvage value or no salvage value is requested, the matter in question shall be approved by the local tax authorities.

"provided that if"意为"如果"，有时也可根据前后文推断出，因此可不译出。

参考译文：对于固定资产的折旧计算，应当估价残值，从固定资产原价中减除。残值应当不低于原价的10%；需要少留或者不留残值的，须经当地税务机关批准。

二、假设性关键词在合同条款中的应用

1. 假设性关键词常出现在合同终止条款中

合同签订后，会因各种情况导致合同终止的情形，在出现这一情况后，对于如何处理相关的事务，常用到假设性关键词。

EG – 7 – 13 In case the contract terminates prematurely, the contract appendices shall likewise terminate.

参考译文：如果本合同提前终止，则合同附件也随之终止。

2. 在合同中约定履行某一义务或享有某一权利时，商定约定的条件

双方在合同履行过程中如果出现某一种情况，常约定前提条件，否则依此享有权利就可不具有效力。

EG – 7 – 14 Either side can replace the representatives it has appointed provided that it submits a written notice to the other side.

"provided that" 在此引导条件句，起但书作用。

参考译文：任何一方都可更换自己指派的代表，但须书面通知对方。

3. 设定引起违约责任的前提条件，以此分清违约责任方

一般在合同中如出现违约责任则涉及追究哪一方责任的问题，因此常用假设性条款引出违约责任方，以此界定合同责任的主体。

由于违约是双方都不愿意发生的事，因此常用 "should" 开头，引导倒装句来说明违约的原因。

EG – 7 – 15 Should all or part of the contract be unable to be fulfilled owing to the fault of one party, the breaching party shall bear the responsibilities thus caused. Should it be the fault of both parties, they shall bear their respective responsibilities according to actual situations.

参考译文：由于一方的过失，造成本合同不能履行或不能完全履行时，由过失一方承担违约责任。若属双方过失，则根据实际情况，

由双方分别承担各自应负的违约责任。

4. 设定索赔事项，以此分清索赔的对象

在合同履行中，会因一方的违约而造成对方的损失，因此可通过假设索赔事项来分清责任的索赔对象。

EG – 7 – 16 In the event of any loss caused by the delay in the delivery, the Representative can claim a compensation from the Manufacturer with a certificate and detailed list registered by the administration authorities of the Representative's site.

"in the event of" 一般引导违约索赔的具体项目。

参考译文：若因任何交货延误导致的代理方损失，代理方可凭代理方所在地行政当局登记的损失清单向制造方索赔，但须出具证明。

5. 设定侵权等合同无关方行为事项，以此确定责任方

在合同履行过程中，可能产生并不属于任何一方的责任，因此可通过约定无关方行为来确定责任方。

EG – 7 – 17 If the third party accuses the Party B of infringement, Party B shall take up the matter...

参考译文：如果第三方指控乙方侵权，乙方应负责……

6. 假设履行合同环境发生变更的条件

合同签订后，履行合同的环境或市场情况会发生变化，因此可通过假设来引出发生变化的情形。

EG – 7 – 18 Should the Seller make delivery on time as stipulated in the contract with the exception of force majeure specified in Clause18 to this contract, the Buyer shall agree to postpone the delivery on condition that the Seller agree to pay a penalty which shall be deducted by the paying bank from the payment under negotiation.

参考译文：如果卖方并非因本合同第18条规定的不可抗力事件而未按合同规定的期限交货，那么只要卖方同意支付罚金，并由付款

行从议付款中扣除，买方便同意卖方延期交货。

7. 设定双方发生争议时的情形，以此确定解决争议的办法或途径

EG - 7 - 19 In case there is any breach of the provisions under this agreement by either Party during the effective period of this agreement, the Parties hereto shall first of all try to settle to mutual satisfaction the matter in question as soon as possible.

参考译文：在本协议有效期间，任何一方对本协议的条款有违背时，缔约双方应首先尽可能迅速友好地解决有关问题，使双方都满意。

EG - 7 - 20 In case no settlement can be reached through consultations, the disputes shall be submitted to the China International Economic and Trade Arbitration Commission for arbitration in accordance with its rules of procedure.

"in case no" 意为 "如果不"，其中的否定词往往是对谓语的否定，而不是对主语的否定。

参考译文：如果协商不能解决，争执事项则应提交给中国国际经济贸易仲裁委员会，根据该会的仲裁程序进行仲裁。

8. 设定拒绝履行义务的前提

EG - 7 - 21 Vessel over 20 years of age shall in no event is acceptable to the Buyer.

参考译文：船龄超过 20 年的，买方概不接受。

9. 设定一方行使权利的前提条件

在涉外合同中有很多条件往往是为一方行使权利而设定的，或者是为一方履行义务而设定的，也就是附条件成交的情形。

EG - 7 - 22 During the term of this contract, in case that the borrower changes the pattern of management or the ownership construction by the means of contracting, leasing, pooling, transforming to stock company, establishing joint venture, separating, merger, foreign investment, transferring of owner-ship, resolving or any other action, the borrower shall seek the lender's consent and ascertain the new source of repayment or provide new security.

参考译文：合同期间，如果借方希望通过协议、租赁、联营、变更为股份有限责任公司、组建合资企业、分立、合并、对外投资、所有权转让、解散或其他行为改变经营方式或所有权结构，借方应当取得贷方的同意，并确定新的还款渠道或提供新的担保。

10. 约定条款效力前提

在合同条款中，有时需要为约定的条款发生效力设定前提，也就是若不出现某一假定的情况则合同条款不发生效力。

EG – 7 – 23 Notwithstanding the completion of the sale and purchase of the ordinary shares in the company, the terms and conditions of this agree-ment shall remain in full force and effect as between the parties hereto in so far as the same are not fulfilled.

参考译文：即使买卖公司普通股已经结束，只要该行为尚未履行完毕，本协议条款对双方仍然完全有效。

三、假设性关键词的作用

1. 为承担额外义务设定前提的关键词

EG – 7 – 24 In case Party B considers it necessary to employ a foreign auditor registered in another country to undertake annual financial verifica-tion and examination, Party A shall give its consent. All the expenses there-of shall be borne by Party B.

参考译文：如果乙方认为需要聘请另一国注册审计师对年度财务进行审查，甲方应予以同意，其所需的一切费用应由乙方负担。

2. 为拒绝履行义务设定前提

EG – 7 – 25 Should any inspected or tested Goods fail to conform to the specifications, the Purchaser may reject the goods, and the Supplier shall either replace the rejected Goods or make alterations necessary to meet specification requirements free of cost to the Purchaser.

参考译文：如果任何被检验或测试的货物不能满足规格的要求，买方可以拒绝接受该货物，卖方应更换被拒绝的货物，或者免费进行必要的修改以满足规格的要求。

3. 为履行义务设定前提条件

EG – 7 – 26 15% of the above contract price, e. g. US MYM ＊＊ shall be paid by Party A to Party B by M/T within 30 days after Party A has received from Party B the following technical documentations and documents and providing that they are in conformity with the contract.

参考译文：甲方从乙方处收到以下技术资料和文件后30天内应信汇乙方上述合同总价的15%，也就是＊＊美元，但该技术资料和文件应符合本合同要求。

4. 设定义务完成的前提

EG – 7 – 27 In case part of or all knowhow of the above – mentioned technical contents have been published by Party B or Third Parties A, obtains evidence of such publication, then Party A shall no longer be responsible for keeping secret and confidential the part already published.

参考译文：如上述专有技术的一部分或全部已由第三方公布，而甲方也掌握了已公布的证据，则甲方不再承担保密义务。

5. 为额外行使权利设定前提

EG – 7 – 28 The Buyer shall have the right to claim against the Seller for compensation of losses within 60 days after arrival of the goods at the port of destination, should the quality of the goods be found not in conformity with the specifications stipulated in the contract after re – inspection by the China Commodity Inspection Bureau and the Buyer shall have the right to claim against the Sellers for compensation of short – weight within 60 days after arrival of the goods at the port of destination, should the weight be found not in conformity with that stipulated in the Bill of Lading after re – inspection by the CCIB.

此句由两个结构相同的并列分句组成，均为主句在前、条件状语在后，在两个条件状语中均含有时间状语。此外，两个并列分句中也都含有时间状语，均为"within 60 days after arrival of the goods at the port of destination"，译成中文时，条件状语应分别置于主句之前，而所有的时间状语均放在各自修饰的动词前面。同时，为了符合汉语句式较短的特点，可以将两个并列分句断开，分解成两个单句。

参考译文：若货物经中国商品检验局复检后发现质量与本合同之规定不符，买方有权于货物抵达目的港后的 60 天内向卖方提出索赔。若经中国商品检验局复检发现货物质量与提单所示重量不符，买方有权于货物抵达目的港后的 60 天内向卖方提出短重索赔。

6. 为丧失权利设定条件

EG – 7 – 29 In any event, the Buyer loses the right to rely on a lack of conformity of the goods if he does not give the Seller notice thereof at the attest within a period of two years from the date on which the goods were actually handed over to the Buyer, unless this time – limit is inconsistent with a contractual period of guarantee.

参考译文：无论如何，如果买方在实际收到货物之日起两年内不将货物不符合合同的情形通知卖方，他将丧失声称货物不符合合同的权利，但这一时限与合同规定的保证期限不符的除外。

第8章

除外关键词：协商一致的利益保护

"除非另有规定"在涉外合同中使用很频繁，其从字面看是一些对例外情况的约定，实际上是对主句约定权利义务的特别强调。其使用得当可以起到强制性效果，但使用不当就可能被对方钻空子。这个概念有多种表达方式，汉语的表达方式主要有"除非合同另有约定"、"除非法律另有规定"、"除非双方另有商定"等。

一、除外条款的常用关键词

英文中除外条款的表达方式主要有"except that"、"provide that"、"except as unless"、"until"、"save"等，法务人员在阅读与审核涉外合同的过程中要特别注意"除外条款"或"但书"的关键词所引导的句子在条款中的位置、起到的实际作用，否则很容易导致阅读与理解上的错误。

以"unless"为例，其可译为"除非"，和"otherwise"连用，且后面接过去分词。除外条款最常用的是"unless otherwise stipulated"和"except as otherwise provided"两种基本句型。"otherwise"后面的动词除上述"stipulate"和"provide"外，还可用"require"和"state"等。

1. save that if

EG – 8 – 1 Subject to Clause 18.4, each party shall bear its own costs arising out of or in connection with the preparation, negotiation and implementation of this agreement save that if this agreement is lawfully rescinded by the Purchaser, the Vendors shall pay to the Purchaser its accountancy, legal and other costs and expenses in relation to the investigation of the company prior to the date hereof and the preparation and negotiation of this agreement.

"save that if"意为"除非"。

参考译文：在遵守第18.4条的条件下，每一方应各自承担其准备、协商和实施本协议所产生的或与之有关的费用，除非如本协议系买方依法解除，则卖方应向买方支付与本协议订立前调查公司以及准备和协商本协议有关的会计、法律和其他花费和支出。

2. save as

EG – 8 – 2 Save as otherwise provided in this contract, each Party shall bear its own legal and other professional costs in relation to the preparation, negotiation and execution.

参考译文：除非本合同另有规定，各方负责自身为准备、谈判和签署合同所花费的律师服务费用。

3. save insofar as

EG – 8 – 3 The contractor shall make his own arrangements for the engagement of all labor, local or otherwise, and save insofar as the contract otherwise provides, for the transport, housing, feeding and payment thereof.

"save insofar as"意为"除……例外"。此条款中，例外显然有两种情况：一是明确约定由业主承担的除外；二是承包人应负责当地和外地劳工的交通、住宿和工资，如果本合同有其他规定，承包商还应承担相应责任，如一般承包合同中有对员工人身意外伤害保险的约定。

这里存在歧义：此处的例外是指责任承担主体例外还是指交通、住宿与工资之外的例外没有说清。

其修改应根据审核者所持立场来分析和判断。

参考译文：承包人必须自行安排雇佣所有当地和外地的劳工，并负责劳工的交通、食宿和工资，除本合同另有规定的例外。

4. unless

EG－8－4 Unless otherwise specified in the credit, banks will reject a transport document issued by a forwarding agent. Provided that unless such transport document is the FIATA combined Transport Bill of Lading approved by the International Chamber of Commerce or otherwise the transport document indicates that it is issued by a forwarding agent acting as a carrier or an agent of a named carrier.

该条款有两个"unless"除外关键词。第一个除外是说明本合同不得与信用证内容相抵触，否则就可能因冲突而失效；第二个除外是标准提单的除外，这就可能存在哪一个优先的问题。显然后一个除外是优先适用的。

这样，本条款就有三层意思：即标准单据是无论如何也不能被拒收的；对于符合信用证规定的运输单据银行也是要接收的；若不符合上述两个条件，则银行就会考虑拒收。

参考译文：除非信用证另有规定，银行将拒收运输行出具的运输单据，但是有"国际运输商协会联合会"的联合运输提单或注明运输行作为承运人或某承运人的代理人出具的运输单据除外。

5. except

EG－8－5 During the lease term of the equipments, any benefit accrued from the possession or use of the leased equipments belongs to the lessee, except otherwise agreed by the contract.

该条款需要通过排除的方式来肯定的显然是"在某种情况下，收益可能归出租人"。

参考译文：在设备租赁期间，因占有、使用该设备而获得的收益归承租人所有，但合同另有约定的除外。

6. except as

EG – 8 – 6 Except as otherwise provided herein, all notices and demands sent by registered airmail shall be deemed received 8 days after they have been sent and notices or demands sent by telex shall be deemed received at the time of the dispatch thereof.

参考译文：除非本合同另有规定，所有通知和请求以航空挂号信寄出后8日应视为送达收悉，以电传形式发出时则以发送时视为送达收悉。

7. except insofar as

EG – 8 –7 The Contractor shall be deemed to have satisfied himself as to the correctness and sufficiency of the Tender and of the rates and prices stated in the bill of quantities, all of which shall, except insofar as it is otherwise provided in the Contract, cover all his obligations under the Contract (including those in respect of the supply of goods, materials, plant or services or of contingencies for which there is a provisional sum) and all matters and things necessary for the things necessary for the proper execution and completion of the works and the remedying of any defects therein.

参考译文：应当认为承包商对自己的投标书以及工程量表中开列的各项费率和价格的正确性与完备性是满意的，除非合同中另有规定，所有这些应包括他根据合同应当承担的全部义务（包括有关物资、材料、工程设备或服务的提供或者为意外事件准备的临时金额），以及该工程的正确实施、竣工和修补其任何缺陷所必需的全部有关事宜。

二、除外条款的表述方式

除外条款常引出以下内容。

1. **除本合同另有明确规定外** (unless otherwise expressly provided for in this contract)

EG – 8 – 8 Unless otherwise expressly provided for in this contract, the Agent shall have no obligations to account to any Bank for any amount received in respect of any loan maintained by the Agent or any of its affiliates or for the profits related to the loan. The Agent and its affiliates may make loans to, accept deposits from, and generally engage in any kind of business with, the Borrower as though the Agent in question were not as an Agent.

参考译文：除本合同另有明确规定外，代理行没有义务向任何银行说明由于它或它的附属机构贷款而收到的金额或其利润。代理行及其附属机构可以向借款人贷款，接受借款人存款，并一般地与借款人进行各种经营活动，如同不是代理行一样。

2. **除双方另有约定外** (unless otherwise agreed by the parties)

EG – 8 – 9 Unless otherwise agreed by the parties to the contract, all expenses and disbursements, such as cabling, traveling and other expenses incurred in connection with the sale of products, shall be borne by the Agent. Provided that the Agent shall also bear the expenses for maintaining offices and other expenses for the performance of the obligations of the salesmen and for the implementation of the instructions given by the Seller.

参考译文：除另有约定外，所有的费用和支出，如电信费、差旅费以及其他有关商品销售的费用，都应由代理商承担。除此以外，代理商还应承担维护其正常办公所需的费用，及其他履行销售人员义务和执行卖方指示而发生的费用。

3. **除非另有规定** (unless otherwise agreed)

EG – 8 – 10 Notwithstanding any reference to arbitration, both Parties shall continue to perform their respective obligations under the Contract unless otherwise agreed.

参考译文：除非另有规定，仲裁不得影响合同双方继续履行合同所规定的义务。

4. 除非引用文件特别授权（unless otherwise specifically specified and authorized in the credit）

EG - 8 - 11 In the case of carriage by sea or by more than one mode of transport including carriage by sea, banks will refuse a transport document stating that the goods are or will be loaded on deck, unless otherwise specifically specified and authorized in the credit.

参考译文：如属海运或多种类型运输中包括海运，除非信用证特别授权，银行将拒收注明货装舱面或要装舱面的运输单据。

5. 除非其他事项中另有明确规定（save as expressly stated elsewhere in the license）

EG - 8 - 12 Save as expressly stated elsewhere in the License, neither party shall be liable to the other party for consequential, indirect, special, exemplary, or punitive losses or damages including loss of use or of profit or of contracts or of data, even if such party had been advised of the possibility thereof.

参考译文：除非许可中另有明确规定，任一方均不就后续、间接、特殊、惩罚性损失或赔偿金（包括使用损失、利润损失、合同损失或数据丢失）向另一方承担责任，即使该方已被告知该等损失发生的可能性。

三、除外条款常用的条款内容分类

在涉外合同中，主要针对以下内容设计除外条款，应引起法务人员的关注。

1. 用于违约金支付的例外

EG - 8 - 13 If Acceptance Standard still fails to be fulfilled in the further tests, Licensor shall pay Licensee liquidated damages as specified in Appendix 1, unless otherwise stipulated in contract. Licensee shall sign the acceptance certificate upon acceptance of the liquidated damages, while Licensor shall not be released from its guarantee obligations.

参考译文：如果在如下的考核中仍不能达到验收标准，除非合同另有规定，许可方应按照合同附件 1 的规定赔偿被许可方违约金，被许可方应在收到违约金后签署验收证书，但许可方的保证义务并没有免除。

2. 用于成本、费用支付的例外

EG - 8 - 14 Subject to clause 18.4, each party shall bear its own costs arising out of or in connection with the preparation, negotiation and implementation of this agreement save that if this agreement is lawfully rescinded by the Purchaser, the Vendors shall pay to the Purchaser its accountancy, legal and other costs and expenses in relation to the investigation of the company prior to the date hereof and the preparation and negotiation of this agreement.

参考译文：在遵守第 18.4 条的条件下，每一方应各自承担其准备、协商和实施本协议所产生的或与之有关的费用，除非如本协议系买方依法解除，则卖方应向买方支付与本协议订立前调查公司以及准备和协商本协议有关的会计、法律和其他花费和支出。

EG - 8 - 15 Unless otherwise agreed by the parties to the contract, all expenses and disbursements, such as cabling, traveling and other expenses incurred in connection with the sale of products, shall be borne by the agent. Provided that the Agent shall also bear the expenses for maintaining offices and other expenses for the performance of the obligations of the salesmen and for the implementation of the instructions given by the Seller.

后一段实质上属于并列条款，相当于所陈述的内容都应由代理商承担，但其应排除了合同的另有约定，也就是说即使合同另有约定，代理商还应承担维护其正常办公所需的费用，及其他履行销售人员义务和执行卖方指示而发生的费用，这些不在除外责任内。对此应引起注意。

参考译文：除另有约定外，所有的费用和支出，如电讯费、差旅费以及其他有关商品销售的费用，都应由代理商承担。除此以外，代理商还应承担维护其正常办公所需的费用，及其他履行销售人员义务和执行卖方指示而发生的费用。

3. 用于标的物风险转移的例外

EG – 8 – 16 The risk of damage to or loss of the goods shall be borne by the Seller prior to the delivery of the subject matter and by the Buyer after delivery, except as otherwise stipulated by law or agreed upon by the parties.

参考译文：货物毁损、灭失的风险，在货物交付之前由卖方承担，交付之后由买方承担，但法律另有规定或者双方另有约定的除外。

4. 用于标的物权利瑕疵的例外

EG – 8 – 17 Unless otherwise provided by law, the Seller shall have the obligation to warrant that no third party shall exercise against the Buyer any rights with respect to the delivered subject matter.

参考译文：卖方就交付的标的物，负有保证第三人不得向买方主张任何权利的义务，但法律另有规定的除外。

5. 对条款效力约定的例外

EG – 8 – 18 This provision shall apply to all documentary credits, including standby letters of credit, to the extent to which the credits in question shall be applicable, and shall be binding on the parties to the contract, unless otherwise expressly agreed by the Parties thereto.

参考译文：本条规定适用于一切跟单信用证，并包括在其适用范围内的备用信用证，除非另有约定，对合同各有关方面均具有约束力。

6. 对相关文件提交日期、方式的例外

提交日期的例外如：

EG - 8 - 19 Unless otherwise specified in the credit, banks will accept a document bearing a date of issuance prior to that of the credit, subject to such document being presented within the time limits specified in the credit and in these articles.

参考译文：除非信用证另有规定，银行将授受出单日期早于信用证开证日期的单据，但该单据须在信用证和本条文规定的时限之内提交。

7. 有关收益归属的例外

EG - 8 - 20 During the lease term of the equipments, any benefit accrued from the possession or use of the leased equipments belongs to the lessee, except otherwise agreed by the contract.

参考译文：在设备租赁期间，因占有、使用该设备获得的收益归承租人所有，但合同另有约定的除外。

8. 对相关文件解释的例外

EG - 8 - 21 Wherever, in the provisions of this contract, any such notice, consent, approval, certificate or determination as are made and issued by any person are mentioned, unless otherwise specified in this contract, such notice, consent, approval, certificate or determination shall be in writing, and the words "notify", "certify" or "determine" shall be construed accordingly. Provided that any such consent, approval, certificate or determination shall not unreasonably be withheld or delayed.

参考译文：本合同条款中，无论何处提及由任何人发出或颁发的任何通知、同意、批准、证明或决定，除合同另有说明者外，均指书面的通知、同意、批准、证明或决定，而通知、证明或决定字样均应据此解释。对于任何此类通知、同意、批准、证明或决定都不应被无故扣压或拖延。

9. 合同义务解除的例外

EG－8－22 Unless otherwise expressly provided for in this contract, the Agent shall have no obligations to account to any bank for any amount received in respect of any loan maintained by the Agent or any of its affiliates or for the profits related to the loan. The Agent and its affiliates may make loans to, accept deposits from, and generally engage in any kind of business with, the Borrower as though the Agent in question were not as an Agent.

参考译文：除本合同另有明确规定外，代理行没有义务向任何银行说明由于它或它的附属机构贷款而收到的金额或其利润。代理行及其附属机构可以向借款人贷款，接受借款人存款，并通常地与借款人进行各种经营活动，如同不是代理行一样。

10. 合同文本本身用词、定义的除外

EG－8－23 In the conditions of contract（"these conditions"）, which include particular conditions and these general conditions, the following words and expressions shall have the meanings stated. Words indicating persons or parties include corporations and other legal entities, except where the context requires otherwise.

参考译文：包括在专用条件和本通用条件的合同条件（"本合同条件"）中，以下措辞和用语的含义如下所述。除非上下文中另有要求，当事人和当事各方所指的词包含公司和其他法律实体。

四、但书条款的常用关键词

除外条款中还有一种专门的形式，那就是但书条款，其常用于对合同的某一条款需要作进一步规定时，或在作规定时语气上表示转折时使用。两者异曲同工，尽管有时从中文看没有但书规定、进一步规定的词语，但在进行英文阅读与理解时应加上"provided that"、"provided (that) /providing (that)"、"on condition that"等均表示实现某结果的前提条件，且一般用于句末。

此外，由于但书条款（如"provided that"）根据上下文可以看出是在同一条款中包含了两个条款，后一句为对前一句的进一步规定，从而在阅读与审核时要注意所持立场方权利与义务的例外情形。

1. subject to the provision

EG – 8 – 24 Legal Proceedings, Injunctions. (a) The Seller, the Buyer and the company shall use commercially reasonable efforts (subject to the provision in Section 5.6 (b)) to cooperate with each other in connection with any claim, action, suit, proceeding, inquiry or investigation with any other person which relates to the execution and delivery of this Agreement or the consummation of the transactions contemplated hereunder.

参考译文：法律诉讼；禁止令。（a）卖方、买方和本公司应竭尽全力（除本合同第5条第6款的但书规定外）（b）互相配合处理涉及本合同履行与交付及本合同项下预期交易完成的与他方有关的索赔、诉讼、案件、诉讼程式、质询或调查。

2. but

EG – 8 – 25 Tenant shall not be required to join in any proceedings referred to in the provision at the end of 4.6 hereof unless the provisions of any law, rule or regulation at the time in effect shall require that such proceedings be brought by or in the name of Tenant, in which event Tenant shall join and cooperate in such proceedings or permit the same to be brought in its name, but shall not be liable for the payment of any costs or expenses in connection with any such proceedings, and Landlord shall reimburse Tenant for, and indemnify and hold Tenant harmless from and against, any and all costs or expenses which Tenant may reasonably pay, sustain or incur in connection with any such proceedings.

需要说明的是，"but"在涉外合同中很少用于但书条款的引导，一般用"provided that"替代。

参考译文：承租人不得被应要求参加本合同第4条第6款最后但书/限制性条款提及的任何诉讼，除非当时生效的法律、法规要求该诉讼应由承租人或以承租人名义提起，此种情况下，承租人应参加配合该诉讼或允许该诉讼以其名义提起，但概不承担与该诉讼有关的任何费用和花费，业主应偿还并保证赔偿承租人合理支付的因该诉讼而产生或遭受的全部费用和花费且确保承租人免于以上责任。

3. however

EG-8-26 In case the quality, quantity, weight of the goods are not in conformity with the provisions of the contract after arrival of the goods at the port of destination, the Buyer may, under survey report issued by an inspection organization agreed by the parties thereto, lodge claim with the Seller, with the exception, however, of those claims for which the insurance company and/or the shipping company shall be responsible.

参考译文：在货物运抵目的港后，一旦发现货物质量、数量或重量与合同的规定不符，买方可以根据双方同意的检验组织所出具的检验证书向卖方索赔，但是应由保险公司或航运公司负责的损失除外。

4. provided that

EG-8-27 In case the products fail to meet the standards of Party A, Party A may refuse the delivery. Provided that Party A may accept the delivery of the products at the discount price to be agreed between Party A and Party B on a cause-by-case basis.

该合同条款显然对乙方不利，其风险点在于：一是甲方标准不具体，不能确定其是企业标准、行业标准还是国家标准；二是甲方根据折扣议价情况予以接受，其折扣比例如何没有确定，显然一旦乙方发货，就任由甲方片面挑剔了。

参考译文：如果出现产品不符合甲方标准的情况，甲方可拒绝收货。但甲方可根据甲乙双方视每次产品交付的具体情况的折扣议价予以接受。

5. provided that if

EG－8－28 An irrevocable credit shall be deemed to constitute a definite undertaking of the issuing bank. Provided that if the stipulated documents are presented and are complied with the terms, conditions and provisions of the credit, and if the credit provides for sight payment, the payment shall be made or shall be guaranteed to be made.

参考译文：不可撤销信用证应被认为构成开证行的确定承诺。在提交了规定的单据并符合了信用证条款时，如系即期付款信用证，则进行付款或保证该款的照付。

6. and if

EG－8－29 If the Seller, in accordance with the contract or this convention, hands the goods over to a carrier and if the goods are not clearly identified to the contract by marking on the goods, by shipping documents or otherwise, the Seller shall give the Buyer notice of the consignment specifying the goods.

第一个"if"是一个条件性关键词，首句嵌入了一个依据性关键词"in accordance with"；而"and if"是一个但书条款，进而再找到本条款的实意性关键词"give sb. notice st."（向某人发出何种通知）。

参考译文：如果卖方按照合同或本公约的规定将货物交付给承运人，但货物没有以货物上加标记或以装运单据或其他方式清楚地注明有关合同，卖方必须向买方发出列明货物的发货通知。

7. while

EG – 8 – 30 Party B shall be liable for any dead freight or demurrage, should they fail to have the quantity of the goods ready for loading in time as stipulated, while the carrying vessel has arrived at the port of shipment as advised.

参考译文：如果乙方没有根据规定及时地把装运货物准备好，而装运船只已经到达所通知的港口，乙方应负责所有的空舱费和滞期费。

"while" 在这里表面上可译为 "当……时"，而实质上其是否具有但书条款的效果需要根据合同其他条款来确定。

前半句说的是：如果乙方没有按照合同约定及时、足额地把货物准备好，应负责所有的空舱费和滞期费。后一句是指：当装运船按照通知要求到达装运港口时。

这里存在三个问题：

一是该装运船是谁通知的，是乙方还是甲方；

二是船到了而货物没有准备好，或者货物准备好了而船没有按照乙方的通知到达的问题；

三是准备货物的承担者用了 "they"，这是指甲方还是乙方并不清楚。

因此，可提出如下合同审核意见：一是根据合同具体情况将 "they" 修改为 "装运货物的责任方"；二是明确 "advised" 的指令者。

如果甲方是供货者而乙方是买方，则可修改为：

EG – 8 – 31 Should party A fail to have the quantity of the goods ready for loading in time as stipulated, Party B shall be not liable for any dead freight or demurrage, while the carrying vessel has arrived at the port of shipment as advised (party A).

如果乙方是供货方而甲方是买方，则可修改为：

EG – 8 – 32 Should party B have the quantity of the goods ready for loading in time as stipulated, and Party A shall be liable for any loss of Party B, while the carrying vessel fail to arrive at the port of shipment as advised (party B).

参考译文：如果乙方依照约定及时为装载准备了足够的货物，而执行运输的船舶没有按照乙方的要求到达装载港口时，甲方应承担乙方的损失。

EG-8-33 Either party may at anytime replace the chairman, deputy chairman or director (s) it has appointed, provided that it gives written notice to the Joint Venture Company and the other party.

参考译文：任何一方可随时更换自己委派的董事长、副董事长或董事，但必须书面通知合资公司和合资的另一方。

五、对关键词"provided that"的重点理解

涉外合同中，"provided that"通常在语气上有转折的含义，不宜翻译为"假如"、"如果"而应译为"但是"，这样才可使译文过渡自然，符合汉语表达的规范。该关键词由于涉及合同条款之间的优先适用，很容易让法务人员明白与引起注意，在英文合同中使用较多。因此，下面对之作专门分析和理解。

1. 常用于双方沟通方面的条款优先

EG-8-34 Instructions given by the Engineer shall be in writing, provided that if for any reason the Engineer considers it necessary to give any such instruction orally, the Contractor shall comply with such instruction.

参考译文：工程师应以书面形式发出指令；但若工程师认为由于某种原因而有必要以口头形式发出任何此类指令，则承包商应遵照执行。

2. 常用于授权方面的条款优先

EG-8-35 A wholly state-owned company has no shareholders'

meetings. The company's board of directors shall be authorized by the state – authorized investment institution or the state – authorized department to exercise part of the powers of the shareholders' meetings, and to decide on the major issues of the company. Provided that if the decisions on merger, division, dissolution of the company, increase or decrease in capital and issue of corporate bonds shall be made and decided, the decisions in question shall be made by the state – authorized investment institution or the state – authorized department.

参考译文：国有独资公司不设股东会，由国家授权投资的机构或者国家授权的部门授权公司董事会行使股东会的部分职权，决定公司的重大事项，但公司的合并、分立、解散、增减资本和发行公司债券必须由国家授权投资的机构或者国家授权的部门决定。

3. 对权利行使条款的优先

EG – 8 – 36 The Engineer may exercise such authority as is specified or necessarily implied in the contract. Provided that if, under the terms and conditions of the appointment by the Employer, the Engineer shall be required to obtain the specific approval of the Employer before exercising any such authority, the details of the requirements in question shall be specified in the contract.

参考译文：工程师可行使合同中规定的或者合同中必然隐含的权利。但是，如果根据业主任命工程师的条件，要求工程师在行使上述权利之前应得到业主的具体批准，则此类要求的细节应在本合同中予以表明。

4. 对各方沟通方式的优先

EG – 8 – 37 Instructions given by the Engineer shall be in writing. Provided that if, for any reason, the Engineer considers it necessary to give any such instruction orally, the Contractor shall comply with such instruction.

参考译文：工程师应以书面形式发出指令。但若工程师认为由于某种原因而有必要以口头形式发出任何此类指令，则承包人应遵照执行。

5. 对现场清理条款的优先

EG - 8 - 38 Upon the issue of any taking - over certificate, the Contractor shall clear away and remove from the site all Contractor's equipment, surplus materials, rubbish and temporary works of every kind, and leave the site and Works clean, to the satisfaction of the engineer. Provided that the Contractor shall be entitled to retain on site such materials, Contractor's equipment and temporary works as are required for remedying any defects in the works until the end of the defects liability period.

参考译文：在颁发任何移交证书时，承包人应从现场清除并运出承包人的全部设备、多余材料、垃圾和各种临时工程，并保持现场和工程清洁整齐，达到工程师满意。但承包人应有权在现场保留为完成在缺陷责任期内的修补工程中缺陷所需的材料、承包人的设备和临时工程，直至缺陷责任期结束。

6. 对合同效力发生变化的优先

EG - 8 - 39 No such variation shall, in any way, vitiate or invalidate the contract, and all such variations shall be valued in accordance with Clause * *. Provided that the Engineer shall issue an instruction to vary the works due to the default or breach of contract by the Contractor, the additional cost attributable to the default in question shall be borne by the Contractor.

参考译文：上述变更不应以任何方式使合同作废或失效，所有上述变更应按第＊＊条估价。由于承包人的违约或毁约，工程师有必要发出指示变更工程，则任何由此类违约造成的附加费用应由承包人承担。

7. 关于标的物接收方面的优先

EG - 8 - 40 If the Seller, in accordance with the contract or this convention, hands the goods over to a carrier and if the goods are not clearly identified to the contract by marking on the goods, by shipping documents or otherwise, the Seller shall give the Buyer notice of the consignment specifying the goods.

第一个"if"是一个条件性关键词，首句嵌入了一个依据性关键词"in accordance with"；而"and if"是一个但书条款，进而再找到本条款的实意性关键词"give sb. notice st."（向某人发出何种通知）。

参考译文：如果卖方按照合同或本公约的规定将货物交付给承运人，但货物没有以货物上加标记或以装运单据或其他方式清楚地注明有关合同，卖方必须向买方发出列明货物的发货通知。

EG - 8 - 41 In case the products fail to meet the standards of Party A, Party A may refuse the delivery. Provided that Party A may accept the delivery of the products at the discount price to be agreed between Party A and Party B on a cause - by - case basis.

"fail to"、"refuse"都隐含否定之意，"at the discount price"意为"折价"。

参考译文：如果出现产品不符合甲方标准的情况，甲方可拒绝收货。但甲方可根据甲乙双方视每次产品交付的具体情况折扣议价予以接受。

第9章

避免冲突："让步"与"保留"
条款的合理描述

在涉外合同的起草过程中常会出现草拟某一条款时需要顾及其会与相关法律、法规、行业惯例或本合同的其他条款所描述的事项或行为相冲突的情形，因此合同起草者需要谋划哪一行为或事项优先适用的问题。在涉外合同的起草过程中，有两种正好相反的思维描述方式：一种表示让步，另一种表示保留。其目的都是要说明某一事项或行为优先适用，由于这两种描述方式的目的具有一致性，当然也就可互换。具体采用哪一种方式完全取决于合同起草者的强调重点或所持立场。

前一种句型称之为让步性条款，以表示该条款所描述的事项或行为优先适用；后一种称之为隔离性条款，以表示该条款所描述的事项或行为不得阻碍其他需要保留或隔离的事项或行为。

一、涉外合同中"让步性"条款的描述

所谓让步性条款的描述，就是当认为该条款所描述的

事项或行为重要，并且可能存在与其他引用法律、法规或同一合同的其他条款所描述的事项或行为相冲突，又要求当前所描述的事项或行为优先适用时，一般用"notwithstanding the foregoing"之类的句子对其他相对次要的事项或行为作某些让步的一种合同条款的组织方法。

就其让步的因素，无外乎法律、法规的规定，合同条款的其他约定、合同条款的具体约定及对特定事项或行为的让步约定等。下面对之作具体的分类描述。

按照英文的思维习惯顺序，需要让步的事项或行为往往已经存在，而需要优先的事项或行为还没有发生而可能要发生，因此"notwithstanding"引导的事项或行为往往放在条款的开头，也就是开门见山地用"notwithstanding"引导出需要让步的事项或行为，或某一事项或行为存在的法律、法规或合同的相关条款。如果需要让步的事项或行为目前并不存在，可采取假设性条件句嵌入"notwithstanding"，以引导可能发生且需要让步的事项或行为。

1. 就相关法律的让步

EG – 9 – 1 Notwithstanding any other provisions of applicable laws, the parties agree that all taxes and duties payable arising from the transfer shall be borne by both the transferor and transferee in equal shares.

上述条款用"notwithstanding"对相关法律的其他规定作了让步，而就费用均摊作了强调，实质上意指无论发生什么情况都不得改变这一分摊办法的约定。

参考译文：尽管相关法律有其他规定，经协议双方同意，因转让而发生的所有应纳税款应由双方均摊。

2. 就本合同其他条款的让步

EG – 9 – 2 Notwithstanding any other provision of the contract, if the Contractor intends to claim any additional payment pursuant to any clause of these conditions or otherwise, he shall give notice to his intention to the engineer, with a copy to the Employer, within 28 days after the event giving rise to the claim has first arisen.

上述条款用"notwithstanding"引导合同的其他条款,以此作出让步,而且就索赔事项的通知要求作了强调,实质上说明了"通知、时间和通知副本提交对象"的重要性。

参考译文:尽管本合同有其他任何规定,如果承包商根据本合同的任何条款或其他有关规定打算索取任何附加费用,他都应在引起索赔的事件开始发生之日后28天内,将其索赔的意向通知工程师,并将一份副本呈交业主。

EG-9-3 Notwithstanding the foregoing, the Buyer's obligation to pay the purchase agreement price, or any other sums due under the purchase agreement, is onto so suspended.

上述条款通过"notwithstanding"排除了前述所有已约定条款的优先适用。

该条款约定了买方的义务为"pay the purchase agreement price"。显然,买方即使在履行合同的过程中发生不可抗力事项,也应按照约定支付合同货款,关键是不可抗力条款是否在该条款之前约定,如果是在该条款之后约定的就可能形成纠纷。因为买方所关注的是让步条款的公平性。也就是说,在此条款中,"Notwithstanding"后面紧跟"the foregoing",表明其后的本条款内容应优先考虑,前述条款不得与之相抵触。当然这并没有排除该条款后的其他约定,如果不可抗力条款在该条款之后,就可能会影响到支付条款的优先性。

参考译文:尽管有前述规定,但买方支付采购订单价格的义务或其他到期款项并不因此推迟。

3. 就合同具体条款的让步

EG-9-4 Notwithstanding the provisions of Article 91 of these Regulations, when a business establishment in charge of consolidated tax filing fails to compute the taxable income of different business establishments appropriately on a separate basis, the local tax authorities may make reasonable apportionment of the taxable income among these business establishments, under their respective proportion of business income, costs and expenses, assets, the number of staff and workers, or the amount of wages.

上述条款用"notwithstanding"引导了本细则某一具体条款的规定,从而强调了税务机关合理计算所得税额的特权不容挑战。

参考译文:虽有本细则第91条的规定,负责合并申报缴纳所得税的营业机构不能合理地分别计算各营业机构的应纳税所得额时,当地税务机关可以对应税所得总额,按照营业收入比例、成本和费用比例、资产比例、职工人数或者工资数额的比例,在各营业机构之间合理分配。

EG – 9 – 5 Notwithstanding IB＊＊, the Owner reserves the right to accept or reject any Bid, and to annul the bidding process and to reject all Bids, at any time prior to the award of the Contract, without thereby incurring any liability to the affected Bidder or Bidders or any obligation to inform the affected Bidder or Bidders of grounds for its action.

该条款对"IB＊＊"的让步显然表明了业主希望保留在招标、评标过程中的某一具体权利,并且不希望因此而承担额外的责任和义务。

参考译文:尽管有IB＊＊款的规定,业主在授予合同前(的任何时间)有保留授受或拒绝任何投标、废除投标程序、拒绝所有投标的权利,而且不承担由此而对投标人造成的不利条件的责任,同时也不承担通知受影响的投标人有关业主作出这一决定的原因的义务。

4. 就相关惯例让步

EG – 9 – 6 The Works shall be measured net, notwithstanding any general or local custom, except where otherwise provided for in the contract.

有时候一些行业可能存在惯例,如果担心惯例影响本条款的适用,就采取让步性描述方式来解除这一担心。

参考译文:尽管有通常和当地的习惯(计量方式),(本)工程计量应该以净值计量,但合同另有规定的除外。

5. 就具体的事项或行为让步

EG - 9 - 7 The Engineer shall, from time to time, have authority to issue instructions on the following matters that: Any works shall, in the opinion of the Engineer, be removed and re - executed, notwithstanding any previous test thereof or interim payment therefor, because the following items fail to meet the requirements and provisions of the Contract.

显然，此处"notwithstanding"引导的是具体的行为或事项，但该行为或事项在该条款约定前并没有发生，所以按照思维习惯放在中间。"notwithstanding"引导了某一行为，说明即使该行为发生也不得对抗本条的特殊规定。该合同条款强调的是工程师就拆除并重新施工指令的优先适用。

参考译文：工程师随时有权依照下列事项签发指令：按照工程师的意见，尽管提前检验或临时支付，但由于下列情况不能满足合同要求或条件的，仍应对任何工程项目进行移动或重新施工：

6. 就市场变化的情形让步

EG - 9 - 8 If the Party A places an order within the time designated in this offer, the price for the goods will remain firm notwithstanding any variation in the costs of producing the goods.

一般以"notwithstanding"引导市场变化的情形，来阐明货物价格的固定性，即表明合同价格不随市场变化而改变。本条款让步的是生产成本的变化不改变货物的价格。

由于市场变化不以人的意志为转移，也并不是合同约定时存在的事项，因此，按照惯常思维方式，"notwithstanding"放在了句中而非句首。

参考译文：如果甲方在要约指定的时间内发出订单，则货物的价格即使生产成本发生变化也维持固定不变。

7. 直接就可能存在的矛盾或冲突情形让步

EG - 9 - 9 Notwithstanding any other provisions to the contrary herein, insurance coverage and limits shall be subject to approval of all the parties.

本条款描述的是合同条款之间的冲突或矛盾，并没有说明具体的条款，当然是对其他冲突或矛盾条款的让步。本条款所描述事项或行为具有优先适用性。这里确定的是"insurance coverage and limits"具有优先性。

参考译文：尽管本合同存在相悖的规定，保险范围及责任限制还是应以各方当事人的确认为准。

EG－9－10 Any dispute between the parties arising out or related to this agreement whether in contract, negligence, but or otherwise shall be finally and exclusively settled by arbitration by three arbitrator in Beijing, china by china international economic and trade arbitration committee (CIETAC) in accordance with CIETAC's rules in force at the date hereof. Notwithstanding the foregoing, the grantor is entitled to seek injunctive relief before the courts in the PRC to prevent or stop any action by the grantee which jeopardizes grantor's or a third party's interests in the information disclosed to grantee under this agreement.

该条款中，"notwithstanding the foregoing"所指显然不是条款前的约定，而是本条款的前半部分所述事项。也就是说，按照"或裁或诉"的原则，双方约定采取仲裁方式解决纠纷就意味着排除了选择诉讼解决纠纷的方式。需要说明的是，本条款的让步并不完全具有排除的意思，而是两种事项或行为可并行。实质上，根据中国的法律，依法向法院申请禁令并不是提起诉讼，而是一种诉讼财产保全或申请采取强制措施等诉前行为。

这里通过一个让步性关键词"notwithstanding"规定了"the grantor"（授权方）的向法院申请禁令的权利。

参考译文：双方之间因本协议或与本协议有关的任何争议，不管是合同的、过失的、侵权或其他都应最终且无例外地提交中国国际经济贸易仲裁委员会。三名仲裁员根据该委员会在协议签订之后一直有效的仲裁规则在中国北京进行仲裁。尽管有前述规定，授权方有权向中国法院申请禁令，以防止或阻止被授权方采取任何行动从而威胁到授权方或第三方对根据本协议披露给被授权方的信息所享有的权益。

8. 就可能涉及的其他情形进行让步

EG – 9 – 11 The indemnity, release, holding harmless, defense and protection obligations assumed in Article × × shall apply in respect of the full liability of the indemnify for claims, notwithstanding the indemnify may be entitled to contribution thereto from any other person and notwithstanding such liability may relate to negligence of a third party, provided that in such event the indemnifying party shall be fully subrogated to the rights of the indemnify against such third party.

该条款使用了两个让步性关键词来说明确保补偿人获得被补偿人全部权利的重要性。其目的是为了防止全部权利因对方认为存在瑕疵而抗辩，这实质上是一种抗辩权的让步。

参考译文：条款中所规定的补偿、免责、免受损害、抗辩以及保护义务适用于向被补偿人主张的全部责任，即使被补偿人有向他人主张的权利，即使这种责任可能与第三方的过失有关，但是在此等情况下，补偿人取得被补偿人向第三方主张的全部权利。

二、对优先适用性事项或行为进行隔离

在涉外合同中，当要求某一条款所描述的事项或行为不得与其他引用法律、法规或同一合同的其他条款所描述的事项或行为相冲突并且不得优先适用时，则使用保留性条款将业已存在的优先事项或行为隔离起来，以防该条款的优先适用会使其他已强调的事项或行为被否定而形成本末倒置的现象。这一条款描述称为条款的保留性或隔离性方式。

需要说明的是，使用该种方式描述的条款并不能说明哪一事项或行为优先，一般应理解为可并行。这也是否定句表述方式的特别所在：否定自我，既不当然地肯定自我之外的事项或行为，也不否定自

我之外的事项或行为。

涉外合同中常用"not be construed"、"not affect"、"without prejudice to"等关键词作为保留或隔离事项或行为的引导。

1. 对相关权利的保留或隔离

EG - 9 - 12 Without prejudice to the foregoing rights, we request and urgent meeting to discuss this problem.

显然,合同起草人担心的是已形成的权利受到本条款的挑战,因此通过"without prejudice to"(在不损害……的前提下,在不影响……的情况下)方式对所担心的事项或行为进行了保留或隔离。

参考译文:在不影响上述权利的情况下,我们要求召开一次紧急会议来讨论这个问题。

EG - 9 - 13 If either party commits any breach of its obligations under this agreement and fails to remedy such breach within thirty (30) days from receipt of a written notice from the other party requiring it to do so, then the party issuing the notice shall be entitled to terminate this agreement. Such termination shall not prejudice any remedy by either party which shall have arisen or shall later arise in relation to this agreement.

关键词"not prejudice"属隔离性引导词,在涉外合同中常用于隔离合同终止时对已发生事项或行为的影响,主要是已经履行合同部分义务的一方因此可能要求保留索赔、已发生债权的清偿等权利。该条款描述了合同的终止不影响已产生的救济权利。

参考译文:合同任何一方如果违反本合同项下任何义务,且在接到另一方要求其补救该违约行为的书面通知后30日内没有进行补救的,则发出通知的一方有权终止本合同。合同终止不影响合同方在本合同下已经产生的救济权利。

2. 对相关责任的保留或隔离

EG - 9 - 14 The provision, use and refund of the deposits shall be without prejudice to the ultimate liability of the contributing parties.

不难理解，该条款是对相关费用分摊责任的保留。

参考译文：保证金的提供、使用和退还不影响各方最终的分摊责任。

3. 约定相关事项或行为优先使用

EG－9－15 However, of the recipient gives notice of another address, communications shall thereafter be delivered accordingly.

这里用"However"、"accordingly"组合说明了优先适用的情形。"accordingly"等同于"according to the address stated in the notice"。

参考译文：然而如果接收人告知了另外地址，则以后的信件必须按所给的（新）地址发送。

4. 对索赔或诉权的保留或隔离

EG－9－16 Termination in accordance with clause ＊. 4 shall not affect or prejudice any right to damages or other remedy which the terminating party may have in respect of the termination event which gave rise to the termination or any other right damages or other remedy which any party may have in respect of any breach of this agreement which existed at or before the date of termination.

"not affect or prejudice"将终止权利隔离起来，将终止条款与索赔及补偿条款隔离起来，以保持其独立性。

参考译文：根据第 ＊.4 条终止协议不应影响终止方就导致该终止的事件有关事项应享有的补偿或其他补救，也不影响在终止之前已经存在的与违反本协议有关的任何一方享有的补偿或其他补救权利。

5. 对某一法律或合同其他条款的保留与隔离

EG－9－17 Party A may terminate this agreement by giving notice to party B in accordance with clause ＊. 3 if party B commits a breach of any of the conditions or any other term of this agreement. The effect of which breach is material (whether or not such breach would otherwise qualify as a repudiator breach at common law), and which is either incapable of remedy, or, if capable of remedy is not remedied within (30) days of service of notice by the party not in breach requiring remedy.

关键词"whether or not"属于隔离性条款。基于英美法中只有达到毁约性的严重程度当事人才有权终止合同,其目的是一旦争议诉诸司法解决,就隔离法官"毁约性违约标准"的适用,引导法官尊重当事人的订约自由。

参考译文:如果乙方违反本协议任何条件或其他条款,违约行为严重(不管这种违约是否达到普通法下的毁约性违约标准),并且这种违约无法补救,或者能补救,但在非违约方发出要求补救的通知后30天内没有得到补救,则甲方有权根据第＊.3条通知乙方终止合同。

6. 对其他事项或行为的保留与隔离

EG – 9 – 18 Nothing in this agreement shall be construed as granting recipient a license under intellectual property rights of disclosing party , or any rights in respect of confidential information other than the restricted use and disclosure rights implied in clause ＊.

Neither party shall be under any obligation or commitment to enter into discussions or any further agreement merely by reason of the execution of this agreement or the disclosure, evaluation or inspection of confidential information, and this confidential agreement shall not constitute nor should it be construed to constitute an offer or commitment to sell or acquire the project.

该条款采用"be construed"的否定形式这种特殊方式对合同起草者所关心的具体事项或行为进行了保留或隔离。

参考译文:除第＊条规定的有限使用各披露权利外,本协议不应被解释为对信息接收方就信息披露方的知识产权或与保密信息有关的任何权利给予任何侵权许可。

任何一方并不仅仅因为签署本协议或因为披露、评价或调查保密信息而有任何义务或承诺进行讨论或签署进一步的协议，本协议并不构成，也不应被解释为构成一个要约或承诺出售或购买该项目。

三、对"subject to"、"notwithstanding"、"without prejudice to"的区别理解

由于这三种表述在意义上有很多相似之处，特此作区别与比较。

（1）签订合同应"依法合规，遵循基本的原则或行业惯例"，而"subject to"就常常用来引导应遵循的法律、法规和合同已达成的一些基本原则或行业惯例，相当于行使权利、履行义务的依据。因此，可以说"subject to"引导的条件是应优先适用的行为准则，一般不可动摇。

在涉外合同中，"subject to"通常用来表示"视……而定"、"以……为条件"，或者是采取某一行为的依据。即某一事项或行为的发生必须优先满足"subject to"所引导的事项或行为，可称之为必要的条件。

EG－9－19 The Seller representative shall be an employee of the Seller. The appointment, change, or any delegation of the authority of, the Seller representative and any terms thereof shall be subject to prior approval by the Buyer, which shall not be unreasonably withheld or delayed.

卖方是否可以任命、变更或授权卖方代表得视买方的批准而定，否则卖方代表的行为将可能视为无效。"买方的批准"即为这里的优先条件。

参考译文：卖方代表必须是卖方的雇员。卖方代表的任命、变更或授权以及任何此方面的条件都必须得到买方的事先批准，但买方不得无故拒绝或拖延。

（2）虽然"notwithstanding"只是一个词，但它和"subject to"使用的效果正好相反。通常情况下，"notwithstanding"表示"尽管……但……"，"notwithstanding"后面所接的内容应放在次要位置予以考虑。

EG－9－20 Neither the Buyer nor the Seller shall be liable one to the other for any delay or failure to perform its obligations under the purchase agreement where and to the extent such delay or failure is caused by Force Majeure. Notwithstanding the foregoing, the Buyer's obligation to pay the purchase agreement price, or any other sums due under the purchase agreement, is not so suspended.

参考译文：买方和卖方对因不可抗力造成的履行迟延或无法履行彼此不承担任何责任。尽管有前述规定，但买方支付采购订单价格的义务或其他到期款项并不因此推迟。也就是说，即使发生了不可抗力，买方照常付款，不得延迟。

（3）有时，"notwithstanding"与"subject to"是可以替换的。

EG－9－21 Subject to the foregoing, the Buyer's obligation to pay the purchase agreement price, or any other sums due under the purchase agreement, is not so suspended.

如此表述，则意思完全相左："买方不得迟延付款，但上述规定除外。"换句话说，如果前例中用"notwithstanding the foregoing"，则表示"发生不可抗力，买方应照常付款，不得迟延"；但如果前例中用"subject to the foregoing"，则表示"如果发生不可抗力，买方就可以迟延付款"。

EG－9－22 Notwithstanding any other provision of the contract, if the Contractor intends to claim any additional payment pursuant to any Clause of these conditions or otherwise, he shall give notice to his intention to the Engineer, with a copy to the Employer, within 28 days after the event giving rise to the claim has first arisen.

参考译文：尽管本合同有其他任何规定，如果承包商根据本合同的任何条款或其他有关规定打算索取任何追加付款，他都应在引起索赔的事件第一次发生后28天内，将其索赔意向通知工程师，并将一份副本呈交业主。

"notwithstanding"后紧跟"any other provision of this agreement"，则表明本条款就其所规定的内容在整个合同中处于最优先考虑的地位，任何其他条款都不得同它抵触，即使抵触了也以本条款为准。如果修改为"subject to any other provision of the contract"并后置，则意思就要靠上下文来理解了，既可能发生冲突，也可能是该条款不能优先考虑。

（4）"without prejudice to"表示"在不影响……的情况下"，比如"without prejudice to the existing rights"就表示"在不影响既有权利的情况下"。该关键词意味着目前描述条款与"without prejudice to"引导的事项或行为具有同等效力，或者说互不影响、互不干涉。

EG-9-23 The contributing parties shall provide security for general average contribution at the request of the parties that have an interest therein. Where the security has been provided in the form of cash deposits, such deposits shall be put in a bank by an average adjuster in the name of a trustee. The provision, use and refund of the deposits shall be without prejudice to the ultimate liability of the contributing parties.

上述通过"without prejudice to"引导最终责任的分摊，说明了提供海损担保和保证金存入银行互不影响，通俗地说就是"各方是各方的事"。

参考译文：经利益关系人要求，各分摊方应当提供共同海损担保。已提供保证金方式进行共同海损担保的，保证金应当交由海损理算师以保管人名义存入银行。保证金的提供、使用或者退还不影响各方最终的分摊责任。

（5）从以上分析可以看出，"subject to"、"notwithstanding"和"without prejudice to"的含义有很大的关联性，通过下述表述能够比较清晰地理解这三个用语：

"subject to"引导的事项或行为优于所处条款事项或行为。

"notwithstanding"引导的事项或行为替所处条款设置事项或行为进行让步，或者说达成某种妥协，处于忽视的地位。

　　"without prejudice to"引导的事项或行为与所处条款事项或行为具有同等重要性，虽不存在哪个条款优先考虑的问题，但其所引导的事项或行为具有重复提示作用，在合同中如果能够被起草者重复提到，可间接说明其重要性不可忽视。

第 *10* 章

权力把握：权力、权利与授权性关键词的理解

在涉外合同中，除了必要的形式或格式要求外，每一条款的设置无不都是围绕权利和义务来设置的，因此法务人员要懂得"权力"、"权利"与"授权"在涉外合同中的基本表述。

一般来讲，"be entitled to"表示"有权做什么"（to give sb. the right to sth.），体现该权利具有法律上的强制性。"power"指与职务相关联的权力，强调的是职务与地位带来的权力。而"right"指与法律义务相关联的权利，是法律或者契约等赋予的权利，与履行义务、承担责任相联系，如"right to possess, use and dispose of the private property"（占有、使用和处分私有财产的权利）。

在涉外合同中，"right"与"obligation"属对义词。"authority"指权威、影响。"authorization"指授权，即指有权的人给无权的人行使合同和法定的权利，并由授权人和授权人所在的单位对受权人的行为承担相应的法律责任，如果指做某事需要别人的同意或许可，对于经济实体

来讲，代表公司签订合同、履行重要合同时一般需要法定代表人或负责人书面授权。如"Party A represents that it has the authority, authorization, power and right to execute this Agreement."（甲方拥有签署本协议的权威、授权、权力和权利。）

一、涉外合同中与权利描述有关的关键词

对于合同权利义务与相关事项的约定，在涉外合同中其描述方式主要有动词性描述、名词性描述与动名词性描述三种。

在涉外合同中，描述有关权利的行使一般以动词性描述为主，也就是说采用动句描述权利的行使最为普遍，即以主谓宾补句型结构较好。

（一）动词性描述

动词性描述主要是指表达权利的关键词处于谓语位置，具有动词的词性，以体现权利的行使具有动态的主观意思。

1. "be entitled to" 意指 "有权做什么"

EG – 10 – 1 When the Buyer is entitled to determine the time within a specified period and / or the place of taking delivery, the Buyer in question shall give the Seller the notice thereof.

上述例句的主旨是随即给通知，虽然关键词"be entitled to"属于分句的谓语，但由于谓语具有较强的突出作用，何况是一个有关时间、期间与地点的分句，这就足以引起合同买卖双方的关注。

参考译文：卖方在规定周期有权决定提货时间和地点，但买方应就上述事项随时给卖方通知。

EG – 10 – 2 This Note means the note mentioned in the loan agreement and is entitled to all the benefits provided therein. This refers to the rights and obligations therein of advance payments, default and acceleration of the maturity in the event of default.

在这里，关键词"is entitled to"意指"有权享有利益"，加之后一主句中用一个静态句意指"the rights and obligations"，足以引起双

方的注意。

参考译文：此票据意为在贷款合同中提到的票据和所有上面提到的相关利益，也意指所含有的预付款、拒付或失效的相关权利和义务。

2. "exercise its powers" 指行使与所授权相对应的权利

EG – 10 – 3 A company limited by shares shall have a shareholders general meeting made up of all shareholders. The shareholders general meeting shall be the company's authoritative organization and shall, in accordance with this Law, exercise its powers.

关键词 "exercise its powers" 在此意指履行法律规定的权利，当然包括公司章程的约定。

参考译文：一个股份有限公司应由全体股东参加股东代表大会。股东代表大会是公司的权力机构，根据本法行使相关权力。

3. "reserves the right to/ have the right to" 指享有相应的权利

EG – 10 – 4 The Leasee shall, at his own expense, keep the commodity in good condition. Provided that the Leasor shall be responsible for the breakdown of the commodity and the Leasee may have the right to lodge claims against the Leasor for any losses occurred therein.

关键词 "have the right to" 在此处于主句的谓语位置，起到了较好的突出作用，该种有权在法律上不是绝对的，而是相对权。相对权是指相对于履行相应的义务，相对于遵守相应的约定。

对于权力的描述一般加情态动词 "may"：一是说明权力的使用是可由权力行使人自主选择的；二是在行使的过程中也是可以与对方协商的。而义务与责任往往用 "shall"，说明是应该的、必须的、不可商量的，否则就存在严重违约问题。

4. "have the right to" 指有权做某事

EG – 10 – 5 The Buyer shall nevertheless have the right to cancel in part or in whole of the contract without prejudice to the 'Buyer's right to claim compensations.

关键词"have the right to"所处的句子具有静态的特征,静态句是突出性最强的句子。同时,"without prejudice to"属于权利义务的隔离,显然该条款对买方有利,也说明买方处于较为强势的地位。

参考译文:尽管如此,买方有权撤销合同的全部或部分,概不妨碍买方索赔权之行使。

5. "have the authority to/have authority to" 指经授权

EG – 10 – 6 The Engineer shall, from time to time, have authority to issue instructions on the following matters that: Any works shall, in the opinion of the Engineer, be removed and re – executed, notwithstanding any previous test thereof or interim payment therefor, because the following items fail to meet the requirements and provisions of the Contract:

"have authority to" 在此强调的显然是经业主合法授权而代表业主的行为。

参考译文:工程师随时有权依照下列事项签发指令:按照工程师的意见,尽管提前检验或临时支付,但由于下列情况不能满足合同要求或条件的,仍应对任何工程项目进行移动或重新施工:

EG – 10 – 7 The Engineer shall, from time to time, have authority to issue to the Contractor such supplementary drawings and instructions as shall be necessary for the proper and adequate execution and completion of the Works and the remedying of any defects therein.

"do sth. at one's option" 一般指某人做某事的选择权;"have the authority to" 强调经合法授权。这里也就是说发出指令的人有权代表单位实施监督权。无论如何选择,只要是经单位授权的,工程师的责任就应由单位来承担。

参考译文:工程师随时有权对承包商适当履行合同完成工程项目和对合同缺陷的弥补签发补充图纸和指令。

6. "grant" 一般指授予他人某些与知识产权有关的权利

EG - 10 - 8 Whereas Party B has the right and agrees to grant Party A the rights to use, manufacture and sell the contract products of patented technology.

If the Licensor grants any other license under the patent or their other responding patents to any third party in connection with the manufacture, use and sale of the licensed products in any place under such conditions as are more favorable to a licensee than those provided herein, the Licensor shall promptly inform the Licensee in written form of the details of such other license and the licensee has the choice to adopt equally favorable conditions.

"control or grant" 为类聚词，意为"同意授权"（实质隐含有权并且在其控制下）。

参考译文：鉴于乙方有权并同意授予甲方使用、生产和销售本专利技术的合同产品。

如果授予方授予的任何专利及专利许可对任何第三方就相关专利的生产、使用或销售的许可产品在任何地方比该协议的相应条件优于受让方那么授让方应立即使用书面形式就这一授予行为的详细情况通知给受让方，在同等条件下，受让方有优先选择受让的权利。

（二）名词性描述

1. "the right of" 一般指因履行法律、契约有关义务而形成的权利

EG - 10 - 9 The Employer shall give the Contractor right of access to, and possession of, all parts of the Site within the time (or times) stated in the particular conditions.

"right of" 作为"give"的宾语，意为"给予某一权利"。

参考译文：雇主应在专用条件中规定的时间（或几个时间）内，给承包商进入和占用场地各部分的权利。

EG – 10 – 10 The right of interpreting the detailed rules and regulations resides in the Ministry of Finance of the People's Republic of China.

"resides" 在这里作"属于"讲，是比"belong to"较为正规的描述。

参考译文：本细则的解释权属于中华人民共和国财政部。

2. "the ownership of"一般指法律赋予某人具有特定不动产或重要资产的所有权

EG – 10 – 11 The ownership of any improved and developed technology shall belong to the party who has improved and developed the technology.

在这里，"The ownership of"表示知识产权的所有权，该权力在法律上具有专属性、绝对性和排他性。一般持有人依据相应法律持有权威部门颁发的权利证书作支撑。当然，这里也可用"owned"强调，从而描述为："The improved and developed technology shall be owned by the party who has improved and developed the technology."

参考译文：技术改进和开发的所有权归属开发和改进技术的一方。

3. "the exclusive property of"一般指法律赋予某人具有特定知识产权方面的专属权

EG – 10 – 12 Any drawings or technical documents interested for use in the construction of the plant or of part thereof and submitted to the Seller by the Buyer prior or subsequent to formation of the contract remain the exclusive property of the Buyer.

"remain"意为"保留"，在此译为"仍为"比较顺畅。

参考译文：本合同订立前后由买方送交卖方用于建筑设备或其部分设备的图纸或技术资料仍为买方的专有财产。

4. "authority"意指权力、权威与权力当局

EG – 10 – 13 Unless otherwise expressly specified in the contract, the

Engineer shall have no authority to relieve the Contractor of any of his obligations under the contract.

"authority" 一般为授权或法定的权力，在承包合同中，工程师一般代表业主督促承包商履行合同，所以无特殊约定一般就不具有改变合同实质性内容的权利。

参考译文：除在合同中明确规定外，工程师无权解除合同规定的承包人的任何义务。

5. "the privilege" 一般指特权

EG – 10 – 14 No one shall have the privilege of transcending the law.

"the privilege" 意为 "特权"，意指一种超越同等条件的权利。该特权并非与生俱来，而是一种人为的规定或法律的赋予。

参考译文：不允许任何人有超越法律的特权。（或：任何人没有超越法律的特权。）

EG – 10 – 15 This contract is made out in two originals, each copy written in Chinese and English languages, both texts being equally valid. In case of any divergence of interpretation, the Chinese text shall prevail.

"prevail" 在这里意为 "优先适用"。其一般指顺序上的优先或位置上的靠前，此外还有 "流行"、"盛行" 之意。

参考译文：本合同由两份正本组成，每一文本用中英文双语写成，每种文本具有同等效力，一旦出现解释上的分歧，应以中文文本为准。

6. "the right of preemption" 一般指优先权

EG – 10 – 16 The right of preemption is a kind of expectant right, which bases on and comes into being when the primary relation setup.

"preemption" 意为 "优先"。其一般指实质上、内容上、实力上的领先，此外还具有 "强制"、"抢先"、"被取代" 之意。

参考译文：优先购买权是一种期待权，始于基础关系成立之时。

EG - 10 - 17 Partial option to purchase refers to the right of preemption for shareholders to purchase part of the shares transferred by the limited - liability company.

"refers to" 一般译为 "意指"、"即"、"是为"，相当于 "be to"。

参考译文：部分行使股权优先购买权意指有限责任公司股东在转让股份时，其他股东希望只优先购买被转让股份中的一部分。

7. "the priority right" 意为 "优先权"

EG - 10 - 18 Provision 286 of the Contract Law in China establishes a brand new system of the priority right to be repaid related with construction.

"be repaid" 意为 "偿还"。

参考译文：中国《合同法》第286条在建设工程合同领域确立了一项崭新的制度——建设工程承包人优先受偿权制度。

(三) 动名词性描述

1. "having jurisdiction" 一般指法律赋予的司法管辖权

EG - 10 - 19 The parties hereto shall, first of all, settle any dispute arising from or in connection with the contract by friendly negotiations. Should such negotiations fail, such dispute may be referred to the People's Court having jurisdiction on such dispute for settlement in the absence of any arbitration clause in the disputed contract or in default of agreement reached after such dispute occurs.

"having jurisdiction" 意为 "具有司法管辖权"。这里用现在分词形式说明其拥有的权力与其法院的性质有关，而无须另行赋予。

参考译文：合同双方当事人应优先通过友好协商解决合同引起的纠纷。一旦协商无果，合同中又无仲裁条款约定或争议发生后未就仲裁达成协议的，可将争议提交有管辖权的人民法院解决。

2. "authorized" 指授权的行为

EG - 10 - 20 The Representatives authorized by the parties to this contract have, through friendly negotiation, agreed to enter into this contract under the terms, conditions and provisions specified as follows.

这里采用过去分词的形式强调代表的授权是已经进行的，从而排除了过期或超越权限的可能，同时也说明了不能先签订合同再去授权。

参考译文：本合同当事人的授权代表，通过友好协商，同意签订本合同如下条款。

二、涉外合同中与权利转让有关的关键词

1. "transfer to" 意指转让

EG - 10 - 21 On the transfer date New Company shall transfer to B , free from any lien or encumbrance created by New Company and without the payment of any compensation, all its right, title to and interest in the infrastructure project, unless otherwise specified in the agreement or any supplementary agreement.

"transfer" 在这里意为 "公司的整体转让"，属完全特权的转让。所以，受让者担心的当然是物权上附加的担保、抵押、留置及权利债务的瑕疵。"free from" 取其所隐含的否定之意，与随后的 "without" 构成平行结构。

参考译文：在转让期，新公司应将对基础设施的权利和利益转让给 B，新公司不应有任何留置或形成的债务，也不能要求补偿，除非协议或补充协议中另有规定。

2. "assign" 意指转让

EG - 10 - 22 The contractor shall not, without the prior consent of the Employer, assign the contract or any part thereof, or any benefit or interest therein or thereunder, unless otherwise specified in the following circumstances.

"assign" 属于合同权利方面的转让，是比较正规的描述。一般来

讲，对于客观物体的转让优先选用 "transfer"，对于非客观物体的转让优先选用 "assign"。

参考译文：未经业主的事先同意，承包商不得将合同或合同的任何部分，或合同中或合同名下的任何利益或好处进行转让，但下列情况除外。

3. "waiver" 意指对权力的放弃

"waiver" 是 "waive" 名词形式，意思是 "弃权"、"权利放弃"，如 "waiver by election of remedies"（因选择救济方式而产生的权利放弃）、"waiver of proof of loss"（损失证明的放弃）、"waiver of right to appeal"（上诉权的放弃）、"waiver of tort"（放弃侵权之诉）等。

EG – 10 – 23 Where a party in the cooperative development declares a waiver of its joint patent application right, the other party may apply by itself, or the other parties may jointly apply, as the case may be.

"joint" 意为 "共享"、"共同"，"jointly" 为其副词形式。

参考译文：合作开发的当事人一方声明放弃其共有的专利申请权的，可以由另一方单独申请或者由其他各方共同申请。

4. "retention of title" 意指对所有权的保留

EG – 10 – 24 If the parties have validly agreed on retention of title, the goods shall remain the property of the Seller until the complete payment of the price, or as otherwise agreed.

当实际物的控制占有权与所有权分离时，才会出现 "retention of title"（所有权的保留）问题。其一般存在于使用、保管、受益权产生了转移或对拥有所有权的物体失去了实际的占有权的情况中。

参考译文：如果双方确实同意对所有权保留，则在完成货款支付前该货物的所有权仍归卖方，或另有规定。

5. "right of access" 意指经特定人许可的一种方便权

EG – 10 – 25 The Employer shall give the Contractor right of access to, and possession of, all parts of the Site within the time (or times) stated in the particular conditions. The right and possession may not be exclusive to the Contractor. If, under the contract, the Employer is required to give (to the Contractor) possession of any foundation, structure, plant or means of access, the Employer shall do so in the time and manner stated in the Employer's Requirements. However, the Employer may withhold any such right or possession until the Performance Security has been received.

参考译文：业主应给予承包商在特定（规定）的时间进入或占用全部或部分工地的权利，该项权利不属承包商专有。如果依照合同，业主要求给予承包商占用的任何基础、构筑物、设备或进出便道，业主可以按照业主要求的方式和时间与承包商享有同等的权利。无论如何，在收到承包商开具的履约保函前，业主可以撤销这一进入或占有的权利。

三、涉外合同中与权利有关的类聚词

1. "power and authority" **意为"授权"**

EG – 10 – 26 Where the Borrower has full power and authority to enter into this agreement, to make the borrowings, to execute and deliver the note and to incur the obligations provided for in this agreement and therein, all the actions in question shall, properly and necessarily, be authorized by legal persons.

"has full power and authority" 一般指经特别授权。其是授权人因职务授权，常为企业或公司的法定代表人或有转委托权的委托代理人行使授权。

参考译文：借款人有权签订本协议，获得借款，签署和交付票据，承担因本协议和票据产生的义务，所有相关的行为是适当且必需的，并经法定代表人的授权。

2. "authorizes and empowers" **意为"授权"**

EG – 10 – 27 Party A hereby authorizes and empowers party B to participate in the action on behalf of Party A which shall be valid till such authorization expires or otherwise is withdrawn or terminated by Party A, as the case may be.

参考译文：甲方谨授权乙方代表甲方参与诉讼，该授权在授权期限届满或被甲方撤回或终止之前（视情况而定）持续有效。

3 "assigned, transferred and conveyed" 意为 "转让"

EG – 10 – 28 Licensee hereby agrees that at the termination or expiration of this agreement Licensee will be deemed to have assigned, transferred and conveyed to Licensor any rights, equities, good will, titles or other rights in and to the name which may have been obtained by Licensee or which may have vested in Licensee in pursuance of any endeavors covered hereby, and that Licensee will execute any instruments requested by Licensor to accomplish or confirm the foregoing.

"equities" 为财务专业术语，意为 "享有权益"；"good will" 为民法专业术语，意为 "善意"，在这里意指经济实体在存在经营期间所特有的无形资产增值能力，即意指商誉。

参考译文：被许可方特此同意本协议终止或届满时，被许可方视为向许可方转让被许可方因该名称可能已获得或经努力已拥有的任何权利、权益、商誉、所有权或其他权利，并且被许可方应在许可方的要求下签署任何文件以完成或确认上述转让。

第 *11* 章
责任把握：尽职、尽责与义务性关键词的理解

　　"legal responsibility and moral duty" 意为 "法律上的责任与义务"。在涉外合同中，对于责任与义务的描述一般是指对某事承担责任、对某事负有责任，或者说有义务做某事。如 "have the legal obligation to do"、"be obliged to"、"shall do"、"be under the obligation to do" 或 "shall be liable to do" 等都具有承担相关责任的意思。"be liable for sth."、"be liable to sb."、"be responsible in accordance with law" 指依照法律对某事或某人负有责任。

一、涉外合同中关于合同各方 "责任" 的描述

　　在涉外合同中常用 "responsibility" 表示 "责任"。该种责任是不可商量的，一般责任方要依相关约定承担所约定的责任。

　　对于责任义务的描述一般有名词性描述、动词性描述和形容词性描述三种方式。

（一）名词性描述

1. "responsibility" 意为"责任"，一般后接"of"或"for"

一般来讲，与"responsibility"相连的"of"引导责任主体。"responsibility"在表示"责任"时，着重强调"职责、义务"（commitment or duty for which a party is responsible）。

EG – 11 – 1 Responsibilities of Each Party to the Joint Venture.

Responsibility of Party A：…

Responsibility of Party B：…

参考译文：合资公司各方的责任。

甲方的责任：……

乙方的责任：……

有时，用"of"引导责任的原因。

EG – 11 – 2 If, in accordance with the provisions of the preceding paragraph, a shareholder fails to pay its subscribed Capital Contribution, the shareholder in question shall bear the responsibility of default to the other shareholders who have fully paid their capital contributions.

该条款中，"of"引导了应承担责任的原因。

参考译文：如果根据前款规定，一个股东没有支付他的股本认购额，该股东应对其他足额支付认缴股本的股东承担责任。

与"responsibility"相连的"for"一般引导承担责任的范围。

EG – 11 – 3 The licensee shall assume full responsibility for the payment of all royalties.

"full"在这里具有强调意味，译为"全部"。"assume full responsibility"具有"承担全部责任"的意思。"for"引导责任范围。

参考译文：对于一切专利权使用费的支付事宜，许可证受让方应承担完全责任。

2. "liability" 意为 "责任"

表示"责任"的单词，一个为"responsibility"；另一个为"liability"。("liability" means to take any liability for being legally responsible for paying or damage or loss.)

EG – 11 – 4 The underwriters refused to take any liability for the losses.

参考译文：承销商对损失拒绝承担责任。

从涉外合同条款的具体构成位置来看，"responsibility"与"liability"几乎等值。不同的是，"liability"在表示责任时主要强调两个方面：一方面指"赔偿责任"；另一方面指"债务责任（一般用复数形式"liabilities"）；而"responsibility"一般不会用来表示赔偿责任，因为该责任是职责或约定所规定的责任，往往与"consideration"对价的许诺有某种关联。因此，在合同中分别约定双方含有权利义务的责任时，常用"responsibility"而不用"liability"；如果描述某一方应就某一具体事项承担确定的责任时，常用"liability"而不用"responsibility"。

EG – 11 – 5 The Seller shall refund to the Buyer such amounts after paying all tax liabilities.

"liabilities"在这里指具体的税务责任，数额一般是明确的、可计算的。

该条款中的责任显然是一种债务责任，或者说是一种应付责任。

参考译文：在付清一切税款后，卖方须向买方偿还这些款项。

因此，"有限责任公司"常被译成"limited liability company"，表示"a company where a member is responsible for repaying the company's debts only up to the face value of the shares he owns"。

由上述条款的分析和比较可见，解释中的"责任"显然是不确定的外国债务，属于合同各方应履行的职责和义务，因此应描述为"responsibility"。

在构词上，"liability"后常接介词"for"以引导责任范围，"of"引导责任主体。这一点与"responsibility"也相同。

EG – 11 – 6 The liability of a party to pay compensation for the breach of a contract shall be equal to the loss suffered by the other party as a consequence of the breach. However, such compensation may not exceed the loss, which the party responsible for the breach ought to have foreseen at the time of the conclusion of the contract as a possible consequence of a breach of contract.

该句中的"liability"（责任）后通过"of"引导责任主体，"responsible"通过"for"引导责任指向或范围。这明显是一种"being legally responsible for paying loss"的含义，所以首句选择"liability"是合适的。而后一句的违约责任并没有确定，十分笼统，因此使用了"responsible for"。

参考译文：一方当事人因违反合同支付赔偿金的责任应相当于另一方因此而遭受的损失，作为对其损失的补偿，但是这一赔偿不应超过当事人在签订合同时对违反损失的预估，尽可能地与违反合同所造成的损失相一致。

（二）动词性描述

合同中经常使用的一个词是"承担"，英文中有"bear"、"accept"、"undertake"、"take"、"respond in"、"shoulder"可供选择，但"承担"在下列不同句子中具有不同的"承担"效果。

（1）"由乙方承担法律上和经济上的全部责任"译为"party B shall bear all the legal and financial responsibility arising there – from"。"bear responsibility"主要表示承担"法律和经济上的责任"（注："法律上和经济上的责任"不译成"law and economic responsibility"）。

（2）"双方承担风险"译为"both parties shall accept the risk"。

（3）"乙方承担后果"译为"party B shall take the consequence"。

（4）"许可方承担赔偿费用"译为"licensor shall respond in damages"。

（5）"承担受让方的赔偿责任"译为"to honor licensee's liability"。

以上例句中如果将"承担"一成不变地译为"bear"，就会令人费解。当然，其他词也具有类似的情况，阅读理解时一定要注意结合上下文仔细推敲词义，勤查专业工具书，做到词不离句、句中辨词。

1. "be fully liable to" 意为 "承担全部责任"

EG – 11 –7 The time as notified by the Buyer, after its arrival at the port of shipment the Seller shall be fully liable to the Buyer and responsible for all losses and expenses such as dead freight, demurrage.

"be fully liable" 意为 "承担全部责任"。该句后面使用 "responsible for" 说明了其损失或赔偿费用的不确定性，不确定性主要在于 "demurrage"。提请注意这是卖方风险控制的关键点。一般来讲，"Chatterer must be responsible for demurrage"（租船人必须对滞期负责）。最好是买卖双方约定过错责任，对于 "demurrage"（滞留费）应分清责任，不能一概由哪一方承担，否则风险将难以承担。因为货船的滞留费的计算是按照满载的延迟启航时间计算的，几天时间就可达数十万美元，如果计划安排不当，几千万美元也可能会因 "demurrage"（滞留费）而被打水漂。

参考译文：在买方通知的时限内，抵达装运港后，卖方应对买方承担全部责任并对诸如空舱费、滞留费等所有损失和费用负责。

2. "be held liable" 意为 "承担（相应）责任"

EG – 11 –8 Seller shall not be held liable for failure or delay in delivery of the entire lot or a portion of the goods under this Sales Contract in consequence of any force majeure incidents.

"be held liable" 与 "be fully liable to"（承担全部责任）有一定的差别。"be held liable" 后接 "for"，一般引导责任的原因。

参考译文：卖方对因任何不可抗力事件导致本买卖合同项下整批或部分货物未能交付或延误概不承担责任。

3. "bear full liability" 意为 "承担全部责任"

EG - 11 - 9 If, in the course of securities trading, an employee of a securities company violates trading rules under the instructions of the company or by taking advantage of his position, the securities company to which the employee belongs shall bear full liability therefor.

在这里，"full"起到了强调作用。

参考译文：证券公司的从业人员在证券交易活动中，按其所属的证券公司的指令或者利用职务违反交易规则的，由所属的证券公司承担全部责任。

4. be liable for

EG - 11 - 10 Should the carrying vessel has arrived at the port of shipment as advised and the Seller fails to have the quantity of the goods ready for loading in time as specified, the Seller shall be liable for any dead freight or demurrage.

"for"引导的是责任原因，在这里是指"空舱费"或"滞留费"。

参考译文：如果买方船只按通知到达装运港，而卖方不能按规定的时间备妥货物以待装船，则由此而产生的空舱费及滞留费应由卖方负担。

EG - 11 - 11 A company may invest in other limited liability companies or companies limited by shares and be liable to the companies which it has invested in to the extent of the amount of capital invested in such companies.

"be liable to"通过"to"引出承担责任的受体，也就是该对谁负责。

参考译文：公司可以向其他有限责任公司、股份有限公司投资，并以该出资额为限对所投资公司承担责任。

EG - 11 - 12 If, in accordance with the Contract, Party B fails to make purchase of the products of compensation trade and Party A fails to deliver the products in question, either Party shall, in accordance with the provisions of the contract, be liable for a breach of Contract, and shall indemnify for all the economic losses.

参考译文：如乙方未能按合同规定购买补偿贸易商品或甲方未能按合同提供商品时，均应按合同条款承担违约责任，赔偿由此造成的经济损失。

5. remain liable to

EG－11－13 The Employer shall not be liable to the Contractor for the matter or thing arising out of or in connection with the contract or execution of the works, unless the Contractor has included a claim in respect thereof in his final statement and in the statement at completion referred to in Sub － Clause ＊＊.

"be liable"后的介词"to"一般引导享有权利的相对方而不是责任方。

参考译文：除非承包人在其最终报表中以及在第＊＊款提及的竣工报表中已经包括索赔事宜，对由合同及工程实施引起的或与之有关的任何问题和事件，业主不应对承包人负有责任。

"be liable under"用来确定责任归属。

EG－11－14 Unless such defect, shrinkage or other fault is the one for which the Contractor is liable under the contract, the Engineer shall, after due consultation with the Employer and the Contractor, determine the amount in respect of the costs of such search incurred by the Contractor. The amount in question shall be added to the contract price and the Engineer shall notify the Contractor accordingly, with a copy to the Employer.

参考译文：除非这一缺陷、缺点或其他毛病依照本合同属于承包商的责任，经承包商与业主协商后决定由承包商发生的这一成本的相关金额，该金额应追加到合同价款之中，工程师应因此通知到承包商，并送达一份复印件到业主。

6. be responsible for

EG – 11 – 15 Both Parties shall protect each other's intellectual property rights. Without prior consent, neither party shall revise copy or transfer to a third party or use for the project other than the project of this Contract any materials and documents of the other party. Under such circumstances, the disclosing party shall be responsible for all the any consequence it resulted and shall bear the relevant compensation. a third party, it shall provide a written notice to the other Party.

参考译文：对方的知识产权，未经对方同意，任何一方均不得对对方的资料及文件擅自修改、复制或向第三人转让或用于本合同项目外的项目。如发生以上情况，泄密方承担一切由此引起的后果并承担赔偿责任。

7. no longer be responsible

EG – 11 – 16 In case part of all know – how of the above mentioned technical contents have been published by Licensor or any third party, Licensee obtain evidence of such publication. The Licensee shall no longer be responsible for keeping the opened parts secret and confidential.

"no longer be responsible" 意为"不再负责"。这里通过"In case"引导出前提条件。按照正常的商务约定，一方不承担保密义务必须有充足的理由，坚持要求时必须出示足够的证据。

参考译文：一旦上述技术所含的全部专有技术的部分内容被许可方或任何第三方公开，被许可方获得这一公开证据，那么被许可方不再对已公开部分承担保密责任。

8. bear its own expenses

EG – 11 – 17 The contents and conclusion of such discussions shall be written in memorandum. The number of attendants of each party shall be no more than five persons. Each party shall bear its own expenses.

参考译文：这一讨论的内容应被写进备忘录中。各方参加的人员不应多于 5 人，各方自费承担相应的费用。

9. not be responsible for

EG – 11 – 18 The Seller shall not be responsible for the delay of shipment or non – delivery of the goods due to force majeure, which might occur during the process of manufacturing or in the course of loading or transit.

参考译文：凡在制造或装船运输过程中，因不可抗力致使卖方不能或推迟交货时，卖方不负责任。

（三）形容词性描述

"responsible" 属于形容词，一般用来修饰责任承担方。

EG – 11 – 19 Upon being indemnified by the Company, subrogate to the Company all the right of recovery, transfer all necessary documents to and assist the Company in pursuing recovery from the responsible party.

本合同条款中，"responsible" 属于形容词，具有对当事人的限定作用。

参考译文：在本公司支付赔款后，被保险人应将向该责任方追偿的权利转让给本公司，移交一切必要的单证，并协助本公司向责任方追偿。

二、涉外合同中有关义务的描述

一般来讲，义务主要有法律义务和约定义务。在涉外合同中，有关义务的描述主要有名词性描述和动词性描述两种。

（一）名词性描述

1. "have legal obligation" 意为 "拥有法定义务"

EG – 11 – 20 The Company has no legal obligation, absolute or contingent, to any other Person to sell any material portion of the assets of the

Company, to sell any material portion of the capital stock or other ownership interests of the Company or any of its Subsidiaries, or to effect any merger, consolidation or other reorganization of the Company or any of its Subsidiaries or to enter into any agreement with respect thereto.

参考译文：本公司没有完全或随附的任何法律义务向任何他人出售公司资产的任何重要部分、出售股本的任何重要部分或本公司或其任一子公司的其他所有权权益，或实现本公司或任一子公司的并购、合并或其他的重组或签订有关以上事项的协议。

2. have any obligation

EG – 11 – 21 The relationship between the Agent and each Bank is that of the agent and the principal only. Provided that the relationship in question shall not be deemed to constitute the Agent a trustee for any Bank or impose on the Agent any obligations other than the obligations specified in the provisions of this Contract.

"have any obligation" 意为"有任何义务"，该义务一般是合同双方约定的。"the agent and the principal" 属对义词，意为"代理人和委托人"。

参考译文：代理行和各行之间的关系仅为代理人和本人的关系，该种关系并非将代理行视为任何银行的信托受托人，或对代理人附加本合同明示条款规定以外的任何义务。

（二）动词性描述

动词性描述就是表达义务的词组以动词形式出现，一般表述为"有义务、有责任做某事"。

1. is obliged/obligated

EG – 11 – 22 In the case of dangerous and/or poisonous cargo (es), the Seller is obliged/obligated take care to ensure that the nature and the generally adopted symbol shall be marked conspicuously on each package.

参考译文：在危险或有毒货物的情况下，卖方有义务照管确保其属性安全且应在每一包装上标注通常采用的标识。

2. be obliged to

EG - 11 - 23 If any event of the Force Majeure occurs which causes damage to the Project or the infrastructure project, then C or New Company shall not be obliged to reinstate the same, or, as the case may be, complete the same, until the parties hereto have agreed upon the terms for such reinstatement or completion.

参考译文：如不可抗力的发生损坏了工程或基础设施，C 或新公司没有义务重新恢复之，或完成其修建，但双方就这种恢复或完成的条件达成一致意见则例外。

（三）权利义务的综合描述

在涉外合同中常采取分别描述的方式确定各方的责任和义务，这样较为公平，也便于理解。如某一设备买卖合同中甲乙方的权利义务约定：

The Buyer's responsibility and obligation：

（a）…

（b）…

…

The Seller's responsibility and obligation：

（a）…

（b）…

…

在分别描述时，一定要注意权利义务的对待。对待并非形式上的，而应关注实质的对等。同时，在描述形式上应尽量采用无主句，甲乙方的权利义务的内容在条款设置上应尽量保持顺序上的一致。

三、涉外合同中责任义务描述的类聚词

1. legal liability and responsibility

EG – 11 – 24 If an arbitrator involved in one of circumstances specified in Item 4, Article 34 of this Law, and if it is serious, or those specified in Item 6, Article 58 hereof, the arbitrator in question shall, in accordance with the law, bear the legal liability and responsibility. The arbitration commission shall remove the name of the arbitrator in question from the list of arbitrators.

参考译文：如果涉及本法第 34 条第 4 款的规定情况之一的和如果问题严重并符合本法第 58 条第 6 款规定的，该仲裁员应依法承担法律责任，仲裁委员会从仲裁员名单中清除该仲裁员的名字。

2. responsibilities and obligations

EG – 11 – 25 The Seller shall to ensure that the Seller of this contract, according to the contract requirements in a timely manner to the right to carry out its responsibilities and obligations of the contract until the completion of the mission.

参考译文：卖方应保证：本合同的卖方依照合同要求，采取适当方式去履行本合同与权利相对的责任和义务，直到完成受托的任务。

3. outstanding claims and liabilities

EG – 11 – 26 The termination of this Contract shall not in any way affect the outstanding claims and liabilities existing between the Parties hereto upon the expiration of the validity of the Contract and the debtor shall continue to be kept liable for paying the outstanding debts to the creditor.

参考译文：一旦合同的有效性消灭，本合同的终止不应以任何方式影响双方之间未决赔偿和已存在的负债，债务人应继续承担对债权人支付未了结债务的责任。

4. the ability and capability

EG – 11 – 27 Neither Party may assign this Agreement, in whole or in part, without the other Party's prior written consent, except to (i) any corporation resulting from any merger, consolidation or other reorganization involving the assigning Party, and (ii) any entity to which the assigning Party may transfer all or substantially all of its assets; provided that the assignee agrees in writing to be bound by all the terms and conditions of this agreement and provides documentation as evidence that the assignee has the ability and capability of meeting all of the obligations under this agreement.

参考译文：任何一方未经另一方事先书面同意，不得转让本协议的全部或部分，除非转让给（i）涉及转让方的因兼并、合并或其他重组而产生的任何公司，（ii）转让方可以向其转让全部或绝大部分资产的实体；但受让方须书面同意受本协议所有条款和条件的约束，并提供文件证明受让方有资格、有能力履行本协议项下的全部义务。

四、涉外合同中要求"某一方有义务尽力做某事"的描述

在涉外合同中，常要求某一方尽力做某事，也就是尽职履行义务或承担责任。对此常用以下方式表达："use all reasonable endeavors (efforts) to do sth."、"make full endeavors (efforts) to do sth."、"exert one's effort (s) to do sth." 或 "exert oneself to do sth." 等，而不用基础英语中的 "try one's best to do sth." 等句型。

1. use commercially reasonable efforts to

EG – 11 – 28 Except as contemplated by this agreement, from the date hereof through the closing date, Mattel shall cause each TLC Subsidiary to use commercially reasonable efforts to conduct its business in the ordinary course in all material respects; and shall use commercially reasonable endeavors to preserve intact its business relationships, keep available the service of its employees and maintain satisfactory relationships with its suppliers and customers.

参考译文：除非本协议预期，从本协议日期到成交日，Mattel 公司应促使 TLC 子公司竭尽全力在所有实质方面按通常程式进行交易；并应尽力来保持其商业关系完整，可获得其员工的服务并与供应商和客户维持良好的关系。

2. make efforts to

EG – 11 – 29 However, both parties shall make efforts to get the ratification within 60 (sixty) days.

参考译文：然而双方应努力在 60 天内获得批准。

3. exert its commercially reasonable efforts

EG – 11 – 30 Each of A and B agrees to exert its commercially reasonable efforts so that B can begin providing instant quotes on ＊＊ in as short a time as the capabilities and technologies of each party will allow.

参考译文：A 和 B 均同意尽其全力使得 B 在各方能力和技术许可的范围内尽快开始向＊＊公司提供即时报价。

4. exert their best efforts to

EG – 11 – 31 Promptly following the Effective Time, the shareholders of tunes who are employed by A or B Sub shall exert their best efforts to cause all employees of C and B Sub to execute in favor of B Sub proprietary rights agreements substantially similar to A's existing employee proprietary rights agreement.

参考译文：生效时间后，被 A 公司或 B Sub 公司所聘的 C 公司股东应立即竭尽全力促使 C 公司和 B Sub 公司的所有员工执行 B Sub 公司控股权协议，该协议实质上与 A 公司现有的员工控股权协议类似。

EG – 11 – 32 If Party B makes decorations or adds ancillary facilities without the written consent of Party A or exceeding the scope and requirements consented by Party A, Party A may request Party B to restore the premises to the original condition and compensate for the losses.

"to restore the premises to the original condition" 意为 "恢复原状"。

参考译文：如果乙方没经甲方同意额外增加辅助设施，或超过甲方同意的要求和范围，甲方可要求乙方恢复原状，并赔偿损失。

EG - 11 - 33 If during the lease term, Party B terminates the lease in violation of the contract, Party B shall pay Party A liquidated damages in the amount of twice the rental for the days to the expiration of the lease term. If the liquidated damages paid by Party B are not sufficient to cover Party A's losses, Party B shall be liable for the difference. Party A may deduct the difference from the security deposit. If the security deposit is not sufficient, the deficiency shall be paid by Party B.

参考译文：如果在租赁合同期间，乙方违反合同终止租赁合同，乙方应从终止租赁合同时起算向甲方支付双倍租金的违约金。如果乙方支付的违约金不够弥补甲方的损失，乙方应承担这一差额。甲方可以从保证金中扣除这一差额，如果保证金不够，乙方还应另行支付不足部分。

第 *12* 章

责任追究：与违约责任
相关的关键词理解

在涉外合同起草、谈判与审核中，合同违约与违约救济条款是双方商务人员与法务人员重点关注的问题。从违约条款的约定可以分析出合同哪一方占强势地位，哪一方占弱势地位。从违约条款与违约救济条款的最终确定也可以看出各方法务人员的专业水准和各方所持态度。

一、违约责任的一般法理问题

在涉外合同的阅读中，主要理解违约责任的追究方式与侵权责任的区别。

1. 违约与侵权的竞合

合同中由于基于公平与自愿原则，一般不会涉及相互的民事侵权问题，即使涉及侵权，相互也会通过免责等条款来相互豁免，但由于产品质量、安全、健康、环保及专利许可等因素，可能会涉及产品或许可技术对第三方的侵权的问题，由于侵权的因素及索赔都具有不确定性，这就会对受让方产生较大风险，应引起重视。

一般来说，因当事人一方的违约行为而侵害对方人身、财产权益的，受损害方有权选择依照本法要求其承担违约责任或者依照其他法律要求其承担侵权责任。这就是受损失的一方可选择是主张违约之诉还是主张侵权之诉的问题。

在合同履行过程中，可能既存在违约问题也出现侵权因素，特别是对于高新技术产品、专利技术转让许可合同等可能会因合同履行存在对第三方的侵权，或者因标的物的质量瑕疵造成对第三方的人身伤害或财产损失。

虽然在合同中可以通过免责条款来规避风险，但无论如何约定，在一方没有过错的情况下，即使约定了免责，也总是需要一方来承担相关损失费用的。这样的竞合约定可以引导损失或费用支付方来选择何种手段有效维护权益，但最难预测也是双方最关注的问题可能还是第三方的主张，这是双方不能通过约定来解决的，即使约定也会被认定为无效，因为依照大陆法系现代民商法理念，除非经第三方的明示同意或担保义务成立，合同双方是不得为第三方设定义务与责任的。

对于违约责任的构成，中国合同法对违约责任的归责原则指有违约行为的存在，一般不包括过错。当然，无论是中国合同法还是英美合同法，对于违约责任都可归因于一般责任和严格责任，同时要区别明示责任与默示责任。

所谓严格责任，又称无过错责任，是指违约发生以后，确定违约当事人的责任应主要考虑违约的结果是否由违约方的行为造成，而不考虑违约方的故意和过失。也就是说，违约方不履行合同义务，不管其主观上是否有过错，均应承担违约责任。因此，法务人员就要判断违约方行为与违约后果之间是否存在必然的因果关系，在举证上只要能够证明某一违约后果系违约方不履行合同或者不完全履行合同的行为引起，即可要求违约方承担违约责任。

当然，实现严格责任的追究并非意味着在任何情况下只要债务人不履行合同债务就必然承担违约责任。法务人员还可结合法律规定的免责事项或合同约定的免责事项或兜底条款来综合分析判断，综合考虑是否应承担完全的违约赔偿责任；同时，作为违约方还享有一定的抗辩权，如能够证明对方违约在先的证据就是最好的免责抗辩，同时也可通过证明违约行为与违约后果之间没有因果关系来推脱责任。

同样，即使合同没有明确约定违约责任追究，当一方明显违反相关规定、行业惯例或交易习惯时，守约方一样可通过默示担保的法理要求来追究对方的违约责任。只是通过默示担保追究对方的责任需要遵循严格的证据开示原则，即既要证明其违反默示担保的规定或惯例，也要证明其违反默示担保的行为，更要通过举证来证明其违约行为所造成的损失，包括直接或间接的损失证据资料。当然，主张默示担保成立的条件是在合同中没有约定不适用默示担保的前提。没有事先确定对默示担保的免责条款，这一点是成文法与判例法的显著区别。成文法主张没有约定则依照法律；判例法主张有约定则依照约定，约定与法律相违背时则约定优先适用。

2. 对于"material breach"（重大违约）的认定

对于涉外合同的条款，一般按照判例法理论区分为"条件"（conditions）和"保证"（warranties）两类。条件是合同中重要的、根本的条款，保证是次要的和附属性条款。违反条件条款的行为构成重大违约，将赋予合同无过错方当事人解除合同的自由；违反保证条款只构成轻微违约，仅赋予无过错方当事人损害赔偿请求权，其并不能免除自己的义务。而实质上，所谓的条件也就是合同约定的实质性义务，具有实质性履行义务的一方如果不切实履行义务，就会构成对他方的重大违约。

对于重大违约的理解也不能光从表面上去区分条件或保证，有些也可能既非条件也非保证，而是属于所谓的中间条款，对条款的违反如果构成对合同目的的实现障碍就属于重大违约。因此，构成重大违约的标准可以从以下几点来参考：一是受害方合理期待的利益被剥夺的程度；二是受害方被剥夺的利益可能获得充分补偿的程度；三是违约方违约的损害程序；四是在全面考虑各种环境条件包括任何担保的情况下，违约方补救违约的可能性；五是违约方的违约行为是否符合诚实信用及公平交易规则。

除此之外，美国联邦法院也总结出了判断重大违约的四个要件：

一是违约是否导致缔约方丧失缔约目的；二是违约行为是否导致守约方利益失衡；三是以习惯和惯例来衡量，该违约行为是否具有重大性；四是违约是否事实上导致了不合理及不公平的后果。

EG – 12 – 1 Avoidance of the contract releases both parties from their obligations under it, subject to any damages which may be due. Avoidance does not affect any provision of the contract for the settlement of disputes or any other provision of the contract governing the rights and obligations of the parties consequent upon the avoidance of the contract.

参考译文：宣告合同无效解除了双方在合同中的义务，但应负责的任何损害赔偿仍应负责。宣告合同无效不影响合同关于解决争端的任何规定，也不影响合同中关于双方在宣告合同无效后权利和义务的任何其他规定。

合同一方当事人没能按照合同条件履行合同义务后，另一方当事人就要依照约定要求对方支付违约金。而主张支付违约的同时也要求受损方举证证明自己到底受到多少损害是一件很困难的事。判例法国家认为违约金是预定的损害赔偿。在订立合同时，当违约金不易确定并难以计算时，如果双方当事人可以合理地约定赔偿范围，为避开举证责任，可约定违约金条款以确定赔偿范围。也就是说，在违约行为发生后，受损害方只要证明对方违约即可，不必再举证自己所受损害的范围。

就目前的合同纠纷审判案例的发展趋势来看，首推损害补偿原则作为合同违约救济的一般原则；一般不承认"惩罚性条款"（penalty）的效力；倡导违约金必须与实际损失相当，避免通过合同获得非法利益。违约金应相当于实际的损失或可预期的损失，否则就带有处罚性了。

由于罚金在性质上违背了救济的补偿原则，同时认为罚金具有刑罚或行政处罚的属性，而企业间或商务主体之间的商务行为不应具有相互惩罚的属性。因此，对违约金的性质要明确约定，并符合主观意思的一致性。

在违约金的表述上，尽量使用"liquidated damages"（违约金），而不要使用"penalty"（罚金），道理也就在于此。

EG – 12 – 2 In case the Seller fails to make delivery ten weeks later than the time of shipment stipulated in the contract, the Buyer shall have the right to cancel the contract, and the Seller, in spite of the cancellation, shall nevertheless pay the aforesaid penalty to the Buyer without delay.

参考译文：卖方延迟交货超过合同规定 10 周时，买方有权撤销合同。此时卖方仍应不延迟地按上述规定向买方支付罚款。

该合同条款有三个问题：

一是"the aforesaid penalty"买方撤销合同是否有权对卖方处以罚款。

二是是否还有相关违约金的描述，卖方没有在合同规定的时间交货属于严重违约，应适用违约责任条款。这里出现罚款显然既不友好，也不专业。

三是"without delay"，没有具体的时间概念，应规定具体的工作日。

建议修改为：In case the Seller fails to make delivery ten weeks later than the time of shipment stipulated in the contract, the Buyer shall have the right to cancel the contract, and the Seller, in spite of the cancellation, shall nevertheless pay the aforesaid liquidated damages to the Buyer within 10 working days.

EG – 12 – 3 In case party B breaches this contract, Party A has right to deduct the default fine, compensation for damage or any other expenses from the deposit. In case the deposit is not sufficient to cover such items, Party B should pay the insufficiency within ten days after receiving the written notice of payment from Party A.

参考译文：因乙方违反本合同的规定而产生的违约金、损害赔偿金和其他相关费用，甲方可在保证金中抵扣，不足部分乙方必须在接到甲方付款通知后 10 日内补足。

EG – 12 – 4 During the lease term, any party who fails to fulfill any article of this contract without the other party's understanding will be deemed to breach the contract. Both parties agree that the default fine will be _____ . In case the default fine is not sufficient to cover the loss suffered by the faultless party, the party in breach should pay additional compensation to the other party.

"default fine" 具有惩罚性质。这里要注意两个问题：一是处罚主体的行政授权，有些国家是禁止经营性单位具有行政执法权的。二是根据英美相关法律，对于处罚性主张需要负举证责任；而违约责任只要合同约定并且不显失公平，就可直接得到法院的支持。

而该条款表述为"default fine"，可能还少于实际损失，显然不具有惩罚性，应改为违约金的表述最好。

建议将"default fine"修改为"liquidated damages"。

参考译文：甲乙双方任何一方在未征得对方谅解的情况下，不履行本合同规定条款，导致本合同中途终止，则视为该方违约，双方同意违约金为人民币_____元整。若违约金不足以弥补无过错方之损失，则违约方还需就不足部分支付赔偿金。

EG – 12 – 5 Should the cooperative venture company be unable to continue its operation or achieve its business purpose due to the fact that one of the contracting parties fails to fulfill the obligations prescribed by the contract and articles of association, or seriously violates the provisions of the contract and articles of association, that party shall be deemed to have unilaterally terminated the contract. The other party shall have the right to terminate the contract in accordance with the provisions of the contract after approval by the original examination and approval authority, and to claim damages. In case Party A and Party B of the cooperative venture company agree to continue the operation, the party who fails to fulfill its obligations shall be liable for the economic losses caused thereby to the joint venture company.

参考译文：由于一方不履行合同、章程规定的义务，或严重违反合同、章程规定，造成合作公司无法经营或无法达到合同规定的经营目的，视做违约方片面终止合同，对方除有权向违约的一方索赔外，并有权按合同规定报原审批机关批准终止合同。如甲乙双方同意继续经营，违约方仍应赔偿履约一方的经济损失。

该合同条款存在两个问题：一是损失赔偿，是对守约方的损失承担赔偿责任，还是对联营公司的损失承担赔偿责任。

二是对于终止合同的描述不清。

"视做违约方片面终止合同"的描述不清。合同终止就是双方同意终止，终止后就可报批；如果视为终止，则说明还没终止，需等报批。这显然难以实际执行。因此，这里应该描述为守约方有权终止合同，并要求违约方承担责任。

EG－12－6 Should all or part of the contract and its appendices be unable to be fulfilled owing to the fault of one party, the party in breach shall bear the liability therefor. Should it be the fault of both parties, they shall bear their respective liabilities according to the actual.

参考译文：由于一方当事人的过错，造成合同和它的附件不能完全或部分履行时，过错一方承担相应的违约责任。双方均存在过错的，应根据实际各自承担相应的违约责任。

3. 违约责任的追究方式

违约责任，又称违反合同的民事责任，是指合同当事人因违反合同债务所应承担的责任。追究违约责任并不以当事人的意志为转移，法务人员应从基本的归责原则中弄清行为人的民事责任的根据和标准，归责原则是追究违约责任和采取相应救济手段的指导方针。

违反了合同就要承担相应的责任，承担责任的方式因不同的国家具有不同的规定和司法实践而略有差异。中国法律规定的承担违约责任的方式通常有继续履行、采取补救措施、停止违约行为、赔偿损失、终止或撤销合同等，此外还有支付违约金及定金的责任形式。当然，对于涉外合同来讲，主要是以双方约定的形式为准。

合同的违约条款一般由违约责任追究条款、违约金确定条款、违约救济条款、违约金支付条款和/或违约赔偿条款等组成。考虑到合同的具体特征以及允诺的性质和允诺履行的情形，英美法发展出"条件理论"。根据该理论，合同的条款区分为条件和保证两类。违反条件条款的行为构成重大违约，将赋予无过错方解除合同的自由；违反保证条款只构成轻微违约，仅赋予无过错方当事人损害赔偿请求权而并不是免除自己的义务。所以，法务人员关注的重点是哪些条款构成条件，哪些条款构成保证。

企业的法务人员应懂得，并不是非得等到对方有违约的事项时才可以主张追究对方的违约责任。根据中国《合同法》第 108 条的规定，当一方明确表示或者以自己的行为表明不履行合同义务的，对方可以在履行期限届满之前要求其承担违约责任。而涉外合同则最好在条款中约定抗辩权行使的前提及事由触发节点。

还有一种是各方本身没有违约行为，但确实有一方存在合同损失的情形。该种情形就涉及依照公平原则实施损失补偿的问题。也就是说，在合同履行过程中可能存在合同双方都没有违约行为，但另一方确实遭受了难以弥补的损失，该损失如何计算与赔偿也因此要在合同中明确约定为好，否则就可能使合同无法履行，从而遭受的损失没有补偿的依据。

以下因素可能导致合同难以正常履行而需要在合同中明确约定：

（1）不可抗力因素；

（2）第三人行为；

（3）政策变化与政府行为；

（4）不可预见因素（主要是合同约定地质资料、气象资料、水文资料的变化与实际相关较大，从而使依靠不可预见因素完成合同目的的成本增加）；

（5）因成果交货期较长而引起的情势变更。

也就是说，合同成立以后客观情况发生了当事人在订立合同时无法预见的、非不可抗力造成的不属于商业风险的重大变化，继续履行合同对于一方当事人明显不公平或者不能实现合同目的，当事人请求法院变更或者解除合同的，法院一般会根据公平原则，并结合案件的实际损失情况确定是否变更或者解除。

二、违约责任追究的几个法律术语

合同签订后，总会因各种不确定性因素或当事人的非善意行为而致合同不能依约得到全面履行，这就要考虑责任追究，就要在合同中事先对可能的违约行为进行界定，并约定责任追究的方式、方法和相应的补救措施。下面重点谈谈违约责任追究的几个法律术语。

1. "penalty"、"liquidated damages" **和** "the liability for breach of contract"

在涉外合同中对于违约责任的描述有两种形式：一种是直接的描述，即"the liability for breach of contract"；另一种是间接的描述，即"liquidated damages"。如是经双方协议一致而不考虑处罚性的加重处罚，一般用"liquidated damages"较为适当。

EG – 12 – 7 The payment of liquidated damages by the Seller shall not release the Seller from its obligation to deliver the delayed Technical Documentation.

参考译文：卖方支付违约金不能免除其继续交付技术文件的义务。

EG – 12 – 8 Where the parties prescribed liquidated damages for delayed performance, the breaching party shall, in addition to payment of the liquidated damages, render performance.

"render" 一般可译为"实施"，在这里译为"持续"、"不间断"较为适当。

参考译文：当事人就迟延履行约定违约金的，违约方支付违约金后还应当履行债务。

EG – 12 – 9 Licensee shall have the right to deduct from any payment the withholding taxes, liquidated damages, and/or compensations, if any, which Licensor shall pay under contract.

参考译文：如果依据合同许可方应支付预提税、违约金和/或赔偿金，被许可方有权从应支付给许可方的款项中扣除。

"the liability for breach of contract"在涉外合同条款中一般多指具体的违约行为；而"liquidated damages"多描述具体的违约金数额，常常列出具体的计算方式，如不列明具体的计算方式则泛指违约行为。因此，"liquidated damages"一般会与支付关键词"pay"或"payment"或相应计算金额、计算方式、方法相配合使用。

EG – 12 – 10 If this Agreement is terminated for any reason attributable Part B before the term expires, Part B will pay ten percent（10%）of the Consultant Fee as liquidated damages.

参考译文：如果本协议在协议期限结束前因B方的任何原因而终止，B方将支付顾问费的10%作为约定的损失赔偿。

EG – 12 – 11 Liquidated damages should not exceed the amount the companies known to workers of trade secrets license price.

参考译文：违约金数额一般不超过职工所知悉的公司商业秘密的许可使用价格。

另外，还有一个常用的词是"penalty"，这个词为"罚款"的意思。由于有些国家不承认企业、商务单位的行政处罚权，因此即使合同约定了"penalty"，也会被法院认定无效。再者，即使被判为有效，也要求主张方提供相应处罚的依据及损失证据。而"liquidated damages"就相对宽容些，因为这是双方约定的违约责任，一般都较为合理，且属于合同内责任性质。法院一般遵循"当事人自治原则"判案，当事人只要能够证明对方有违约事实，即可主张要求对方支付违约金。

EG – 12 – 12 Contract awarding units and contractors should fully fulfill their contractual obligations. Failure to fulfill contractual obligations is subject to contract – breach responsibilities under the laws.

参考译文：发包单位和承包单位应当全面履行合同约定的义务。不按照合同约定履行义务的，依法承担违约责任。

"the liability for breach of contract" 是一个意群性法律关键词，即"违约责任"。

EG – 12 – 13 The contract shall expressly provide the amount of the loan, the use, the term, the interest rate, the procedures for settling accounts, the liability for breach of contract and other similar terms.

这里没有对违约责任进行具体的计算，如涉及详细计算，就要应用到"liquidated damages"。类似的表述还有"default responsibilities for"、"the default liability"等。

参考译文：合同中，应明确规定贷款的数额、用途、期限、利率、结算办法和违约责任等条款。

EG – 12 – 14 If a Party breaches this contract, it shall bear the liabilities arising from such breach in accordance with the relevant laws and regulations of China.

参考译文：如果本合同一方违约，该方应按中国有关法律和法规承担违约责任。如属双方违约，则由双方分别承担各自违约所引起的责任。

2. "infringement"和"tort"

在英美法系国家使用的法律术语中，被译为"侵权"的"infringement"与同样被译为"侵权"的"tort"有着完全不同的含义。前者包含一切民事侵害行为，与之相应的民事责任应当是中国《中华人民共和国民法通则》第 134 条的全部，再加上"其他"。后者则仅包含需要负财产损害赔偿责任的侵害行为。

在英美法系国家的法院中，认定"infringement"（侵权）从来不需要去找"过错"、"实际损失"这类"要件"，只要有侵权事实即可。从语源上看，当初判例法选择的这个英文术语本身正是"只需认定侵权事实"之意。"in"表示"进入"，"fringe"表示特定范围。任何人如果未经许可进入法定的他人权利范围，即构成侵权。而"tort"含有"错误"、"过失"的意思，只有错误或过失存在，"tort"才可能产生。

英国法律把"infringement"与"tort"作清晰划分的典型是版权法。早在 1936 年的一则有名判例中，高等法院就指出"infringement"覆盖了"tort"；"tort"仅仅是"infringement"中需要确认过错并负赔偿责任的那一类。英国现行版权法中，哪一类行为要负"infringement"的相应责任、哪一类要负"tort"的相应责任更是泾渭分明。

"tort"问题即侵权赔偿责任的确认在通常情况下需要以过错为前提。而作为"tort"的严格责任，亦即侵权赔偿的严格责任，则不需要以过错为前提，这只是各国（包括中国）民法在侵权篇（实质应是侵权赔偿篇）中专门列出的诸如高危作业之类的特例。对此，国内多数人是比较了解的。

"infringement"意指"侵权"，它包含了"物权请求权"、"知识产权请求权"、"人身权请求权"之类绝对权的请求权相对应的侵害。这种侵害的行为人所应负的民事责任包括（但远不限于）损害赔偿，但更包括与赔偿（乃至财产利益）无关的其他责任（如停止侵害、赔礼道歉）。这类侵权构成的确认在通常情况下未必以过错为前提。它的通例是无过错责任（即严格责任），只要有侵权事实就必须负"停止侵权"责任，反倒是非严格责任或过错责任在这里成了特例。

实际上，"tort"是一种"错误的行为"或者"民事的过错"。美国词典《Merriam – Webster's Dictionary of Law》将该词解释为"合同法违约以外的不当行为"。换言之，"tort"是一种既非刑法也非合同法领域中的民事过错，即"civil wrong"。"tort"这个词来自于拉丁文的"tortum"后者为"不公"、"过错"的意思。

EG – 12 – 15 The service provided for this project shall not violate or infringe any industrial property right or intellectual property right or right of any third party.

"violate or infringe"属类聚词，直接译为"侵犯"即可。

参考译文：为本项目提供的服务不得侵犯任何工业产权或知识产

权或任何第三方的权利。

3."compensate"和"indemnify"

从字面看，两个单词都有"补偿"、"赔偿"的意思，"compensate"指的是给予别人付出的劳动或者损失相应的报酬或弥补。而"indemnify"是为他人的行为所造成的损失进行赔偿或实质恢复原状的行为，是法律英语尤其是合同中的一个常用单词，意思是"补偿"、"赔偿"，要比"compensate"（补偿）的含义广泛。

EG - 12 - 16 Each party shall indemnify the other from any and all losses that may arise out of breach by such party of any of the warranties set forth in this Article.

参考译文：一方如果违反其在本条中的任何保证而使另一方发生损失，应向损失方作出赔偿。

"indemnification"用于赔偿条款或独立的赔偿协议中时指的是一个广义的过程，包括索赔、赔偿、对赔偿的限制、救济等一切与赔偿相关的行为。

"indemnification"的英文意指：

（1）"a sum of money paid in compensation for loss or injury"；

（2）"an act of compensation for actual loss or damage or for trouble and annoyance"。

"indemnify"在涉外合同中结合具体的语境有时可翻译为"免于承担责任"，这应引起法务人员的特别关注。在合同中表述为"要求甲方承担责任"或"甲方免于乙方承担责任"实质上是一种方式的两种表达形式，也就是翻译中的正话反说或反话正说的技巧问题。但需要引起注意的是，在翻译中主语与宾语的位置不能颠倒。

EG - 12 - 17 The Consignor shall be deemed to have guaranteed to the Carrier the accuracy, at the time the goods were taken in charge by the Carrier, of the goods' description, marks, number, quantity, weight, and/or volume as furnished by him, and the Consignor shall indemnify the Carrier against all losses, damage, and expenses arising or resulting from inaccuracies in or inadequacy of such particulars. The right of the Carrier to such indemnity shall be in no way limiting his responsibility and liability under this bill of lading to any person other than the Consignor.

参考译文：双方应认为发货人在承运人接管该批货物时已向其保证所供货物的品种、唛头、编号、数量、重量和/或体积的准确性，对因此类细节不准或不足而产生的任何损失、损害及费用，发货人应对承运人实行免责。但承运人享受的此种免责权不得限制其在本提单项下对发货人以外的任何人所承担的责任和义务。

4. 三种描述方式

（1）名词性描述

EG - 12 - 18 If such appointment results in loss to the agent, it may seek indemnification from the principal.

参考译文：因此给受托人造成损失的，受托人可以向委托人要求赔偿损失。

EG - 12 - 19 If product could not reach quality standard, the seller would make an indemnification loss to the Buyer.

参考译文：如果产品达不到质量标准，卖方会对买方的损失作出赔偿。

EG - 12 - 20 The warranty and indemnification provisions of this agreement shall survive the termination hereof.

参考译文：本协议中的担保与赔偿条款就此终止。

（2）动词性描述

在涉外合同中，"indemnify"侧重于给相对方造成损失的赔偿。"indemnify"这个动词与"hold harmless"经常搭配使用，如"Party A agrees to indemnify and hold Party B harmless against any and all..."其实

两者含义相同，译成"A 方应当赔偿并使 B 方不受……的侵害"、"赔偿"即可。

（3）形容词的描述

"indemnifiable losses"指的是"应赔偿损失"。

"应赔偿损失"是指累计损失，还包含因此提起诉讼而发生的相关费用。

还有一点需要指出的是，"compensate"（补偿）在合同中作为补偿更多地是通过友好协商或公平原则，而"indemnify"是基于违约方的过错或过失而形成。因此，要求"compensate"（补偿）时，一般要求主张己方的损失并限于成本或实际产生的损失；而主张"indemnify"的一方就不一定造成了损失，也无须主张自己已形成的损失的证据。当然，在具体条款的描述中，如果都约定为某一具体的计算方法，则两者无实质差别，均可理解为"赔偿"和"补偿"。

EG – 12 – 21 I'm afraid you should compensate us by 5% of the total amount of the contract. The damages are designed to compensate victims for their direct losses.

参考译文：贵公司要赔偿我方合同全部金额的 5%。该赔偿金是用来补偿受害人的直接损失的。

一个经常与"indemnify"同时出现于赔偿条款或赔偿合同中的词是"defend"。其一般与"indemnify"和"hold harmless"相同，即"保护，不受……侵害"之意。其也常与"against"搭配，表示"使其免遭损害或损失"。当然，其有时也可作"辩护"或者"答辩"、"抗辩"理解。

"claim"一词在法律语境中作为名词使用时，通常表示"索赔"或"权利主张"、"赔偿请求权"、"提出要求"、"声称"、"索赔"、"断言"。

EG – 12 – 22 Should either joint – venture fails to pay the contribution on schedule according to Clause 5, the default party should pay the other 10% of the interest one month after the dead line. The other party shall hold right to terminate the contract or to claim the damage against ／ to him according to Clause 53 thereof, if the default party has not done so three months after the deadline.

"claim"在这里就有"索赔"之意。

参考译文：如果合资一方未能按本合同第 5 条规定按期付款，违约方应在逾期后 1 个月付给另一方 10% 的利息。如果违约方逾期 3 个月仍未如资，合同另一方根据本合同第 53 条规定有权终止合同并向违约方索赔损失。

三、对关键词"indemnify and hold harmless"的详细分析

本书通过笔者十多宗涉外专利技术转让合同审核的体会，结合精读陶博［美］所著的《中英双语法律文书中的语义歧义》一书的学习笔记，拟就"indemnify and hold harmless"在专利技术转让合同特定法律语境中进行辨析，并重点谈谈"indemnify"和与之相同的"hold harmless"所搭配的介词和/或宾语不同，就可能产生赔偿范围的差别和合同主体各方法律风险的分担责任的大小，以此提高涉外合同的起草与审核能力。

（一）正确理解"indemnify and hold harmless"

"indemnify and hold harmless"是由连词"and"连接的两个同义词，是典型的类聚词，大意为"赔偿和不要求承担债务"。其经常用于各种不同的合同中，如用于涉外技术工艺包引进合同时，主要是基于被许可方担心第三方主张被许可方所用的技术侵犯了第三方的专利或其他权益并对其提出诉讼而免遭索赔之患。因此，被许可方会要求许可方的赔偿是广义的，从形式来讲包括违约责任与侵权责任，从范围来讲包括损失、成本、债务或涉诉费用支出等，从表达方式来讲包括动词"to indemnify"或"to hold harmless"或"to save harmless"。赔偿条款一般用于赔偿一方因另一方的行为，或由另一方控制的具体情况，或另一方理应负责的，如许可方负责的技术许可安排方面，所遭受的损失，包括可预料的或有负债。

"indemnify clause"不仅指合同一方承诺承担某方面的责任和/或损失，而且指使合同相关方免于承担相应的责任和/或损失。

一般的英语词典对于"indemnify"的解释有两种：一是"to keep free from or preserve, protect from"；二是"to compensate"。"to compensate for damage or loss sustained"是"indemnify"一词现在最常用的意思。

"indemnify"的两种意思：（1）"indemnify against loss"。"indemnify against loss"意为"赔偿协议中可能产生的损失或损害"。赔偿合同中的损失和损害必须在受偿方确实受到损失时才能发生。赔偿的义务在支付求偿权、支付求偿权的判决或支付求偿权的理赔时才形成。也就是说，只有当受偿方实际付出金额后，赔偿方才有义务赔偿受偿方。（2）"indemnify against liability"。按照美国法理学说，"indemnify against liability"意为"在赔偿债务的合同中，债务一旦成立，即可采取行动"。也就是说，如果合同不仅仅是赔偿损失，而且还赔偿债务或索赔，则损失的计算根据是所发生的债务而不是实际遭受的损失。显然，"indemnify against liability"的赔偿范围广于"indemnify against loss"。

"harmless"基本上和"indemnify"相同，都是"free from liability or loss"，也就是说，"hold harmless"的主要意思不是"赔偿损失"而是"免除承担债务"。

在专利技术转让合同中，如果被许可方遭起诉并被判决向专利遭到侵犯的第三方支付金额，那么判决一旦下达，许可持有人就有义务支付金额。届时，如果赔偿条款是赔偿债务，那么赔偿方必须付款；如果是赔偿损失，那么赔偿方可以等到被许可方实际支付后才付款。

显然，赔偿损失和赔偿债务之间的主要区别是时差问题。所谓时差，也就是赔偿方何时付款，是在判决时支付还是等受偿方实际付出后支付。但是，凡牵涉金钱，"以后付"可能就是"不付"。例如，受偿方破产，不用为判决付费了。如果契约是赔偿损失，赔偿方可能就永远不需付钱了，因为只有等受偿方支付后他才有义务赔偿，受偿方不付，他也就不用付了。如果是赔偿债务，即使受偿方破产了，赔偿方也必须支付，因为赔偿方的债务是根据受偿方的债务形成的，也就是在判决下达之时形成的，无论受偿方是否破产。因为赔偿的支付义务是建立在受偿方的债务上而不是受偿方的付款上。假若法院判决所涉及的赔偿条款是赔偿损失而不是赔偿债务，因为受偿方破产了，赔偿方得以免除付款。这样，对于专有技术许可方来讲，赔偿损失条款比赔偿债务条款对其更为有利。反之，对于被许可方来讲，赔偿债务契约对其更有利。

（二）"indemnify" and "hold harmless" 之辨析

《美国法律百科全书》讲道："赔偿契约究竟是赔偿债务还是赔偿损失和损害在于其契约的真正意图和意思；如果契约只涉及赔偿，那就是赔偿损失和损害，如果契约要求赔偿方采取某种行动或支付款项，而且该行动和付款得以阻止受偿方受到损害或损伤，那就是赔偿债务。"在起草法律文书中该用什么语言来说明与澄清契约的意思呢？

在英文表述中，赔偿条款一般由四部分组成，其用意差别较大，详细辨析经笔者总结整理如下表：

动词	介词	介词的宾语	表示因果关系的修饰短语	用意
indemnify	against for （较优）	losses/*damages/charges/expenses/cost*	arising from this contract/in connection with this contract	表示赔偿损失的事项
hold harmless/ save harmless	against	liabilities/ debts		表示尚未支付的债务
indemnify/ hold harmless	from/ against	losses/*damages*/liabilities	arising from this contract/in connection with this contract	可在具体条款中选用，形成不同的意思，分开表述可达到消除歧义的目的
说明	1. 有时"indemnify"与"reimburse"相同。而"reimburse"后一般用"for"，所以"for"相对于"against"较优。 2. 宾词组"for losses/*damages*/liabilities"的列举不以泛指结尾，最后一个并列成分前没有"other"一词，这样就不会出现类别推定的错误。			

在实务中常会犯搭配上的错误。例如，在专利技术许可协议中："Licensee shall indemnify licensor and hold it harmless against and from any liability, claims or damages, and expenses whatsoever in any way arising out of licensee's manufacture, use or distribution of the products …"此条款中有"liability"一词，应该是"赔偿债务"，但是这种债务表达方法不理想，也会引起对立的解释。因为有四个词的列举，而"liability"没有用"and"或其他词分开，所以联想理解推定可能会适用。如果该推定适用，"liability"会被解释为"discharged liability"，即"loss"。

再如，在专利技术许可协议中："Licensee shall subject to the provisions of Section 8.4 hereof, protect, indemnify and hold harmless licensor and, upon licensor's request therefore, defend licensor from and against any and all losses actually incurred or suffered by licensor …"这里没有提到债务，所以不能理解为赔偿债务，但"protect"一词让人费解。根据合同，许可人可要求"protection"，但"protect"又难以理解为"辩护"，究竟指什么并不清楚，可能是要求相关保护的费用由对方承担的意思，但表述不清反而可能引起歧义。这就可能被对方认为是一个多余的词而被要求删除掉，而不是按照其意思去增加新内容。合同谈判中，删除一个不易理解的词组容易，扩充一个词组以达成一致是相当难的。

（三）法务人员在审核法律文书时如何判断赔偿的范围

法务人员在审核法律文书时究竟应如何判断或界定赔偿的范围呢？

在合同审核中，"liability"一般指未付债务，即法律上债权人还没有拿到钱，债务人有义务向债权人赔偿。"undercharged liability"是一项债务，而"discharged liability"是一笔费用或开支。可以在"liability"前加合适的形容词来表示债务和损失之间的区别，例如，用"discharged liability"来代替"loss, claim, damage, cost or expense"；用"undercharged liability"指未偿还的债务；用"indemnify discharged liability"表示赔偿损失；用"hold harmless against undercharged liabilities"表示赔偿债务。

在专利技术转让合同的审核中，下列措施有助于正确表达是赔偿债务还是赔偿损失。其一，把"indemnify and hold harmless"拆开使用，让各自的介词和宾语直接跟在动词后面。其二，只用表示损失的词语作"indemnify"后介词的宾语；只用表示债务的词语作"hold harmless"后介词的宾语。其三，避免使用"claims"、"suits"等容易引起歧义的词语。其四，把"indemnify"和"hold harmless"的次序根据其引发事件的先后排列，因债务发生的损失在前，故"hold harmless"就应放在"indemnify"前面。

（四）法务人员起草和审核专利技术转让合同时应重点关注的问题

在起草和审核有关专利技术转让合同中的赔偿条款时，应考虑相关的背景资料，了解合同的目的，并在充分理解上下文的基础上决定采用何种搭配形式。通过实务总结，笔者认为应重点考虑以下几点：

（1）要明确合同条款约定的归责原则。条款约定的归责原则是指追究对方的违约责任还是侵权责任。一般来讲，违约责任限于损失或成本支付，精明的预期违约方会要求限定为直接责任所导致的损失或成本支付。而侵权责任不仅涉及损失或成本支付，可能还涉及债务追究，包括涉诉费用和预期的或有债务的承担，特别是可能涉及对第三方侵权时债务会扩大。因此，如何选用"indemnify"和/或"hold harmless"就十分重要了。

（2）要明确合同条款设置的目的。就赔偿目的而言，如果目的不是债务而是赔偿损失，就不应用"hold harmless"，也不应用"liability"、"debts"、"obligation"、"to which [he] may be subjected or become liable"、"to which [he] may be liable"等词，如"indemnify against losses, costs, expenses, damages, charges and judgments"等。

如果目的包括债务、损失和涉诉费用，就应用两式词，并加"辩护"等词。其次序是"defend"、"hold harmless"、"indemnify"。例如"defend [licensee] against claims, actions, demands and suits"、"hold [licensee] harmless against liability"、"indemnify [licensee] against losses, costs, expenses, damages, charges and judgments"等。

特别需要注意的是，枚举出现多组词语时一定要注意事件发生的先后次序、事件的发生引起的严重性以及客户所关注程度，还要关注到词性的联想所引起的推定。

（3）法务人员的立场。如何选用动词与介宾词组的搭配可能导致扩大或缩小赔偿条款的范围，这一行为要考虑是否符合客户利益最大化原则，这与法务人员所持的立场有关。如果是为赔偿方起草或审核文件，就应把赔偿范围限制在损失方面，一般应用"loss/discharged liability"一词作"indemnify"后面的介词"for"的宾语；如果是代表受偿方，就应扩大赔偿范围，一般应用"liability"一词作"hold harmless"后面的介词"against"的宾语，因为"hold harmless"一般指债务。根据先债务后损失的次序，"hold harmless"应放在"indemnify"的前面。例如："...hold harmless against liability and indemnify against loss，..."。

（4）从风险防范角度考虑词语间的搭配。任何词语的搭配都可能形成解释上的歧义，歧义就是法律风险的根源所在，所以需要防止这一问题的出现，并尽量避免不同词性的词组枚举，同时还应与合同标的额的大小和其他影响风险程度的因素和赔偿条款紧密关联进行思考，防止小的疏忽形成较大的风险。

（5）注意词组列举的局限性和排他性。一定要注意同一文本中同一词组的意思不能存在两种以上的解释，否则就可能形成语境歧义。

（6）适当地做好三种推定：一是联想理解推定，即列举一组相关的词语时，对与狭义词组组合的广义词一般作狭义的解释，如"liability"与"loss"、"cost"、"damages"等词一同枚举时，往往会理解为对已产生的损失承担某种特定的责任，而非债务性责任；二是类别推定，即列举一组相关词语时，紧随特义词后的泛指词一般应推定为特义，在英文中主要是要对"or any other"、"or other"、"whatever"、"whatsoever"、"e. g."、"such as"、"etc."、"so on"等表述特别关注；三是否定含义推定，即要正确理解未被包括的列举是否意味被排除、肯定一方是否意味否定另一方等。例如，列举中有"including"一词，就不排除其他没有包括在内的项目。否定含义推定要对"all"、"any"、"excluding"、"including but not limited to"、"including without limitation"等词特别关注。对此一般应解释为范围限定，不能否定之中得出必然的肯定。排除适用于刑事辩护，如某一词语理解为对控方有利，就必然推出对辩方不利，在合同文本与民事代理中就得不出必然的推定。而在其他领域，特别是在合同文本的审核与起草中一般只作限定，意味着所列举已穷尽，而其他再多余的排列就可能存在另类解释。

（五）专利技术转让合同中有关赔偿条款的常用范本小结

在专利技术转让合同中，赔偿条款可参照如下范本起草或审核。

1. 考虑赔偿债务和损失的简单条款

EG - 12 - 23 "Licensor shall hold harmless licensee against liability, and indemnify licensee for , in each case arising out of..."

"Licensor shall hold harmless licensee against undischarged liability, and indemnify licensee for discharged liability, in each case arising out of..."

2. 包括辩护的赔偿条款

EG - 12 - 24 "Licensor shall defend licensee in any judicial or arbitral proceeding, hold harmless licensee against any liability, and indemnify licensee for any loss, in each case arising out of..."

"Licensor shall defend licensee in any judicial or arbitral proceeding, hold harmless licensee against any undischarged liability, and indemnify licensee for any discharged liability, in each case arising out of..."

四、涉外合同中风险控制的基本关键词

笔者最近几年参与了几份涉外工艺包专利技术转让合同的谈判和审核，从对方提供的合同文本中可以看出，licensor（外资方）对风险的控制十分严格。在条款设计上，无论是对违约责任还是因专利侵权形成的赔偿责任都设定了可控制的风险点。其风险控制都限定在可获得利益的范围内。也就是说，最大的风险不超过其预计可获得的利益，同时考虑成本的可补偿性，而不像国内一些公司，只要能够拿到订单或有可获得的利益，就从来不考虑可承受的风险控制点，即使其风险控制超过了注册资金或企业可承受的能力也不加思考和控制，最

后损失惨重，甚至被一份简单的合同或合约拖到破产清算的边缘。下面以一份涉外专利转让合同的谈判和审核为例，抽取七个法律关键词为审核线索进行分析，借鉴老外同行对风险点控制的设置，并以此考虑应对措施，从而进一步提高涉外合同的谈判与审核能力。

1. **法律关键词：**"all direct cost"

对于因违约给 licensee 造成损失的，licensor 承担的责任以直接成本损失为限，并约定不超过相关专利转让费用总额的40%。这就避免了 licensee 间接损失难以估计而给 licensor 形成的潜在商务风险。合同条款如下：

EG－12－25 The total liability of Licensor for all direct cost of Licensee as stipulated in Articles 6. 6, 7. 3 and 7. 4 shall not exceed forty percent (40%) of the license fee and technical documentation fee and APC fee in sections 3. 1A and B and E. The assessment of liability and exact amount of payment shall be evaluated and agreed by Licensee and Licensor via friendly discussions and provided that such claims or demands from Licensee shall be made no later than thirty (30) days after the acceptance date of contract plant.

对法律关键词"all direct lose"的审核分析："all direct cost"中的"成本"（cost）显然在财务上有专门的定义，而法律上的损失与财务上的成本不可同语，应改为"all direct lose"较符合法律惯用语的要求。

2. **法律关键词：**"the total payment"

对于与专利技术转让有关的相关技术参数（除特别参数外）考核达不到约定的，"product quality warranty"控制在相关专利转让费用总额的11%；对于特别参数达不到约定的，"product quality warranty"控制在相关专利转让费用总额的4%；同时约定，各项技术参数（包括特别参数）考核不达标的，"the total payment to be made by Licensor"不超过相关专利转让费用总额的35%。合同条款如下：

EG－12－26 If any grade fails any parameter of the product quality warranty except for A＊＊＊＊ or F＊＊＊, Licensor shall continue to improve the contract plant and bear all direct costs until the contract plant passes the warranty, or shall pay liquidated damages of 11% of the license fee, technical documentation fee and APC fee per failed grade, at Licensor's choice.

EG－12－27 If any grade fails the A＊＊＊ or F＊＊＊ parameter of the product quality warranty, Licensor shall continue to improve the contract plant and bear all direct costs until the contract plant passes the warranty, or shall pay liquidated damages of 4% of the license fee, technical documentation fee and APC fee per failed grade, at Licensor's choice.

The total payment to be made by Licensor under Articles 6.7 and 7.7 hereof shall not exceed an amount equal to thirty－five percent (35%) of the license fee and technical documentation fee and APC fee in Sections 3.1A and B and E.

对法律关键词"the total payment"的审核分析："the total payment"条款为转让方总的赔偿或补偿设定了限额，一定要考虑是否约定已支付合同款的返还，否则就可能形成即使对方违约也还有利益可赚的局面，这对于受让方来讲很可能血本无归。这是很多同行容易忽视的问题。也就是说，一般约定应在合同总价100%以上加一谈判约定数，或者在以合同中已支付款项的返还为前提下另有约定。

3. **法律关键词**："the aggregate liability"

"aggregate"多作形容词使用，意思与"total"相同；但也可作名词使用，指"累计金额"。

对于给对方造成损失的赔偿限于直接成本损失（all direct cost, damages, claims or demands of Licensee, the aggregate liability of Licensor），并不超过相关专利转让费用总额的50%。同时，限额还包括了因单位与员工（Licensor or Licensor's personnel）的任何疏忽而应承担的责任。合同条款如下：

EG－12－28 Except as set out in Sections 7.9, 8.3 and 9.2, the aggregate liability of Licensor all direct cost, damages, claims or demands of Licensee shall not exceed fifty percent (50%) of the license fee and technical documentation fee and APC fee in Sections 3. 1A, B and E. This limitation shall apply regardless of any alleged negligence of Licensor or Licensor's personnel except to the extent that such claim or liability arises from the gross negligence or willful misconduct of Licensor, Licensor's personnel, Licensor's affiliate (s) and/or Licensor's affiliate's personnel.

对法律关键词"the aggregate liability"的审核分析：该条款为转让方设定了总的赔偿或补偿限额。关键是责任主体除单位外还扩大到了单位员工（Licensor or Licensor's personnel），并定义为员工的任何疏忽，这对于授让方来讲显然是不可接受的条款。因为单位员工的责任应由转让方去追究，否则容易引起主体不明确的问题；同时，总的限额也应考虑合同已支付款项是否应返还的问题。

4. **法律关键词**："indirect or consequential damages or losses"

要求"Licensee"或"Licensor"相互免除对方间接和不可预见的损失。由于专利技术转让对于 Licensor 造成的间接损失或不可预见的损失很少，而对 Licensee 造成的间接损失和不可预见的损失难以估计，因此显然互免对于 Licensor 有利而对于 Licensee 不利。合同条款如下：

EG – 12 – 29 No Party shall be liable for another Party's indirect or consequential damages or losses, such as loss of production, or loss of profit.

对法律关键词"indirect or consequential damages or losses"的审核分析：对于知识产权转让、技术服务类合同，提供技术方或服务方一般都会要求约定此条款。由于技术与服务是应用在受让方设备与工艺上，受让方受损失的概率远大于转让方，也就是说转让方受间接损失的可能性小，而受让方受间接损失的可能性大。显然这对于受让方来讲是形式上的公平而实质上的不公平。特别是对于货物、工程建设、承揽类合同所包括的知识产权转让，更要注意专门进行定义或约定间接损失的范围，不可不将之作为受让方谈判和审核的要点。

5. **法律关键词分析**："infringement"

对于因专利侵权而造成索赔或纠纷的，Licensor 的最大责任为相关专利转让费用总额的 75%，其他部分由 Licensee 承担。合同条款如下。

EG – 12 – 30 Licensor shall protect, defend and indemnify Licensee as indicated in this Article 8 from any claims or cause of action for infringement of a third party's patents in existence as of effective date of this contract lodged by a third party against Licensee as described in Article 8. 2.

In the event that such an above claim is made against Licensee for infringement of such third party's patents, Licensor shall be obliged to handle the claim and make the defense against the accuser at its own cost in Licensee's name. All the legal and financial responsibilities which may arise in such defense or settlement of such claim shall be borne by Licensor. Licensor shall indemnify Licensee from any damages or other sums that may be assessed in or become payable by Licensee under any final decree or judgment by any court which results from such claim; provided that the maximum payable by Licensor for such indemnification shall be 75% of the License and know – how fee and technical documentation fee and APC fee.

对法律关键词"infringement"的审核分析：对于知识产权的受让方来讲，不仅要注意违约责任的追究，更要关注侵权责任条款的设置，防止受让方因其所接受的技术所采用的工艺、设备等侵权而形成使用受限甚至被禁止使用。"the maximum payable by Licensor for such indemnification"不仅要注意已支付款项的返还，还要注意不能为转让方承担侵权责任。对于受让方来讲，这就可能形成风险敞口，因此宁愿在"no material breach"、"liquidated damages"条款上让步也绝不可以在"infringement"条款上得益（承担 35% 的责任与 75% 相比好像得益了）。

此外，双方还以成果交付与履约保函、预付款保函的设定来保证资金的安全与作为成果提交的保证。

从以上分析可以看出，Licensor（外方）从各方面考虑了自己可承担的风险责任限额，排除了给对方造成间接损失或不可预见损失应承担的责任；并要求对方以银行履约保函的形式提供支付担保，确保了相关专利转让成果提交后相关专利转让费用能够得到回收。当然，对于专利技术转让本身而言，专利权持有方处于绝对强势，被授予专利权方处于劣势。因此，在风险分担与责任分配上，作为授予专利权方就要据理力争，在风险分担上注意专利的可利用性与专利责任的瑕疵担保来确保利益或风险分担的均衡。在该合同中，Licensee（中方）通过设计一些与专利技术转让有关的工期保证、验收条款、技术培训、质量担保条款来达到授让专利技术的目的。只有合同双方都注意到了风险分担的均衡，其所签订的专利转让合同才可能容易执行。

6. limitation on liability（**责任限制**）

EG - 12 - 31 Notwithstanding any other provision of this contract, neither Party shall be liable to the other Party for damages for loss of revenues or profits, loss of good will or any indirect or consequential damages in connection with the performance or non – performance of this contract. The aggregate liability of a Party for all claims for any loss, damage or indemnity whatsoever resulting from such Party's performance or non – performance of this contract shall in no case exceed United States Dollars（USMYM）or the RMB equivalent thereof.

参考译文：无论本合同其他条款有何规定，任何一方均不向对方承担因本合同的履行或不履行而造成的收入或利润丧失、商誉丧失或任何间接或附带性损失的赔偿责任。在任何情况下，一方因本合同的履行或不履行而造成的损失、损害或补偿索赔所承担的责任累计总额不得超过 ［ ］美元（US￥［ ］）或等值的人民币。

五、常用类聚词

1. damage or injury

"damage" 一般指对物的损害，"injury" 一般指对人的伤害。

EG - 12 - 32 If while in the possession of the lessee, the lease item caused personal injury or property damage to any third person, the lessor is not liable.

参考译文：承租人占有租赁物期间，租赁物造成第三人的人身伤害或者财产损害的，出租人不承担责任。

EG – 12 – 33 If a substandard product causes property damage or injury to others, the manufacturer or Seller shall bear civil liability according to law.

参考译文：因产品质量不合格造成他人财产、人身损害的，产品制造者、销售者应当依法承担民事责任。

2. bind and obligate

"bind"和"obligate"应该说是近义词，前者指"约束"，后者指具体负有什么样的义务，二者经常同时出现，表示"使……有义务做"。

EG – 12 – 34 Both Parties hereto hereby agree willingly to bind and obligate themselves to act and perform as follows.

参考译文：双方在此同意受本协议约束，执行以下条款。

3. cost expense and charge

EG – 12 – 35 All the cost, expense and charges related to the provision of service by Party B to Party A in accordance with the instructions of Party A shall be borne by Party A, notwithstanding the fact the Party B advance the said payment.

参考译文：根据甲方指令，所有因为甲方服务的乙方发生的相关成本、损失和费用应由甲方承担，不管该支付事项是否属乙方事先支付的。

4. joint and several liability

"joint and several liability"意为"民法中的连带责任"，经常与"contribution"（违约责任份额）和"relative fault"（相对过错）相关联。

EG – 12 – 36 Where there are two or more guarantors, they shall undertake joint and several liabilities.

Joint tortfeasors should assume joint and several liabilities, the mode of assumement coincide with general tort.

参考译文：保证人为 2 人以上的，保证人之间承担连带责任。

共同侵权行为人应承担连带赔偿责任，责任承担的方式同一般侵权责任承担方式。

EG – 12 – 37 Where there are two or more guarantors, they shall undertake joint and several liabilities. Joint tortfeasors should assume joint and several liabilities, the code of assumement coincide with general tort.

参考译文：两个以上的保证人应承担连带责任的，连带侵权人应承担连带责任，以符合一般侵权保证的法典。

第 *13* 章

责任限定：涉外合同违约责任的具体描述

一个完整的违约责任条款一般有四个部分的描述：一是一方应当做什么，不应当做什么；二是指出违反了哪些约定（一般会列出具体的事项或适用的合同条款）；三是违反约定所导致的后果；四是如何计算违约责任和弥补的最大责任限度。在具体的约定中也可省略前三项。

一、违约金具体计算方式的描述

对于违约金的计算没有统一的规定，一般依照当事人的约定确定。

1. 以天按比例计算

EG – 13 – 1 Contractor shall pay to the employer at the rate of ＊＊ per day liquidated damages for such default.

该条款显然是以天按约定比例计算损失作为需承担的违约责任。该条款没有说明是以什么作为比例的计算依据，从而风险关注的重点是可能形成纠纷的债权一方会认为以总合同金额计，而债务一方会认为应以违约涉及的合同金额计。

参考译文：承包方应当为这种违约向发包方支付按每

天＊＊％的比例计算的损失。

2. 按照贷款（费用、合同价款）等总值计算

EG－13－2 Party B shall, if it fails to comply with this agreement to make purchase of the goods delivered by Party A as reimbursement, or Party A shall, if it fails to comply with this agreement to deliver the goods it is due to provide, be deemed liable for a breach of agreement and shall compensate the non－breaching Party for the loss caused thereupon and shall pay the non－breaching Party a fine accounting for _____ % of the total value of the goods in question.

"a fine accounting for" 在这里译为"违约金"较为合适。

参考译文：乙方不按合同规定购买补偿商品或甲方不按合同规定提供商品时，均应按合同条款承担违约责任，赔偿由此造成的经济损失，并向对方支付该项货款总值_____％的违约金。

EG－13－3 If the cotton fails to be shipped as scheduled due to the Seller's reasons, the Seller shall pay the Buyer a delayed delivery fee equivalent to ＊＊％ of the value of the commodity for the delay incurred in the contracted latest shipment date from the eleventh day after the month the cotton was due to be shipped.

参考译文：由于卖方原因造成不能按期装运的，则卖方应从合同规定的最晚装运日的第 11 天起，按照实际延迟的天数，每月付给买方货值金额＊＊％的迟装费。

3. 以延期交付货物的总价计

EG－13－4 In case that Buyer delays in paying the payment according to this contract, Buyer shall pay liquidated damages to Seller for each delay day, which is equal to ＊＊％ of total amount.

In case that Seller fails to deliver the products to Buyer in accordance with this contract, except for the force majeure, Buyer should agree to

Seller's late delivery on the condition that Seller agrees to pay delay liquidated damages.

该合同中卖方违约金计算方式没有约定清楚的最大可能是有专门的延期交付违约金的计算方式。否则，卖方一旦违约，则买方无法主张延期违约金。

参考译文：买方未按合同规定日期付款，每延期一天，应偿付卖方延期付款总额＊＊％的违约金。

如果卖方不能按合同规定及时交货，除因不可抗力者外，若卖方同意支付延期违约金，买方应同意延期交货。

4. 按延期天数的约定比例计算

EG – 13 – 5 If Party B causes any delay to the completion of this project, then Party B must pay to Party A a fee of 0. 1‰ (in words: 1/ 1000) of the total overall project fee for each day beyond the scheduled completion date.

参考译文：由于乙方原因逾期竣工的，每逾期一天，乙方向甲方支付工程造价0. 1‰（大写：千分之一）的违约金。

5. 按照约定以某一固定金额计算

EG – 13 – 6 The Purchaser shall indemnify the Seller for all costs incurred by it as a result of any delay in the delivery of the metal building system caused by the Purchaser, including, without limitation, the cost of storage which shall be charged at the rate of RMB ＊＊ per ton per day.

参考译文：买方应赔偿或补偿卖方因买方造成的交货延误所受到的所有损失，包括（但不限于）货物储存的费用，该费用以每天每吨人民币＊＊元计算。

EG – 13 – 7 Party A shall hand over the leasing items to party B on the date as prescribed in this contract, otherwise giving twice of the rent as liquidated damages by the day.

参考译文：甲方应按合同签订的出租日期将出租的房屋交乙方使用。如甲方逾期不交房屋的，则每逾期一天应向乙方支付租金双倍的违约金。

6. 笼统地描述支付违约金

EG – 13 – 8 If either party of this contract fails to perform its obligation as stated in this contract, other than by reason of force majeure as per Clause ＊＊, The concern party shall pay 2% liquidated damages to the other party. The liquidated damages must be paid within 30days.

"pay 2% liquidated damages" 比较笼统，没有说明是依照合同总额还是依照未履行合同的部分，一旦发生纠纷会产生争议。

参考译文：如果本合同的一方未依照合同约定履行他的义务，除本合同第＊＊条由于不可抗力原因外，责任方应向另一方支付2%的违约金，违约金应在30天内支付。

7. 综合描述

可综合各方情况，结合上述 1～6 的描述，组合成综合的违约金计算方式。

二、违约救济条款的描述

1. 约定一方有权取消、撤销或终止合同

EG – 13 – 9 Buyer has the right to cancel this contract in case that Seller delays in delivering the products over 10 weeks. Seller must immediately pay to Buyer the above mentioned liquidated damages after Buyer's cancellation of this contract.

参考译文：如果卖方交货延期超过合同规定船期 10 星期时，买方有权取消合同。尽管取消了合同，但卖方仍须立即向买方交付上述规定的违约金。

2. 约定守约方有权要求违约方赔偿

EG – 13 – 10 If Party B makes any unauthorized changes to load bearing walls or building pipelines and such changes result in damages or loss, it shall be the responsibility of Party B to pay for such loss.

Party A shall be responsible for any extra costs incurred due to his use of the property before the final completion meeting and signing of the "Engineering Quality Acceptance" document.

参考译文：如果乙方未经授权而对承重墙或建筑管线进行了变更，且这些变更导致了危害或损失，乙方应因此承担这些损失或危害的支付责任。

在最终竣工和签署"工程质量接收证"文件之前，如果甲方擅自动用，应负责承担由此产生的额外成本。

3. 约定适用定金、保证金条款

EG – 13 – 11 Party A, if fail to deliver vehicle, should pay breach fine reference to bank's prescription on delayed payment according to party B's paid sum from the date of delay to actual delivery. In case fail to deliver excess * * days party B is entitled to cancel this contract and require party A pay breach fine by % of paid sum or apply clause of earnest money.

参考译文：甲方未按时交付车辆的，自延期之日起至实际交付日止，按乙方已付款依银行迟延付款的规定向乙方支付违约金。延期交付车辆超过 * * 日的，乙方有权解除合同，并要求甲方按相当于已交车款的 % 支付违约金或适用定金条款。

4. 约定适用保函条款

EG – 13 – 12 The Licensor shall, within * * (* *) calendar days after signing of the contract, furnish a performance bond to the Licensee, issued by the Bank of China, Beijing against the counter – guarantee issued by a foreign bank to the Bank of China, Beijing: in the amount of ten (10) percent of the total contract price. The performance bond shall remain valid until the acceptance of the contract products and expiration of the guarantee period of the contract equipment.

The performance bond shall be furnished by the Licensor by a bank guarantee in the form as stipulated in annex ＊＊ to the Contract. The cost thereof shall be borne by the Licensor.

In case the Licensor fails to perform any of his obligations under the contract, the Licensee shall have the right to have a recourse from the performance bond.

参考译文：合同双方签字后＊＊天以内，让与人应提交金额为合同总价10%的履约保函，该保函应由北京中国银行根据外国某一银行向北京中国银行提交的反担保开具。该履约保函的有效期将持续到合同产品验收和合同设备保证期结束以后。

让与人应按合同附件＊＊的格式提交履约保函，由此产生的费用由让与人承担。

如果让与人未能履行合同规定的某项义务，引进方将有权对该保函行使追索权。

5. 约定提出索赔的具体条件

EG－13－13 Subject to ＊＊% franchise against B/L weight, Buyer shall have the right to send claim concerning the quantity and quality of the material within ＊＊ days from the date of B/L.

参考译文：按照提单重量＊＊%的免赔质量，买方有权在提单之日起 ＊＊ 天之内提出有关材料数量和质量的索赔要求。

6. 约定收取滞纳金或利息

EG－13－14 In case of delay in paying rent or fees of property management beyond the prescribed period, party B shall undertake belated payment 4‰ more of rent by the day. For fees of power or water, it shall be 1‰ more by the day.

参考译文：乙方逾期交付租金及物业管理费的，除如数补交外，按日支付逾期租金款项的 4‰的滞纳金。逾期交付水电费等其他费用的，按逾期交纳款项的 1‰支付滞纳金。

7. 明确给予损失方补偿

EG - 13 - 15 If Party B fails to make full payment of labor remuneration of Party A's staff on time (including but not limited to pay and overtime payment), and therefore Party A suffers any liquidated damages, claim or loss, Party B shall make full compensation to Party A.

参考译文：因乙方未及时足额支付甲方员工劳动报酬（包括但不限于工资、加班工资等），导致甲方遭受任何处罚、索赔、损失的，均应由乙方向甲方作出足额补偿。

8. 延期交付货物或成果

EG - 13 - 16 The Employer should pay charges for design to the Designer at the amount and date provided in this contract. For each day of overdue payment, 2‰ of the overdue payment shall be paid as damages for overdue payment and the time for delivery by the Designer shall be extended accordingly. Where the delay of payment has exceeded 30 days, the Designer shall have the right to suspend the performance of the work at the next stage and give written notice to the Employer. In case the higher authority or competent department of design approval would not approve the design documents or the engineering construction of this contract is suspended or stopped, the Employer should pay the payable charges for design.

参考译文：发包人应按本合同规定的金额和日期向设计人支付设计费，每逾期支付 1 天，应承担应支付金额 2‰的逾期违约金，且设计人提交设计文件的时间顺延。逾期超过 30 天以上时，设计人有权暂停履行下阶段工作，并书面通知发包人。发包人的上级或设计审批部门对设计文件不审批或本合同项目停缓建的，发包人均应支付应付的设计费。

9. 模糊地约定有权提出索赔

EG – 13 – 17 Within the guarantee period stipulated in Clause ＊＊ hereof should the quality and／or the specifications of the goods be found not in conformity with the contracted stipulations, or should the goods prove defective for any reasons, including latent defect of the use of unsuitable naterials, the Buyers shall arrange for an inspection to be carried out by the Bureau and have the right to claim against the Sellers on the strength of the inspection certificate issued by the bureau.

"on the strength of" 意为 "依据"。 "including" 在这里属典型枚举。

参考译文：在合同第＊＊条规定的保证期限内，如发现货物的质量及/或规格与本合同规定不符或发现货物无论任何原因引起的缺陷，包括内在缺陷或使用不良的原料，买方应申请商检局检验，并有权根据商检证向卖方索赔。

10. 模糊约定为损失赔偿

EG – 13 – 18 If by reason of delay on the part of the Purchaser or Purchaser's agent or representative, any payments due to Corporation are not made in accordance with the agreed payment schedule, Corporation reserves the right to apply a late payment charge of one and a half percent (1.5%) per month (19.56% per annum) on all overdue amounts and Purchaser agrees to promptly pay any such late payment charges which are properly due hereunder. In the event that one or more payments are delayed for sixty (60) days or more, Corporation shall have the right to stop all work under this agreement and shall also have the right to claim such period of work stoppage and the effects thereof as excusable delay pursuant to Article ＊＊ hereto (Excusable Delay). Purchaser agrees to reimburse Corporation for those additional reasonable costs incurred by Corporation resulting from such work stoppage (s) and restart (s). Should one or more payments by delayed for one hundred and twenty (120) days or more, this agreement may, at Corporation's option, be deemed to be cancelled under the provisions of paragraphs（＊＊）through（＊＊）of Article ＊＊ hereof（Termination for Insolvency & Cancellation）.

该条款看似复杂，实质上只要弄清"if"、"in the event"与"should"构成平行结构，就会清晰地明确买方违约的三个层次，即三种处理的办法，其中第二种情形较为模糊。

参考译文：如果由于买方或买方代理商或代理人的延迟，不能按议定的付款时间支付公司业已到期的款项，公司保留收取延付费的权利，延付费月率为到期未付款的 1.5%（年率为 19.56%），买方也同意即刻交付本协议所规定的此种费用。如一次或数次延迟付款达 60 天或以上，公司有权停止本协议所规定的工作，并有权根据本协议第＊＊条（可谅解的延迟）称此段工作停顿及其产生的后果为可谅解的。买方同意对公司因停工和重新开工的额外费用作合理补偿。如一次或数次延迟付款达 120 天或以上，根据本合同第＊＊条（因无力清偿债务而终止和撤销）第 ＊＊~＊＊ 款规定，按公司的意愿，本协议可视为被撤销。

11. 模糊表述为承担法律与经济上的损失

EG – 13 – 19 The Licensor shall guarantee that the Licensor has lawful ownership of all the technical know – how, the technical documentation and software supplied by the Licensor to the Licensee in accordance with the contract, and that the Licensor has the right to transfer the technology and supply the contract equipment and the parts to the Licensee. In case any third party brings a charge of infringement, the Licensor shall take up the matter with the third party and bear all legal and financial responsibilities, which may arise.

"take up the matter"意为"商谈的相关事宜"，"financial responsibilities"意为"经济责任"。

参考译文：让与人保证对根据本合同向引进方提供的一切专有技术、技术资料和软件拥有合法的所有权，并有权向引进方转让该专有技术和合同设备。如果发生第三方指控侵权，让与人应负责与第三方交涉，并承担由此引起的法律上和经济上的责任。

12. 约定按照实际成本补偿

EG – 13 – 20 In the event of cancellation in accordance with paragraph (b) of this Article, Corporation shall be entitled to reimbursement for all actual costs which shall be properly allocable or apportionable under recognized accounting practices to the performance of this agreement and its cancellation, plus a profit which shall be computed at the rate of ten percent of the said actual cost. Payments previously made hereunder by the Purchaser shall be credited against such reimbursement.

参考译文：如按本条第 2 款规定撤销协议，公司有权获得按公认的会计惯例合理计算的因本协议的履行和撤销而发生的一切实际成本费用的补偿，外加为实际成本 10% 的利润。买方以前根据本协议所付款项必须从补偿费中扣减。

13. 综合各方情况，提出解除合同及其他附加赔偿要求

EG – 13 – 21 Should the Sellers fail to make delivery on time as stipulated in the contract, with exception of force majeure causes specified in Clause * * of this contract. The Buyers shall agree to postpone the delivery on condition that the Sellers agree to pay liquidated damages which shall be deducted by the paying bank from the payment. The liquidated damages, however, shall not exceed 5% of the total value of the goods involved in the late delivery. The rate of liquidated damages is charged at 0. 5% for every seven days. Odd days less than seven days should be counted as seven days. In case the Sellers fail to make delivery ten weeks later than the time of shipment stipulated in the contract, the Buyers shall have the right to cancel the contract and the Sellers, in spite the cancellation, shall still pay the aforesaid liquidated damages to the Buyers without delay.

该条款通过 "should" 前置倒装条件句与 "in case" 引导的条件

句构成平行结构，采用两个层次描述了迟交货引起的后果。

参考译文：如果卖方未能按合同规定及时交货（除了本合同＊＊条款所言的不可抗力外），买方同意在卖方付违约金的前提下迟交货。违约金的金额不超过迟交货的合同货物部分的价值的5%，违约金按每7日0.5%计算，少于7日的增加天数按7日计。如果卖方未能于合同规定的交货期之后的10周内发运，买方有权取消该合同，除此之外，卖方仍要将有关违约金不加拖延地付给买方。

三、责任限额与免责约定的描述

在合同谈判中，双方就责任分担与违约问题谈到节骨眼时，总会有一方提出一些免责与限制条款。如果法务人员对此不熟悉，即使是看似平等或公正的互免条款实质上也隐含着风险与危机，这些条款一旦发生争议或纠纷而闹到法庭，则很有可能被法院判为无效。对于弱势方来讲，一旦免责情形发生，完全按照免责条款执行就可能给其造成难以预料的风险。

因此，审核合同的法务人员要清醒地利用以下三点在合同中合理设计互免责或限制权利使用条款，从而使本企业的法律风险降到可接受的程度。

（一）违背或规避国家强制性法律的免责条款无效

在合同中，双方通常会就过失责任、产品瑕疵责任、不可抗力事件、不可预见事件、误述责任、人身伤亡责任、后果性责任进行互免责和限制权利使用的约定。例如，在专利技术转让许可协议中，许可方总会提出在专利技术使用过程中双方互免因专利技术使用不当给对方造成的财产或员工人身伤害损失。该条款看似平等，但由于许可方发生免责的几率远大于被许可方，所以相对来讲，被许可方存在法律风险的几率就远大于许可方。因此，相对弱势方要在对方提出免责条款时合理利用中国《合同法》第53条来保护自己。

中国《合同法》第53条规定：合同中的下列免责条款无效："（一）造成对方人身伤害的；（二）因故意或者重大过失造成对方财

产损失的。"

在违约条款约定中，如果有一方提出就某一条款互免责任，提出互免责任的一方往往是合同强势方，同时很可能是违约几率较大的一方。例如，笔者在审核一份工艺包技术许可合同时，对方提供的合同文本内容主要为："双方互免因履行本合同或与本合同有关而造成的对方员工的死亡或事故或伤害承担责任，也不承担另一方或另一方员工的任何财产损失或损坏的责任。"该条款看似平等，实质上也是不公平的。因为被授予方是接受工艺包成果并向对方支付价款，而接受过程或支付价款过程存在给授予方造成人身伤害或财产损失的几率几乎为零；而授予方提供的工艺包在应用于生产过程时，因技术设计缺陷而给被授予方造成人身伤害或财产损失的几率是很大的。这样的条款从发生的几率来讲对于被授予方是不公平的，显然也是违背合同目的的。

由于笔者所持立场方属于被许可方，而风险的评估标准是与发生几率大小有直接关系的。因而，笔者在谈判中就提出，由于《合同法》第53条有不得就员工伤害或因故意或者重大过失造成对方财产损失的互免责的强制性法律规定，建议对许可方提出的合同文本条款作如下修改：

（1）因本合同造成的死亡、伤害而引起的经济损失和/或损害赔偿由当地政府授权的事故认定小组认定的责任方承担。

（2）尽管如此，被许可方或技术许可方按照何种比例承担上款所述责任，都不应为另一方员工因本合同或与本合同有关而造成的死亡或事故或伤害直接承担责任，也不直接承担另一方或另一方该员工的任何财产损失或损坏的责任。

修改后的第1条意在发现较大事故时以政府认定为准，显然该条款对被许可方有利。第2条意为单位互免为对方员工负责赔付，各自单位员工的人身伤害损失由本单位承担，且无论该种责任由哪方承担，都要适当地在其他条款中约定好员工保险，从而界定为双方对于本单位的员工各司其职、各负其责。虽然该条款对员工（合同第三方）是没有法律效力的（详见下面叙述），实际的诉讼中也出现过员工因此而起诉非员工所在单位方的伤害责任而胜诉的案例，法院在审判中并不接受双方的约定而免除责任方的义务，但是对于被许可方来讲，能够以此替换修改前的条款，风险控制也算降到了可以接受的程度。一般来讲，合同中约定对第三方造成的伤害免责对于第三人来讲是没有约束力的。

（二）是否免责还要看具体的损失是否合理、公平

对于过失责任，合同有约定的一般会依约定，但并不是注定就会产生具有约束力的效力，因为法官在审理案件时还要考虑免责必须有合理的标准，且不能超过预期收益或预期损失，否则就可能得不到法官的认同。

对于免责条款是否具有合理性，法官在审理中通常是看合同整体条款是否体现公平，法官不会把不合理的某一条款或条款的某一部分隔离出来认定其无效，而是直接认定整个免责条款无效。对于合同来讲，一般要分析标的的大小、既得利益的实现预期，有的还要跳出合同来分析社会效果，因为中国《合同法》还有一条基本的原则就是第5 条："当事人应当遵循公平原则确定各方的权利和义务。"如果显失公平，法官就可能引用《合同法》第 54 条第 1 款："下列合同，当事人一方有权请求人民法院或者仲裁机构变更或者撤销：（一）因重大误解订立的；（二）在订立合同时显失公平的。"

虽然《合同法》第 55 条规定撤销权消灭的除斥期间是 1 年，但由于违约与侵权的责任是当事人难以知道或不可预料的，因此所谓的知道或应当知道也只能是在事情发生后，这样就可能不受除斥期间和短期时效的限制。对于质量瑕疵担保的约定就可能还要因当事人知道或应当知道而引用《中华人民共和国产品质量法》的规定。如该法第41 条第 1 款规定："因产品存在缺陷造成人身、缺陷产品以外的其他财产（以下简称他人财产）损害的，生产者应当承担赔偿责任。"第45 条规定："因产品存在缺陷造成损害要求赔偿的诉讼时效期间为两年，自当事人知道或者应当知道其权益受到损害时起计算。因产品存在缺陷造成损害要求赔偿的请求权，在造成损害的缺陷产品交付最初消费者满十年丧失；但是，尚未超过明示的安全使用期的除外。"这

样就不可能是除斥期间问题了，进而演变成诉讼时效问题，根本上是利益的公平、合理保护问题。

最典型的、看似公平的免责条款是不可抗力条款，即合同各方各自承担因不可抗力给自己造成的不利后果和间接损失，这属于相互免责条款。这一条款看似平等、合理且符合惯例，实质上，不可抗力条款对于产品制造商或工程施工方来讲是比较有利的，因为不可抗力对产品制造商或工程施工方来讲是致命的。而对于支付对价、接受标的物方来讲，不可抗力的影响就微乎其微了。特别是对于大型工程建设来讲，现在很多总承包商都希望将不可预见事件形成的损失列入互免责条款。因为工程的不可预见事件的概念十分广义，如恶劣气候条款、地质资料错误、原材料价格大幅波动、人工成本增高等都可人为归入不可预见事件，这对业主来讲就显得不公平了。合同双方本着友好协商的宗旨，可能不仅对间接损失相互免责，对某些直接损失也经双方约定相互免责，主要是各自承担自己一方的人员伤亡责任、财产损害责任、间接性损失和自己一方资产造成的污染损失，即使这些责任因合同另一方的过失导致产生也不例外。该种约定的效力如前所述，对第三方责任的约定不会产生实质性的约束力。当然，合同条款不是独立的，也不是孤立的，要结合合同的整体性来考虑风险分担与免责的具体事项，万不可因为是互免就掉以轻心。

很多时候，处于谈判强势地位的合同一方总是希望最大限度地免除己方或限制对方主张权利的责任，或者增加对方的责任，这会使得合同条款看似有违常规，以致合同条款的合理性不够，这时候，弱势方就要明确地表达出自己的真实意图。笔者在审核有关新产品采购合同、专利技术转让许可合同、工艺包采购合同等的过程中，通常要用较大篇幅的"鉴于条款"来说明采购目的，这样就可能形成对弱势方的保护，以确保合同标的物受让方实现所预期的利益。万一发生较大损失，也可通过鉴于条款来说明采购目的，证明损失分担是否公平合理，从而为诉讼纠纷中主张免责条款无效设下依据，同时还可充分通过"条款换条款"达到整体的风险分担的均衡。

（三）责任限制及责任免除的描述

1. 最大责任限制为合同总值的比率

EG – 13 – 22 Except for force majeure or a failure by the Buyer to perform its obligations under this contract, if the Seller fails to complete on time any of its tasks set forth above, it shall pay a liquidated damages of 0. 1% per day on the late amount, commencing on the fourth day of such delay, provided that such liquidated damages shall not exceed 3% of the contract price.

参考译文：除天灾人祸等不可抗力因素及因买方未尽本合同责任之情形以外，如卖方逾期完成以上任何一项义务，须从逾期第 4 天起按日支付该笔逾期款项 0.1% 的违约金，但该违约金不应超过本合同总价之 3%。

EG – 13 – 23 In the event of any repeat of a performance test failing for reasons imputable to the Contractor, and there being no mutual agreement to continue re – testing, the results of the final test will be measured and the Contractor will be liable to pay to the owner liquidated damages on the scale set out in appendix （…） up to a maximum of （…）% of the contract price.

参考译文：如果由于承包商的原因导致性能测试的再次失败，而双方并无继续重新测试的协议，则对最后一次测试的结果进行评估。承包商将根据附录×的规定向业主支付违约赔偿费，费率不超过合同价格的××%。

EG – 13 – 24 If the Contractor is unable for reasons within his control to obtain a final acceptance certificate for the whole plant by （…） months from the effective date of this contract, he shall be liable to pay to the owner for each month's delay liquidated damages of （…）% of the contract price up to a maximum of （…）% of the contract price in accordance with appendix（...）.

参考译文：如果承包商因自身的原因未能在合同生效后的×个月内获得整个工厂的最后验收合格证书，承包商须根据附录×的规定向业主每月支付相当于合同价格××%的拖延赔偿费，但最多不超过合同价格的××%。

2. 以支付合同金额或固定金额为限

EG－13－25 If the verification tests fail with the responsibility lying with Party B , as there suit, Party A cannot start normal production with the contract having to be terminated, Party B shall refund all the payments previously made by Party A to Party B together with the interest at the rate of...percent per annum.

参考译文：如因乙方原因，产品性能试验没能达到合同的规定，且甲方不能依照合同正常开工生产产品时，依此甲方有权终止合同，乙方应返还甲方已支付给乙方的预付款项，并按年＊＊%利率支付相关的利息。

EG－13－26 Limitation on Liability

Notwithstanding any other provision of this contract, neither Party shall be liable to the other Party for damages for loss of revenues or profits, loss of goodwill or any indirect or consequential damages in connection with the performance or non－performance of this contract. The aggregate liability of a Party for all claims for any loss, damage or indemnity whatsoever resulting from such Party's performance or non－performance of this contract shall in no case exceed United States Dollars (USMYM) or the RMB equivalent thereof.

参考译文：无论本合同其他条款有何规定，任何一方均不向对方承担因本合同的履行或不履行而造成的收入或利润丧失、商誉丧失或任何间接或附带性损失的赔偿责任。在任何情况下，一方因本合同的履行或不履行而造成的损失、损害或补偿索赔所承担的责任累计总额不得超过 [　] 美元（US￥ [　]）或等值的人民币。

3. 限定违约责任以承担直接损失为限

EG – 13 – 27 Liability

C or New Company shall be under no responsibility or liability to compensate any damages except direct damages incurred due to material breach of its obligations under this agreement.

In circumstance provided above in Clause 14. 1 C or New Company shall, at its sole option and discretion, be entitled to transfer to B all or part of C or New Company's proprietary rights and ownership of the infrastructure project, under construction or after completion date, as liquidated damages, in lieu of computing and compensating the actual damages provided that such transfer shall be conducted of C's own free will or rendered in the arbitration award as stipulated in clause ＊＊. However, any transfer shall be subject to the confirmation and approval of the People's Insurance Company of China and the lending bank.

In above case, C or New Company's liability to B shall be limited to transfer of the proprietary right and ownership of the infrastructure project and B's claim against C or New Company demanding the damages shall be extinguished and nullified.

参考译文：赔偿责任

C 或新公司对任何损失均不负赔偿责任，但由于严重违反本协议规定的义务而造成的直接损失除外。

在第 1 款所述情况下，C 或新公司有权将 C 或新公司对建造中或已竣工的基础设施的拥有权和所有权作为违约罚金全部或部分转让给 B，以替代对实际损失的计算和赔偿。这种转让应是 C 自愿的或仲裁第 ＊＊ 款裁定的。在贷款本息偿还期中，任何转让须经 ＊＊ 保险公司和贷款银行确认并批准。

在上述情况下，C 或新公司对 B 的赔偿责任仅限于将其对基础设施的拥有权和所有权转让给 B，B 向 C 或新公司的索赔一律无效。

4. 约定免于承担责任

EG – 13 – 28 Patent infringment

Subject to the conditions hereinafter set forth, Corporation will indemnify and protect the Purchaser against any payments made by Purchaser in discharge of its liability, excluding any liability for consequential or incidental damages as enumerated in Article 14 hereof (Limitation of Liability), resulting from any infringement or claim of any infringement of any American patent, but no other patent or rights, by the Equipment purchased hereunder, except that Corporation's only patent indemnify with respect to accessories, equipment or parts which are not manufactured exclusively to Corporation's detailed design shall be that specifically set forth in paragraph (b) hereof.

Corporation shall only indemnify the Purchaser in respect of the infringement, or claim of any infringement, of patent by the accessories, equipment and parts not manufactured exclusively to Corporation's detailed design, but incorporated into the equipment, to the same extent and with the same limitations as the respective manufacturers of such accessories, equipment and parts indemnify Corporation there for and provided, in each case, that the indemnify obtained by Corporation from the manufacturer shall be assignable to the Purchaser. Corporation shall use all reasonable efforts to obtain from its venders and suppliers the most favorable indemnity protection for the Purchaser hereunder.

参考译文：侵犯专利

公司将按以下所规定的条件，保护买方免于承担因按本协议购买设备而侵犯或被指控侵犯美国专利（非其他专利或权利）的任何赔偿责任，本协议第 14 条（责任范围）所罗列的间接损害或意外损害责任除外，只属公司所有，且涉及没完全按公司设计详图制造的附件、设备或零件的专利保护由本条第 2 款另行具体规定。

对于没完全按公司设计详图制造，但安装在本设备上的附件、设备或零件，公司只能按这些附件、设备及零件的制造商所能提供的免责方式、范围和限度来使买方免责，在这种情况下，公司从制造商处所得的免责的保护应转让给买方。公司必须尽可能地为买方从公司的卖方和供方处争取最优惠的保护补偿。

5. 约定承担限定范围的侵权责任

EG – 13 – 29 Respect to any actual or alleged infringement unless：

（a）Suit is commenced against the Purchaser for infringement or the Purchaser receives a written claim alleging infringement, and the Purchaser gives notice in writing to Corporation within ten （10） days after the receipt by the Purchaser of such written claim, as the case may be.

（b）The Purchaser shall assist Corporation and shall use all diligent efforts, in full cooperation with Corporation, to reduce （otherwise than by non – use of the article in respect of which infringement is claimed） royalties, claims, damages and expenses involved and promptly furnishes to Corporation copies of all data, papers, records and other documents within the Purchaser's possession, material to resistance or defense against such claim or suit, and the Purchaser refrains from making any payment and from assuming any obligations, expenses, damages, costs or royalties for which Corporation may be asked to respond.

（c）Corporation shall be enabled and entitled to conduct negotiations concerning, or defend any action in respect of, any claim or allegation and may choose to negotiate and defend either in its own name or that of the Purchaser.

参考译文：公司对买方任何实际或被指控的侵权概不负责，除非：

（a）买方被诉侵权或收到指控侵权的索赔书，且在收到此种索赔书后 10 天之内将情况书面通知公司。

（b）买方必须协助公司且与公司通力合作，以便减少（或不使用被指控是侵权的物品）专利权使用费、索赔费、损害赔偿金及有关费用，并及时向公司提供买方掌握的可用在此种索赔或诉讼中作为辩驳材料的所有资料、文件、记录及其他文据副本，对于可能要求公司承担的任何义务或支付的任何费用、损害赔偿金、诉讼费或专利权使用费，买方概不承担或支付。

（c）公司有权进行任何有关索赔指诉或指控的谈判或辩护，且可以本公司名义或以买方名义参与谈判和进行辩护。

6. 一方为另一方全部免责

EG – 13 – 30 Subject to the conditions hereinafter set forth, Corporation will indemnify and protect the Purchaser against any payments made by Purchaser in discharge of its liability, excluding any liability for consequential or incidental damages as enumerated in Article 14 hereof (Limitation of Liability) resulting from any infringement or claim of any infringement of any American patent, but no other patent or rights, by the Equipment purchased hereunder, except that Corporations only patent indemnity with respect to accessories, equipment or parts which are not manufactured exclusively to Corporation's detailed design shall be that specifically set forth in paragraph (b) hereof.

参考译文：公司将按以下所规定的条件，保护买方免于承担因按本协议购买设备而侵犯或被指控侵犯美国专利（非其他专利或权利）的任何赔偿责任，本协议第 14 条（责任范围）所罗列的间接损害或意外损害责任除外，只属公司所有，且涉及没完全按公司设计详图制造的附件、设备或零件的专利保护由本条第 2 款另行具体规定。

（四）在考虑损失与违约追究相当时，关注风险敞口问题

在审核合同违约条款时，无论是哪一方的法务人员，都要既关注损失与违约责任是否相当，又要关注风险是否可控。一般来讲，双方商务人员及法务人员都十分关注合同总价款的敞口问题，而容易忽略违约敞口问题。一是违约责任条款尽量在同一处排列，不要零星分布

在权利义务条款或支付条款中；二是违约责任尽量设置兜底条款，避免一方违约时超过合同预期。

所谓"兜底条款"，就是在所有违约金表述之后再另设一条款，约定违约方的最大赔偿责任或支付责任。如对于发货方或成果提交方来讲，可要求约定为："上述所有违约金、损失支出不超过合同总额的＊＊％"；约定累计违约金比例后还要补充一句："违约金的支付不影响合同目的的实现，并不影响支付违约金方对产品或服务质量瑕疵的弥补。"对于货款或服务费支付方来讲，可要求约定为："滞纳金的支付不超过未支付款的＊＊％"；约定累计违约金比例后，还要补充上"违约金的支付不影响应支付款项的支付"。

EG – 13 – 31 Notwithstanding any other provision of this contract, neither party shall be liable to the other party for damages for loss of revenues or profits, loss of goodwill or any indirect or consequential damages in connection with the performance or non – performance of this contract [except for breach of confidentiality obligations or infringement of the other party's IPR]. The aggregate liability of a party for all claims for any loss, or damage or indemnity whatsoever resulting from such party's performance or non – performance of this contract shall in no case exceed [＊ ＊] united states dollars USMYM [＊ ＊] or the RMB equivalent thereof [except for breach of confidentiality obligations or infringement of the other party's IPR].

参考译文：无论本合同其他条款有何规定，任何一方均不向另一方承担因本合同履行或不履行而造成的收入或利润丧失、商誉丧失或任何间接或附带性损失的赔偿责任（但该方有违反保密义务或侵犯知识产权情形的除外）。在任何情况下，一方对因本合同的履行或不履行所致的损失、损害或补偿索赔的责任累计总额不得超过 [　] 美元或等值的人民币（但该方有违反保密义务或侵犯知识产权的情形的除外）。

一般来讲，对于交货方或提供服务方的违约金的最大限额应以大于质量保证金的 1 ~ 3 倍为宜，如质量保证金为 5%，则违约金累计不应超过 10% 或 20%，最小不得低于质量保证金，否则违约金就失去了意义；对于支付货款方应不高于价款日 4‰，累计最大违约金限额以 5% ~ 10% 为宜（一般不得低于银行同期货款利率的 3 倍），否则就可能存在风险或失去了违约金约定的意义。

（五）在违约金计算时，避免与合同价格计算方式联动

在合同审核时，合同的计价模式一定要固定，即使是数量难以确定的约定单价模式，也一定要提前锁定单价。千万不要在违约条款中约定违约行为对于价格条款的调整，这样就可能造成合同难以实质履行，因为合同的价格组成与一定权利义务相匹配，而合同的计价条款与违约救济条款是两个相对独立的子模块，不可混为一谈，否则就可能形成执行过程中的循环指向的死结，最终造成纠纷。

第 *14* 章

特殊条款：重点关注其特殊所在

在涉外合同中，有很多能够独立于一般权利义务的特殊条款，这些条款都是基于某一方对风险关注的不同，随着语言、文化、法律的发展而来的，法务人员对之一定要小心谨慎，逐一分析，并且要综合合同的整体条款去关注风险所在。

一、持续性条款

所谓合同条款的持续性是指执行合同某一条款时不影响其他条款的执行，或者某一条款无效或失效或履行完毕时不影响某一特定条款的持续效力。特别是对于合同条款的变更、解除、终止、中止等重大事项的出现，为保证某些合同条款的持续效力不受影响，需要通过特定的方式将其独立出来，以确保其效力的持续性。因此，持续性条款也可称之为独立性条款。如因一方违约导致合同终止时，为避免已履行合同一方的利益受到损害，就会约定哪些条款持续有效并还将继续约束合同违约方。比较常见的独立条款有争议解决条款、保密条款、结算条款、清算条款等。这些条款相对比较独立，且直接涉及当事人特别是善意方的利益，与其他条款不能形成联动，具有相对独立性。

EG – 14 – 1 When any dispute occurs and is the subject of friendly consultations or arbitration, the Parties shall continue to exercise their remaining respective rights and fulfill their remaining respective obligations under this contract, except in respect of those matters under dispute.

"continue to exercise rights and fulfill obligations" 意为"持续享有权利，承担义务"，这是本条款主旨句的实意性关键词。"remaining respective obligations" 意为"其余相关条款"。

参考译文：当某一争议已发生并且正在通过友好协商或仲裁解决时，双方可继续行使其各自在本合同项下的其他权利，同时应继续履行其各自在本合同项下的其他义务，但与争议事项有关的权利和义务除外。

EG – 14 – 2 Expiry or termination of this contract shall not in any way affect accrued rights and/or obligation hereunder on or before the date of above expiry or termination, and/or any and all provisions of this contract relation to unresolved disputes, resolution of disputes and /or indemnification which shall survive any expiry or termination of this contract.

本条款的主旨关键词是"not in any way affect"（不以任何方式影响），同时用关键词"shall survive any"（持续有效）作了强调。这样就将已产生的权利和义务和争议解决条款及赔偿条款从合同的期满或终止事项中独立了出来。

参考译文：本合同期满或终止不应以任何方式影响本合同项下在前述期满或终止合同之前已经产生的权利和/或义务，以及/或与本合同未决争议、争议的解决和/或赔偿有关的所有条款，这些条款在本合同期满或终止后应继续有效。

EG – 14 – 3 The obligation contained in this clause confidentiality shall survive the expiry or termination of this agreement for any reason, but shall not apply to any confidential information which is or becomes publicly known at the time of disclosure to the receiving party.

"survive" 本是 "存活" 的意思，在这里可译为 "持续有效"，是一个独立性条款的关键词。

参考译文：不管出于何种原因，保密条款中规定的义务在本协议到期或终止后仍然有效，但并不适用于在向接受方披露时已为公众知晓的信息。

EG - 14 - 4 The various provisions of this agreement are severable and if any provision is held to be invalid, illegal or unenforceable by any arbitration tribunal or court of competent jurisdiction then such invalidity, illegality or unenforceability shall not affect the remaining provisions of this agreement.

"severable" 意为 "可分割性"，实质是阐明各条款是相对独立的。"not affect" 意为 "不影响"。

参考译文：本协议各个条款是可以分开的，如果其他任何一个条款被仲裁庭或管辖法院认为无效、违反法律或不可执行，则这种无效、违反法律或不可执行并不影响协议其他条款的效力。

EG - 14 - 5 Subject to the amendments herein provided in this amendment, those parts of the articles which have not been amended shall continue to be in full force and effect.

"continue to be in full force and effect" 意为 "继续有效"。

参考译文：除本变更协议所作变更外，未变更的协议其他条款继续有效。

二、完整性条款

所谓合同的完整性条款，是为了说明与合同有关的洽谈纪要、事先的协议或多份协议之间的关系而强调相互间构成整体的意思表示的约定。

合同完整性条款的设置目的是为了防止人为的解释歧义、解释依据或解释顺序的不同，并确保所有双方当事人事先达成的文本、阶段性成果或所作的沟通都是围绕一个整体的目标而实现的，防止出现多目标的情形。

EG – 14 – 6 This contract constitutes the entire agreement between the parties hereto and supersedes all prior negotiations, representations or agreements whether oral or in writing relative to the subject matter of this contract.

This contract shall be altered or supplemented only by mutual consent in writing between the owner and the contractor.

"the entire agreement" 意为 "完整的协议"。"constitutes" 意为 "构成"。"supersedes" 意为 "取代"。

参考译文：本合同是合同方之间的完整协议，它取代了以前所有与本合同事项有关的洽谈、说明及口头或书面协议。对本合同的任何修改或补充，须经业主或承包商双方的书面同意。

EG – 14 – 7 This purchase agreement constitutes the entire agreement between the Buyer and the Seller and supersedes all prior negotiations, representations or agreements related to this purchase agreement, either written or oral except to the extent they are expressly incorporated.

关键词 "supersedes" 意为 "替代"。

参考译文：本采购协议构成买卖双方之间的全部协议，并取消合同方之前就与该协议有关事项所作的口头或书面谈判、陈述和协议，但本协议有明确规定的除外。

EG – 14 – 8 This agreement hereby cancels all prior agreements between the parties (if any) relating to the subject matter hereof and also cancels and nullifies all rights (if any) of either party arising against the other by virtue of all or any of the said prior agreements, or any of the provisions thereof, notwithstanding the existence of any provision in any such prior agreement that any such rights or provisions shall survive its ter-mination.

"cancels" 意为 "取消"。"cancels and nullifies" 为类聚词，意为 "使其无效"。

参考译文：本协议在此取消合同方之间就合同有关事项在之前达成的所有协议（如有），并使所有根据任何这些之前签订的协议或条款而获得的所有权无效，即使之前的协议规定了这些协议终止后仍然有效，这样的条款也不例外。

三、厘清性条款

厘清性条款指在合同条款的描述中，为防止一方过度行使权利或滥用权利或错误理解权利，需要在合同条款中说明合同行使的权利范围或责任限定，并约定因过度行使或滥用权利而发生的损失不应由义务方承担责任。

厘清当然是厘清某种特定的法律关系。一般是要厘清不因某一事项的发生而连锁引起其他事项的发生或理解为其他特定法律关系的存在。因为其他特定的法律关系意味着不确定的风险，这是其中一方所所特别关注的风险。

1. 厘清对相关受让技术、信息过分依赖的责任

EG – 14 –9 Other than as a result of a breach of the representation and warranty in section ＊. ＊, disclosing party will have no liability with respect to the use of or reliance upon the confidential information by the receiving party or its affiliates.

"no liability with respect to the use of or reliance upon" 意为 "对相关使用或依赖不承担责任"。其实质目的是要厘清信息提供方不承担信息使用者对信息的过度使用或不当使用所引起的实质性后果。

参考译文：除了因为第＊＊节产生的后果外，信息披露方对信息接收方及其关联公司使用或依赖该保密信息概不负责。

2. 厘清对因违反保密协商所产生的后果不承担责任

EG – 14 – 10 Both parties shall be liable for the breach of this confidential agreement. Nevertheless, neither party shall be liable in an action initiated by one against the other for special, indirect or consequential damages resulting from or arising out of this agreement, including, without limitation, loss of profit or business interruptions.

参考译文：双方应对违反保密协议承担责任。但是，任何一方对于另一方就本协议产生的各种特殊的、间接的或后果性损失提起的诉讼索赔不承担任何责任，包括但不限于利润损失、商业中断。

3. 厘清对超过所提供货物、服务范围之目的而引起的额外损失不承担责任

EG – 14 – 11 Unless other specified, Seller warrants that the goods will be fit for the ordinary purpose for which such goods are normally used. Seller does not warrant that the goods are suitable for any particular purpose for which they may be required, whether or not Seller has reason to know of any such requirements. There are no warranties which extend beyond the description hereof. Except as expressly set forth herein, Seller makes no warranties, express or implied. Seller will assist in obtaining compliance with any warranties of the manufacturer and in effecting prompt settlement of any just claims, but without responsibility or liability for any such compliance or effecting such settlement. Seller shall not be liable for consequential damages.

本条的主旨条款是一个保证性条款，通过一个"not warrant"、两个"no warranties"、一个"without responsibility or liability"厘清性关键词的使用，将通常使用之目的外的责任排除在外，也厘清了卖方应承担哪些责任、不应承担哪些责任，条理十分清晰。

如果合同使用"warranty"，则当货物出现瑕疵时，买方可以直接起诉卖方违反该保证条款，从而要求损害赔偿。如果买方直接对其进行维修，则很可能卖方对此维修费用不予认可，从而导致索赔失败。

而如果合同使用"indemnity"，则当货物出现瑕疵时，买方必须先进行损害赔偿，然后再向卖方索赔该维修所花费的费用。

参考译文：除非另有规定，卖方保证货物符合该类货物通常使用之目的。但卖方并不保证货物符合买方要求货物满足的任何特定目的，卖方是否有理由知晓该要求都无例外。卖方也不保证超出本协议产品描述的部分。除非在合同中明确指出，卖方对此未作任何明示或暗示的保证。卖方将协助让供应商满足任何保证，并协助迅速解决任何正当的索赔，但对供应商是否遵守或解决索赔问题不承担任何责任和义务。卖方对任何间接损失不承担责任。

4. 厘清违约方与非违约方的责任范围

EG – 14 – 12 If the Buyer is of the opinion that emergency remedial work or repair is urgently necessary for security, safety or any other purpose which justifies immediate action, where it is practicable to do so, the Buyer shall notify the Seller of the urgency and require the Seller to perform such work as may be necessary.

If the work or repair so performed by the Buyer or any contractor retained by the Buyer is not part of the work, the Buyer shall issue a change order making any adjustment to the purchase order price.

Where the Seller is unable or unwilling to perform that work, then the Buyer may do whatever word or repair that the Buyer considers necessary.

If the work or repair so performed by the Buyer or the above – mentioned contractor is part of the work, the Buyer shall be entitled to recover from the Seller all costs incurred by the Buyer in so doing and shall issue a change order making any adjustment to the purchase order price.

该条款约定违约方或非违约方都有权采取补救措施，但规定非违约方采取补救措施所产生的一切费用也应由违约方承担。

参考译文：如果买方认为，紧急补救措施或修理是为安全防范之正当的当务之急，那么买方可采取相应的行为，但买方应通知卖方这一紧急事项和要求卖方应履行义务的必要性。

如果买方所做的相关事项或修理不是卖方所应服务或工作的范围，买方应签发变更单去调整相关订单的价格；

如果卖方不能或不希望去承担这一工作，买方认为必要的话，可以采取任何适当的方式补救或修理。

如果通过买方补救或修理的事项或上述属于卖方补救的一部分，那么买方应有权要求卖方补偿所有因此发生的成本和通过签发变更单对采购订单价作出变更。

5. 厘清相互之间不构成合伙、代理或雇佣等关系

EG – 14 – 13 Nothing in the agreement and no action taken pursuant to it shall constitute or be deemed to constitute the parties a partnership or constitute one party an agent for the other for any purpose whatever.

关键词"Nothing shall constitute or be deemed to constitute"厘清了双方不是合伙或代理关系，从而避免了承担额外的合同责任或侵权中的连带责任。

参考译文：无论出于什么目的，本协议所作约定或根据本协议采取任何行动都不构成或被视为构成合同方之间是合伙关系或一方是另一方的代理人。

EG – 14 – 14 Nothing in this contract shall constitute a partnership or establish a relationship of principal and agent or any other relationship of a similar nature between or among any of the parties.

参考译文：本合同的任何规定均未在各方之间形成合伙关系或者建立委托人和代理人的关系或者任何其他类似性质的关系。

EG – 14 – 15 The agreement shall not create a partnership, joint venture, agency, employer / employee or similar relationship between company and sales representative. Sales representative shall be an independent contractor. Company shall not be required to withhold any amounts for state or federal income tax or for FICA taxes from sums becoming due to sales representative under this agreement. Sales representative shall not be considered an employee of company and shall not be entitled to participate in any plan, arrangement or distribution by company pertaining to or in connection with any pension stock, bonus, profit sharing free to utilize his time, energy, and skill in such manner as he deems advisable to the extent that he is not otherwise obligated under this agreement.

参考译文：本协议不得在公司与销售代表之间形成合伙、合资、代理、雇佣或类似关系。销售代表应为独立承包商。不得要求公司从销售代表依本协议规定到期应得的金额中代扣代缴任何州和联邦所得税，也不得要求公司代扣代缴任何 FICA 税费。不得将销售代表看做公司雇员，销售代表不得参加公司与公司决定给予雇员的与津贴、股票、资金、利润分配或其他利益相关的计划、安排和分配。本协议义务中未有其他规定时，销售代表应自主利用时间精力，发挥自己万有引力可取的技能。

EG – 14 – 16 During this agreement, the contractor shall be an independent contractor and nothing contained herein shall be construed as creating an employer – employee relationship between the company and the contractor.

参考译文：协议期间，承包人应为独立的承包人，不得将本条文的任何规定理解为在公司与承包人之间确立了雇佣关系。

6. 厘清特定的权利或利益关系

EG – 14 – 17 Nothing in this agreement shall be considered or construed as conferring any right or benefit on a person not a party to this agreement and the parties do not intend that any term of this agreement should be enforceable, by virtue of the contracts (rights of third parties) act 1999, by any person who is not a party to this agreement.

参考译文：本协议不得被认为或被解释为赋予本协议以外的任何人权利或利益。协议各方无意让本协议以外的任何人根据 1999 年的

《合同法》（和第三方权利）实施本协议项下的任何条件。

四、隔离性条款

隔离性条款是指在涉外合同中约定因一方构成违反某一条款时可能形成对其他条款的影响，因此通过约定将受影响的条款隔离起来，从而不受违反条款的影响。隔离性条款实质上是独立性条款的另一种表达方式。独立性条款是正说，隔离性条款是换种说法而已，其实二者的目的是一致的。

EG－14－18 Any failure either in whole or in part by purchaser to comply with its payment obligation shall be a breach of condition. On the occurrence of such a breach and for as long as such breach is continuing the Seller may at any time by notice to purchaser forthwith：

Terminate this contract；and/or

Without prejudice to the right to terminate，suspend all or any supplies of the product.

Termination hereunder shall be without prejudice to any right of action or claim accrued on or before the date of termination.

前一个"without prejudice to"将终止权利隔离出来；后一个"without prejudice to"将起诉或索赔的权利隔离出来。这样的结果是暂停产品供应，可能会导致终止权利，而终止权利可能导致起诉和索赔，且三项权利互不影响、相互独立。

参考译文：购买方全部或部分违反支付义务应构成违反条件。一旦发生违约尚存持续，卖方有权在任何时候通知买方立即：

终止合同；和/或

暂停任何产品供应而不影响其终止权利。

合同终止并不影响终止前产生的起诉或索赔权利。

EG－14－19 Party a may terminate this agreement by giving notice to party b in accordance with clause ＊.3 if party b commits a breach of any of the conditions or any other term of this agreement. The effect of which breach is material (whether or not such breach would otherwise qualify as a repudiator breach at common law), and which is either incapable of remedy, or, if capable of remedy is not remedied within 30 days of service of notice by the party not in breach requiring remedy.

关键词"whether or not"属于隔离性条款。英美法中，只有达到毁约性的严重程度当事人才有权终止合同，目的是一旦争议诉诸司法解决，就会隔离法官对"毁约性违约标准"的适用，从而引导法官尊重当事人的订约自由。

参考译文：如果乙方违反本协议任何条件或其他条款，违约行为严重［不管这种违约是否达到普通法下的毁约性违约标准］，并且这种违约无法补救，或者能补救，但在非违约方发出要求补救的通知后 30 天内没有得到补救，则甲方有权根据第 *. 3 条通知乙方终止合同。

EG – 14 – 20 Termination in accordance with clause *.4 shall not affect or prejudice any right to damages or other remedy which the terminating party may have in respect of the termination event which gave rise to the termination or any other right damages or other remedy which any party may have in respect of any breach of this agreement which existed at or before the date of termination.

"not affect or prejudice"属于隔离性关键词。

参考译文：根据第 *.4 条终止协议不应影响终止方就导致该终止的事件有关事项应享有的补偿或其他补救，也不影响在终止之前已经存在的与违反本协议有关的任何一方享有的补偿或其他补救权利。

EG – 14 – 21 If at any time any provision of this agreement is or becomes illegal, invalid or unenforceable in any respect under the law of any jurisdiction, that shall not affect or impair: The legality, validity or enforceability in that jurisdiction of any other provision of this agreement; or the legality, validity or enforceability under the law of any other jurisdiction of that or any other provision of this agreement.

关键词"not affect or impair"意为"不影响或损害"。

参考译文：如果本协议任何时候某个条款根据管辖法律违反法律、无效或不可执行，这不应影响或损害：本协议其余条款在本管辖范围内的合法性、有效性和可执行性；或本协议该条款在其他管辖范围内以及其他条款的合法性、有效性和可执行性。

五、不放弃条款

"不放弃条款"实质上是为了防止对默示行为的错误理解，即某一方依照法律应行使某一权利时，基于成本、时间等因素的考虑而没去主动行使某些特定的权利（这些权利往往是非实质性的程序性要求），这样一来，另一方就会认为自己也因此不应承担其他相关的责任或放弃履行应有的义务。为防止这一事项的发生，权利方（一般是合同的强势方）就会特别约定不放弃条款，从而打消义务方对默示行为放弃方的误解，要求其依照合同约定毫不影响地履行合同的义务。

EG - 14 - 22 Failure of any party to exercise its right or take any action against the other party for any breach of contract shall not be deemed as a waiver or such breach. No waiver of any party to any right shall be deemed as a waiver to any other rights. Waiver of any party to any of its right shall be sent to the other party in writing.

"not be deemed as a waiver"意为"不被视为放弃"。

参考译文：任何一方没有行使其他权利或未对另一方的违约行为采取任何行动不应被视为放弃追究违约方责任的权利；任何一方对某一项权利的放弃不应被视为是对任何其他权利的放弃。一方对某项权利的放弃均应以书面形式送交对方。

EG - 14 - 23 The failure of either party to enforce at any time any of the provisions of this agreement, or to require at any time the performance by the other party of any of the provisions hereof, shall in no way be construed to be a waiver of such provisions, nor in any way affect the validity of this agreement or any part thereof, or the right of the said party thereafter to enforce each and every such provision.

"in no way be construed to be a waiver" 意为 "不得被解释为放弃"。

参考译文：不论何方在何时未执行本协议的任何规定，或未要求另一方履行合同任何规定项下的权利，都不得解释为放弃这些权利，也不得影响本协议或其任何部分的效力，以及上述一方此后执行任何和全部此种规定的权利。

EG – 14 – 24 The guarantor shall have no right of subrogation reimbursement, exoneration, contribution or any other rights that would result in the guarantor being deemed a creditor of Seller under the law or for any other purpose, and the guarantor hereby irrevocably waives all such rights, the right to assert any such rights and any right to enforce any remedy which guarantor may now or hereafter have against Seller, and hereby irrevocably waives any benefit of and any rights to participate in any security now or hereafter held by Buyer, whether any of the foregoing rights arise in equity, at law or by contract.

参考译文：担保人不应具有代位权、求偿权、免除权、补偿权或者其他任何根据法律或为任何其他目的会导致担保人被视为卖方债权人的权利，担保人据此不可撤销地放弃上述权利、主张上述权利的权利以及强制执行担保人现在或今后可能针对采购的任何救济措施的权利。担保人据此不可撤销地放弃由买方现在或今后持有任何担保所带来的利益并放弃任何分享该担保物的权利，不论上述任何一种权利源于衡平法、普通法或合同。

EG – 11 – 25 No omission or delay on the part of any hereto in requiring a due and punctual fulfillment of the obligation by the other party hereunder shall be deemed to constitute a waiver by the omitting or delaying party of any of its rights to require such due and punctual fulfillment of the obligation and of any other obligations of the said other party, or a waiver of any remedy it might have hereunder.

参考译文：任何一方没有要求或迟延要求对方适当及按照履行其在本协议项下的义务，不能视为构成没有要求或迟延要求的一方放弃要求对方适当及按时履行该义务以及任何其他义务的权利，也不能视为其放弃本协议项下可采取的任何补救措施的权利。

六、禁止性条款

禁止性条款就是指在合同条款中约定某一方不得因合同关系从事对方特别关注的事项。这一事项可能造成对关注方的利益损害。禁止性条款一般用"no"这一特别强调形式来表述。

禁止性条款一般涉及以下事项。

1. 对外公告、新闻发布或商务行为的广告利用（No announcement）

EG – 14 – 26 Within the term in this agreement, no party, without the prior written consent of the other, shall make any public announcement, or issue any press release, with respect to any aspect of the activities taking place or to take place under this agreement.

参考译文：在本合同有效期内，未事先经另一方书面同意，一方不得就本协议正在开展的或将要开展的活动相关事项对外公告或发布新闻稿。

EG – 14 – 27 It is expressly understood and agreed that all rights to copyright are reserved unto Corporation and that all such publications, documentation, manuals and data in whatever form supplied hereunder by Corporation to the Purchaser shall not be transmitted, disclosed or used by the Purchaser except as herein expressly permitted.

Except as herein provided, it is further expressly understood and agreed that the provision of publications, documentation, manuals or data does not permit, nor provide a license to, manufacture or to have manufactured any part, component, system or element of the equipment.

参考译文：双方清楚知道和同意所有版权均属公司所有，买方不得传播、公开或使用由公司提供给买方的一切出版物、文件、手册和任何形式的资料，本协议明文规定的除外。

双方还清楚知道和同意，提供出版物、文件、手册或资料并不是准许或特许制造或让他人制造本设备的任何零件、部件、系统或元件，本协议另有规定的除外。

2. **不得招聘对方工作人员** (Non – solicitation)

EG – 14 – 28 Neither party shall, during the term or within one (1) year after the expiration date, directly solicit for employment the other party's personnel who are engaged in the performance of this contract without the prior written consent of the other party.

参考译文：在本合同有效期内以及合同期满日后 1 年内，任何一方未经另一方事先书面同意均不得直接向另一方参与本合同执行的雇员发出招聘要约。

EG – 14 – 29 Neither Party shall directly solicit for employment the other Party's personnel who are engaged in the performance of this contract, during the term of this contract and within one (1) year after the expiration date, without the prior written consent of the other Party.

参考译文：在本合同有效期内以及本合同终止后 1 年内，任何一方均不得直接向另一方参与本合同执行的雇员发出招聘要约，经另一方书面同意的除外。

3. **不得转让合同项下的利益或转包、分包合同**

EG – 14 – 30 Subject to any provisions contrary to the agreement, no party shall be entitled to assign or transfer any of its interests, rights or obligation under this contract without the written permission of the other.

参考译文：协议任何一方未经另一方书面同意，不得转让或转移其在合同项下的利益、权利或义务，但合同另有相反规定的除外。

EG – 14 – 31 Neither party hereto may be free, at any time, assign all or any part of the benefit or its rights under this agreement.

参考译文：本协议任何一方都不可在任何时候将其在本协议项下的全部或部分利益或权利进行转让。

EG – 14 – 32 The Buyer shall not assign or transfer its rights or obligations hereunder to any third party without the prior written consent of the Seller.

参考译文：未经双方事先书面同意，买方不得将其在本合同项下的权利或义务转让给任何第三方。

EG – 14 – 33 The lender may at any time assign any of its rights, transfer or novate any of its rights, benefits and obligations under this agreement to a group company. The borrower may not assign, transfer or novate any of its rights or obligations under this agreement.

参考译文：贷款人可在任何时候将其本协议项下的任何权利、利益和义务转移或转让给一个集团公司。借款方不得将其本协议项下的任何权利和义务进行转让或转移。

4. 禁止泄密或披露（No publicity）

EG – 14 – 34 The existence of this Contract, as well as its content, shall be held in confidence by both Parties and only disclosed as may be agreed to by both Parties or as may be required to meet securities disclosure or export permit requirements. Neither Party shall make public statements or issue publicity or media releases with regard to this Contract or the relationship between the Parties without the prior written approval of the other Party.

双方应对本合同的存在及其内容保密，只有在双方均同意的情况下，或者根据有关证券市场规定须披露或为获得出口许可证须披露的情况下，方可向有关方披露。未经对方事先书面同意，任何一方均不得就本合同或双方的关系发表公开声明或发布宣传或新闻稿。

5. 禁止留置 (No security Clause)

EG - 14 - 35 The Owners shall not have a lien on the cargo and on all sub - freights payable in respect of the cargo, for freight, dead freight, demurrage, claims for damages and for all other amounts due under this Charter Party including costs of recovering same.

参考译文：船舶所有人得因未收取的运费、亏舱费、滞期费和滞留损失和所有应付费用包括为取得该笔收入所花的费用而对货物和该批货物的转租运费有留置权。

6. 禁止构成竞争 (Non - competition)

EG - 14 - 36 During the continuance of the employment, the employee shall not be employed by, be engaged in or take an interest in any other business, unless a prior written consent of the partners is acquired.

参考译文：在劳动合同存续期间，受雇佣人不得从事其他任何有偿商务活动，除非事先依照要求经合伙人的书面同意，否则不得被雇佣。

EG - 14 - 37 In consideration of my being employed by ＊＊＊ company, I, the undersigned, hereby agree that upon the termination of my employment and notwithstanding the cause of termination, I shall not compete with the business of the company or its successors or assigns, to wit: ＊＊＊ and shall not directly or indirectly, as an owner, officer, director, employee, consultant, or stockholder, engage in the business of ＊＊＊ or a business substantially similar or competitive to the business of the company.

The non – compete agreement shall extend for a radius of ＊＊＊ miles from the present location of the company, and shall be in full force and effect for ＊＊ years, commencing with the date of employment terminations.

参考译文：因受聘于＊＊＊公司，在此同意，我无论因何故终止合同后，不得与公司其继承人或受让人的经营相竞争，即＊＊＊。此外，还同意，不得以公司所有人、官员、董事、员工、股东等身份直接或间接从事与公司业务类似或相竞争的＊＊＊业务。

本竞争禁止协议在公司坐落地方圆＊＊＊英里范围内有效，有效期间为＊＊年，自劳动合同终止日起生效。

7. 对特定事项的限制或不得限制

EG – 14 – 38 Any and all payments under this guarantee shall be made free and clear of any restriction, counterclaim, set – off, deductions or withholdings (except to the extent required by law) seeing that the payments may be contingently deduced due to any tax or expenses charged, imposed, levied, collected, withheld or assessed by any person.

参考译文：鉴于支付款项可能被他人征收、收取、代扣、评定了税费而抵押，本保函特规定所有付款不得设定限制条款，或者存在反诉、抵消、抵扣、代扣代缴，法律另有规定者除外。

EG – 14 – 39 Injunctive Relief Notwithstanding the foregoing, the Parties agree that each Party has the right to seek injunctive or other similar relief in any court of competent jurisdiction in respect of any claims of breach of confidentiality or IPR infringement.

参考译文：申请禁制令的司法救济权利无论本合同前述条款有何规定，双方同意如果一方提出对方违反保密条款或侵犯知识产权的指控，则提出指控一方可向任何一个有管辖权的法院申请发布制止侵权、违约行为的禁制令或采取其他类似救济措施。

EG – 14 – 40 The chairman shall be the legal representative of the jv company. Should the chairman be unable to perform his duties and responsibilities, he shall empower the vice chairman or other director to act on his behalf.

The directors, chairman and vice chairman shall not be compensated by the JV company in their capacity as directors, chairman or vice chairman.

参考译文：董事长是合营公司的法定代表人。若某位董事在其任期中被撤换，接替董事的任期应为离任董事的剩余任期。

董事、董事长和副董事长不得因其担任的董事、董事长或副董事长职务而从合营公司领取报酬。

第 *15* 章

道不清的事：涉外合同中精确与
模糊的合理并用

在涉外合同的阅读与理解中，可能最难把握的是一些说不清的事，但还想努力表述清楚，从而心烦意乱。这就涉及用词的精确与模糊问题。也就是说，在涉外合同的起草、审核及谈判过程中，在某一用词上要表达清晰、精确，尽量避免含糊其辞；但在实际的过程中，又不得不依靠精确用词和模糊用语的共同使用来描述某一事项。特别是在合同谈判中，双方会因翻译上的不能一一对应或用词上的习惯与偏好不同而产生严重分歧，目的都是为了避免歧义，所以不得不精确中掺杂模糊、模糊中掺杂精确，从而使词义更确切。

一、必要的逻辑知识

要想在涉外合同中不出现描述上的歧义，就得具备基本的逻辑知识。

1. 概念的内涵和外延
概念的内涵就是概念对事物的特有属性的反映。概念所反映的是对象的本质属性，而不是非本质属性。属性是事物自身的性质和事物之间的关系。本质属性是决定一类事物之所以成为该类事物并使其与其他类事物相区别的属性。从逻辑学的角度看，内涵和外延是概念的两个基本逻辑特征。

内涵就是反映在概念中的对象的本质属性，即概念的质的规定性。其作用是表明对象"是什么"。

外延是指具有概念所反映的本质属性的全部对象，即概念的量的规定性。其作用是表明对象"有哪些"。

内涵是事物区别于他物的内在本质，而外延是指事物的范畴（概念所反映的一切相关事物）。二者成反比关系：即内涵越小，则外延越大；内涵越大，则外延越小。

明确概念就是要明确概念的内涵和外延。那么怎样才能使概念的内涵和外延明确呢？定义是明确概念的内涵的方法。

在定义时要注意以下几点：一是被定义的概念与其定义的内容前后两部分的外延必须完全一样；二是被定义的概念与其定义的内容不能形成循环定义；三是定义概念的内容不能包含含混不清的概念，也不能用比喻；四是定义概念的内容与被定义的概念之间不能形成并列概念、反对概念等。

在涉外合同中为防止歧义，需要注意用词概念之间的内涵与外延的一致性。

2. 类聚关系

在人类情感的发展过程中，"物以类聚，人以群分"的根本原因在于人的意识里有了属种概念和/或源种概念。事物皆因"同属、同源或同质"才能归于一类而成为同一种类。

所谓属种概念是指一个概念的外延正好落在另一个概念的外延间，两概念的外延存在包含与被包含的关系。外延较大的概念称为属，外延较小的概念称为种。属与种之间存在 1 对 N 的关系，也就是说一个属里面可能存在多个种。这种情况可表述为，A：a1，a2，a3，…，an。

所谓源种概念，是指一个概念的处延可能存在于多个概念的外延之间。那个外延较小的概念称为种，那几个外延较大的概念称为源。源与种之间是 n 对 N 的关系。源种关系的逻辑图就相当于交。这种情况可表述为，A：a1，a2，a3，…，an；B：b1，b2，b3，…，bn；等等。其中，A、B 之间的子项有一个以上是等值的。如父亲属下的子女与母亲属下的子女之间就存在源种关系。如果父亲与母亲不属再婚，则子女是一一对应等值；如果父亲或母亲再婚，则子女间不会是一一对应的等值。

对涉外合同当事人行使权利或履行义务的描述一般是利用属种关系的描述来把握相关的概念。如甲方有权行使接受货物、退还货物和要求赔偿等权利。权利与接受货物、退还货物和要求赔偿之间显然是 1 对多的属种关系。

对涉外合同当事人的责任方面的描述一般是利用源种关系的描述来把握相关概念。如甲乙双方应各自承担违约责任、各自承担因不可抗力发生的损失、因过错给对方造成的额外支出或因自身原因对第三方造成侵权的索赔。显然，各方责任与"承担违约责任、各自承担因不可抗力发生的损失、因过错给对方造成的额外支出或因自身原因对第三方造成侵权的索赔"构成 2 对多的关系。

3. 逻辑运算

还有一点需要明白的是，人的思维在运行过程中具有运算的功能，即对概念之间进行相互连接，并确认其可能存在的真假情况。这一连接方式所表述的逻辑运算方式有"not"、"or"和"and"三种情况。它们分别是"not"（逻辑非）、"or"（逻辑或）、"and"（逻辑与）。逻辑运算用来判断一件事情是"对"的还是"错"的，或者说是"成立"还是"不成立"，判断的结果是二值的，即没有"可能是"或者"可能不是"，这个"可能"的用法是一个模糊概念。

一般来讲，在涉外合同中，"逻辑与"相当于生活中说的"并且"，就是两个条件都成立的情况下"逻辑与"的运算结果才为"真"。用"and"连接两个或两个以上概念的，往往形成一个完全的概念，常可用"all"来描述。

"逻辑或"相当于生活中的"或者"，当两个条件中任一个条件满足，"逻辑或"的运算结果就为"真"。用"or"连接两个或两个以上概念的，往往形成两个以上的概念，常可用"any"来描述。

"逻辑非"相当于生活中的"不"，当一个条件为真时，则"逻辑非"的运算结果为"假"。在涉外合同的描述中，如果某一事项在特定语境下可分或可独立成种时，一般可用"any"修饰，如时间、可数的数额或以"or"相连接的事项等；如所描述的事项为不可数且只能作为一个整体来描述，则一般使用"all"来修饰。

EG – 15 – 1 The Contractor shall provide the plant and contractor's documents specified in the contract, and all contractor's personnel, goods, consumables and other things and services, whether of a temporary or permanent nature, required in and for this design, execution, completion and remedying of defects.

"all"是整体性描述，在这里只能是对人的修饰，而不能理解为对其他事，否定就会将人、物、行为混为一谈了。"other things and services"是泛指。

EG – 15 – 2 The Works shall include any work which is necessary to satisfy the Employer's Requirements, or is implied by the Contract, and all works which (although not mentioned in the Contract) are necessary for stability or for the completion, or safe and proper operation, of the Works.

"any"显然是为了强调与接后的"or"一致，即满足二选一的条件或两条件都具备。"all"强调的是"words"应具备后面所有特征时才具备的整体性。

参考译文：工程项目包括任何满足要求所必须的工程施工，或者合同所暗示，和所有稳定、完全、安全和正确的操作而必须的工程施工（尽管合同没有提示到）。

4. 基本的推定

在人们的思维中，对概念的理解之所以会出现歧义，还由于人的思维的复杂性。这种复杂性就产生了四个基本的推定：同源推定、同属推定、类聚推定和反对推定。

所谓同源推定：就是当一组词连接在一起，对其中的某一个具有歧义的概念应按与其他一同连接的词所具有的相同源种来解释其属性，而不能与其他不相关的源种相关联，即使被解释的概念与其他源具有更明显的特征。如在描述为属于合同双方责任的组词连接时，即使某一个词可能归属于另一个源，但也应按照合同双方责任的划分来理解。

同源推定就是人们提起属于某一源的事项具有特定属性时，往往会联想到属于同一源的其他事项是否也同样具有这一特定属性。

如属于 A 的 a1、a2、a3 与属于 B 的 b1、b2、b3：如果 a3 与 b3 同质，那么描述为所有属于 A 的某些事项包括 a1 和 a2 是否就意味着应该包括 a3，或者是应排除 a3 呢？

一般来讲，根据同源推定，由于 a1、a2、a3 同源于 A，因而具有相同属性，没有提到包括 a3，但不能排除 a3，由此可以根据同源推定应包括 a3，从而可以得出结论。当提到某些事项属于特定事项的范围时，如果没有对其他事项进行排除，那么具有相同源和相同属性的其他事项类推应属于特定事项的范围。

所谓同属推定：就是当一组词连接在一起，对其中的某一个具有歧义的概念应按与其他一同连接的词所具有的最相同属种来解释其属性，而不能与其他不相关的属种相关联，即使被解释的概念与其他属更具有明显包含与被包含的特征。

EG – 15 – 3 All contracts for the sale or disposal of real property, tangible personal property, equipment or other items owned by or under the control of the county commission shall be let by free and open competitive bids.

"disposal" 可理解为 "处置"，包括买卖、租赁、报损等，显然，由于其与 "sale" 用 "or" 连接，因此应推定其与 "sale" 同属，而不能理解为 "出租"、"报损" 等。

同样，如果描述为所有属于 A 的事项包括 a1、a2 和其他 b3，那么是否应包括 b1、b2 呢？显然，由于 b3 与 a3 同质，而 a1、a2、a3 同源，具有相同属性，因此 a1、a2 和 b3 同源同属性，这样就应排除

b1、b2 了。

所谓类聚推定，就是当某一泛指词的概念与其他具有特定含义的词相连接在一起而产生歧义时，应推定有歧义词的属性应类聚于具有特定含义词的属性。理解中出现歧义，往往是具有歧义的词属于泛指词，如果通过"相邻、相近、相似"原则来扩大概念的内涵或减少其外延，则容易与其他相邻、相近或相似的概念通过类聚而归属于同属、同源。

所谓反对推定，就是当同源、同属的概念产生枚举时，一般对没有枚举的同源、同属的概念反对同样适用，除非其他概念与被枚举的概念同质而不可分时才不会被反对。

如果描述为：所有属于 A 的某些事项不包括 a3，是否意味着也不包括 a1 和 a2 呢？显然，明确指出只不包括 a3 当然不能排除 a1、a2，也就是说，同属的事项包括其中一项并不排除其他具有相同属性的事项，而明确排除其中一项同样也就肯定了其他项的存在，而不能借以排除其他没明确反对的事项。

在理解上述四个推定时，应注意以下几点：

第一，前三种推定的词之间用"or"相连接时可能不完全适用。

第二，从逻辑角度来看，"一个概念的内涵越大越丰富，则其对应的外延就越小"。产生歧义一般是由于某个词具有广义的理解或者概念的外延过小，因此推定的目的是扩大其外延，与相邻的词作类聚而限制其内涵，作狭义的理解，也就是用特定词限制泛指词。

第三，前三种推定与第四种推定之间可能会存在混淆，应具体分析或通过其他限制来确定。在涉外合同中，"include"一词出现在枚举的最后，没有被枚举的概念一般不会被反对适用。若在枚举最后出现"and all other…whatsoever"之类的短语，一般不适用反对推定。

第四，在各具属性概念的枚举中，如果排除枚举的某些概念适用，那么没有被排除枚举的概念不应适用反对推定。也就是说，部分否定不能推定全部否定；部分肯定不反对全部肯定，但也不能完全肯定。

第五，一般认为用"and"连接两个以上概念时会形成类聚推定，因此在类聚推定中就要注意：一是分析这些枚举是否建立了一个类聚推定；二是枚举是否穷尽了一个类聚；三是这些枚举是否仅仅包括若干独立的项目。

EG - 15 - 4 Whereas, licensor possesses certain technical information and knowledge relating to the development, production, and sale of automotive parts.

显然，"development, production and sale" 并没有建立一个类别，后面也没有跟有歧义的泛指词，其实这些词只是程序上的三个步骤，即开发、生产与销售，不可能产生类推或联想。

EG - 15 - 5 Licensee expressly assumes the risk of, and shall hold licensor harmless from, and shall indemnify licensor against, any liability, expense, claim, demand, or cause of action arising out of or resulting from any property damage, personal injury or death.

上述五个词语都非常类似，而起草所用的类似词语越多，否定含义的推定适用的可能性也就越大。

EG - 15 - 6 The employees shall devote their best efforts and substantially all of their business time and attention for the duties as outlined in the statement of secondment (except for the usual vacation periods and reasonable periods of illness or other incapacity) to the business of the foreign subsidiary.

上述未能构成类别，只能按照两个独立的项目。因为只有一个例外从句，否定含义推定适用于括号中的短语，任何不包括的事物被视做排除在外。

例如："person means any individual, partnership, firm, corporation, association, trust, unincorporated organization or governmental authority." 列举越多，招致否定含义推定的可能性就越大。

"Government order means any order, writ, judgment, injunction, decree, notice, directive, stipulation, determination or award entered by or with any governmental authority." 这都是招致否定推定的独立项目，没有建立起类别，最后也没有泛指词。

二、涉外合同中对四个模糊性关键词的理解

通过掌握上述基本逻辑知识，对于涉外合同中的四个关键词 "any"、"all"、"including"、"such as" 就便于结合上下文或语境来推定了，以此就能够完整地表述清晰的思路。

1. 有关 "all" 的理解

"all" 作 "全部" 讲，但 "全部" 在具体的语境中又如何定义清楚呢？总有一方会认为 "全部" 是否会扩大解释。如 "all expenditure"，按照解释可作 "支出，花费；经费，消费额" 讲。而支出、花费又有合理与不合理的问题；经费有与合同有关的，又有与合同无关的。"all" 在理解上显然对权利方是有利而对义务方是不利的，但按照否定含义解释又会对义务方有利。也就是说，义务方会认为只有合同中有明确约定的支出与花费才是 "all"，否则就不属于定义的范围。

在推定过程中，应根据 "同源、同属、同本质与同种类" 类聚原则适用类别推定，而不能扩大解释。

"and all" 放在句末是很口语化的词，意思是 "及其他的"、"等等"，表现了说话者满不在乎多余的事项，但又不得不提。

2. 有关 "any" 的理解

"any" 作 "任何" 讲，属泛指，应根据 "同种类、同本质" 原则适用类别推定。

如 "any apparatus"、"any equipment" 等，上述设备只能指同种类型的设备，当然是与通过枚举同质、同种类的设备。

"any other" 与任何具体的事项具有类似的语义。如在总承包合同中，如果列举了动产，那么就包括所有动产；如果列举了部分机动设备，那么就包括所有同质的、同种类的机动设备。

再如，列举任何到现场服务的人员的计酬服务费用，如设备工程师、工艺工程师等任何工程师，那么其他非工程师人员就另计，而不在本列举范围。这就要说明其他非工程师人员的现场服务费用计算标准，否则，就存在歧义，容易产生纠纷。

同样，在特指后的泛指词"whatsoever"同样具有相同的表达意义，如"other equipment whatsoever"等同于"any other equipment"，而不能将泛指扩大到"非同质、非同源、非同属"的人与事去理解或翻译。

EG – 15 – 7 All tools, implements, instruments, and contractor's property whatsoever, that equipment should be cast insurance.

显然，所有承包商的财产都要投保，应限定与施工有关的设备，而不能是与设备无关的属施工方的其他资产。这里用"and"加上"all"的强调共同组成了一个新概念，那就是属于"property"的范畴，从而形成了一个需要投保的整体。如果这里将"all"改成"any"、将"and"改成"or"，那就会产生歧义了，后果是承包商会因此可选择性地认为那些需要投保的事项而自主选择投保了。

3. 有关"including"的理解

"including"一般来讲有四种含义：

（1）B是对A的枚举。这里的逻辑B与A应是属种关系。

（2）B属于A的一个组成部分，与A不可分割。这里的A与B部分同质。

（3）B被视为A的一种或一部分。这相当于上述（1）和（2）的选择，也就是既可理解为（1）的情形，也可理解为（2）的情形，都无大碍。如"repair the water piping, valve, including the tap"实质上可理解为"water lines, valve and the tap"。因为维修供水系统不可能将水管线与阀门进行维修后却留下漏水的水龙头。

（4）B组成A，A就是由B组成的，A与B完全同质。也就是说，第四种情形作了限制性解释。

上述（1）~（3）种情形中，"including"（包括）的意思是"not limited to"（不限于）。

如"the contractor's Construction tools, including providing service to the construction site for mobile devices"中的"including"（包括）只起一种定义与解释作用，不能作扩大解释，应属——对应关系，翻译时可作"就是"或"等同于"理解。

一般都认为："including"如果作扩充解释，则其后带不带"without limitation"或"but not limited to"，其所表述的含义都差异不大。但上述扩充解释只能是相似的类别内解释，而不能是不同质、不同源、不同属的不同种类范围的任意扩充。

EG - 15 - 8 Remedy including but not limited to costs, losses, liabilities, liquidated damages and directly compensation in connection with this contract (or arising from this contract).

因侵权责任的处罚显然不应包括在内，因为侵权处罚与上述五项中的任何一项都不是同源、同属、同质的，因此完全可以排除在外。

参考译文：承包商应向业主赔偿包括但不限于与本合同有关的（或由本合同引起的）费用、损失、负债、违约金和直接补偿。

EG - 15 - 9 Owner shall indemnify, defend, and hold contractor harmless against any and all claims, suits, action, demands. proceedings, losses, damages, liabilities, costs, and expenses, including, without limitation, interest and reasonable attorneys fees arising out of relating to or resulting from the product.

"any and all"显然在这里强调的是各种赔偿既可单独存在，也可一同要求，以防止出现歧义，可理解为其中之一。

该条款中的赔偿提到了费用、成本、补偿、赔偿等，并没有特别说明含惩罚性的罚款，那么罚款就应排除在外。同时，限定是与产品有关的，所以与产品无关的损失或赔偿就不应包括在内了。

参考译文：业主应赔偿承包商相关损失，并使其免于承担由产品导致或引起的索赔、诉求、诉讼、要求、行动、损失、损害、债务、成本、费用，包括但不限于利息和合理的律师费用。

EG - 15 - 10 The contractor remedial measures, including but not limited to, the contractor shall be made up for direct costs, compensation and liquidated damages.

该补救措施显然不应包括带有惩罚性措施的罚款，如"penalty"。

因为在民商法中罚款属于惩罚性赔偿，与补偿及成本弥补是两种不同质的补偿。也就是说，在理解上，如果没有注明适用的惩罚性条款，这是不适用的，关键是前述都只需合同约定，而惩罚性的措施还需举证证明。

4. 有关"such as"与"such...as"的理解

"such as"较为常见的含义是"举例说明"，如同"for example"或"similar to"，用做"相似"含义时可以导致类别推定的适用。

涉外合同力求严密、准确，为避免误解和歧义，常用"such...as"作关系代词来引导从句，把所修饰的词或短语放在"such"和"as"之间来明确含义。涉外合同中，也常用这种方式引起相关人员的重视。

EG – 15 – 11 The Engineer shall have authority to issue to the Contractor, from time to time, such supplementary drawings and instructions as shall be necessary for the purpose of the proper and adequate execution and completion of the works and the remedying of any defects therein.

本条款强调的是"补充图纸和指令"。

参考译文：工程师有权随时向承包人发出合理和恰当施工、竣工及修补工程缺陷所必需的补充图纸和指令。

EG – 15 – 12 Shall provide such information and data as useful and necessary for the negotiation and appoint a person to cooperate with the representatives from C or New Company and the People's Insurance Company of China in charge of the negotiation.

"such information and data as"在本条款中强调的是"资讯"。

参考译文：乙方应向丙方或新公司和主管该谈判的中国人民保险公司提供谈判所需的有用资讯材料并指定人员与上述各方进行配合。

EG – 15 – 13 The packing of the goods shall be preventive from dampness, rust, moisture, erosion and shock, and shall be suitable for ocean transportation/multiple transportation. The Seller shall be liable for any damage and loss of the goods attributable to the inadequate or improper packing. The measurement, gross weight, net weight and the cautions such as "do not stack up side down", "keep away from moisture", "handle with care" shall be stenciled on the surface of each package with fadeless pigment.

"such as" 在这里起强调作用。一般来讲，"such…as" 属于完全枚举，没有例外情形；而 "such as" 属于典型枚举，相当于 "例如" 的意思，表示列举，相当于 "for example"，除已列举之外还会有例外情形，对此应足够注意。

参考译文：货物应具有防潮、防锈蚀、防震并适合于远洋运输的包装，由于货物包装不良而造成的货物残损、灭失应由卖方负责。卖方应在每个包装箱上用不褪色的颜色标明尺码、包装箱号码、毛重、净重及 "此端向上"、"防潮"、"小心轻放" 等标记。

EG – 15 – 14 Party A agrees to acquire from Party B and Party B agrees to transfer to party A the patented technology for contract products. The patented technology in question shall be the same technology as the technology of Party B's latest products.

这里用 "same as" 强调 "technology"，要注意 "same as" 同 "such as" 的区别。前者为 "一样" 的意思，后者只具有 "列举" 的意思。

参考译文：甲方同意从乙方获得，乙方同意向甲方转让合同产品的专利技术。这种技术应与乙方最新产品的技术完全一致。

"such as" 前后放逗号，就表示是指以某为例，而不具有 "类似" 的意思；或者直接用括号将 such as A 括起，即 "（such as A）"，那就表示只是以 A 为例，相当于 "for example"，否则 "such as" 就可作为 "类似" 讲了。

"et" 等于 "et cetera"，意思为 "其他同种类物"。使用这个词语会暗示合同双方都不想一一列举，或者双方都暂时难以界定清楚。而实质上，"etc"只能描述事物而不能描述人物，否则就会给人以不尊重的感觉。其实质有"多余"的意思，谁愿意自己被描述为多余的人物呢？即使理解为"相似的人"，也难以让人有快感，所以还不如用"and so on"或"and so forth"（用于事物）或"and others"（用于人物）。

同样，在合同中如果选用了"etc"，那就只能是同源、同属、同质、同种类的推定。

如"all personal property including clothing, daily essentials, etc"，当然只能解释为"与衣服和日常用品有关的私人财产"，而不能扩大到个人拥有的代步交通工具。

5. 推定小结

为防止理解上的歧义，在阅读与理解涉外合同时，应注意是否列举穷尽，是否同源、同属与同质列举而构建了一个类别，是否列举为解释性的定义，是否列举构成了对全面的子项的涵盖。前两种在翻译时一般可译为"等"或者"等等"，后两种情形中一般可将"等"省略。

如："与我随同的家庭成员包括父母、哥哥、姐姐"是否就意味着不包括弟弟与妹妹呢？

为此，应注意以下几点：

（1）在"including"一词后用"without limitation"或"among other things"，以避免否定含义的推定。

（2）用上下词代替列举，以定义解释的语句形式来避免否定含义的推定。

（3）用穷尽列举的方式，以避免否定含义的推定。

（4）如何避免否定含义的推定：在"including without limitation"后加由"similar"修饰的并列成分，如"and similar events"。

（5）用上下词加例外，以避免否定含义的推定。如列举后，加上枚举出不应包括的范围。如果枚举不全，就可能形成前后语句的循环推定错误。这一用法要么能够枚举全包括部分，要么能够枚举全不包括部分。

三、条款分析：涉外合同中精确与模糊的把握

EG – 15 – 15 In the conditions of contract（"these Conditions"），which include particular conditions and these general conditions, the following words and expressions shall have the meaning stated, except where the context requires otherwise：

（a）Words indicating persons or parties include corporation and other legal entities, except where the context requires otherwise；

（b）Words indicating one gender include all genders；

（c）Words indicating the singular also include the plural and words indicating the plural also include the singular.

由于"include"后跟了"all"，因此应属特指性别。通过前后相同指代"genders"，从而消除歧义。但由于所有性别本身不能形成一个完整的性别，笔者认为将"all"修改为"any"更符合思维的逻辑运算，即无论男性、女性都应属于本合同所指性别，亦即提到一种性别就意味着包含提到另一性别。

上述"include"显然属特指，即通过相同语序使人一看就将"the singular"与"the plural"等质，从而消除歧义。

上述第一个"include"显然枚举了全部"particular conditions and these general conditions"，可作"否定排除"理解。也就是说，除所包括的两种情形外，可否定其他任何被解释在"these Conditions"范围内。

第二个"include"并没枚举全部，但由于有"other, except—otherwise"除外条款，因此基本可消除歧义。

参考译文：依照合同条件（以下称这些条件），包括通用条款和特殊条款，下列字和表述应有特定的意思，含有人的字包括公司和其他法人，除文本另有要求外。

文字人或当事人包括公司和其他法律实体，除非文本另有其他约定；

文字单一性别包括所有性别；

文字单数也包括复数，文字复数也包括单数。

EG – 15 – 16 "Contract Agreement" means the contract agreement referred to in Sub – Clause ＊＊［Contract Agreement］, including any annexed memoranda.

上述"including"及"any"显然都属特指而非泛指，也就表示必须是与合同前所符的"annexed memoranda"包括在内，否则就应排除在外。

参考译文：合同协议意指被合同第＊＊条（合同协议）提到的合同协议，包括任何备忘录附件。

EG – 15 – 17 "Performance Guarantees" and "Schedule of payments" mean the documents so named (if any), as included in the contract.

上述"included"应限定在合同规定的范围内，不能泛指。

参考译文：履约保函和预付款保函意为以此命名的文件（如有），应包括在本合同之中。

EG – 15 – 18 "Employer's Equipment" means the apparatus, machinery and vehicles (if any) made available by the Employer for the use of the contractor in the execution of the works, as stated in the Employer's requirements, but does not include plant which has not been taken over by the Employer.

上述条款采取了否定的形式，因此属特指本合同所指"plant"，而非其他合同或其他地方的"plant"。

参考译文：业主的设备意指为业主有用的装置、机械和交通工具（如有），因履行本合同按照业主要求的规定为承包商使用的，但不包括不被业主接收的装置。

EG – 15 – 19 "Variation" means any change to the Employer's requirements or the works, which is instructed or approved as a variation under Clause ＊＊［Variation and Adjustment］.

该任何变更应属泛指，但由于有"as a variation under Clause 13"的进一步限定，所以不会发生歧义。"any"在这里强调了"or"所具有的逻辑计算作用，也就是说任何一种或多种情况的出现都是约定的变更。

参考译文：变更意指依据本合同"变更与调整"条款（第＊＊条），按照业主的要求或经业主指令或批准的工程的变更。

EG－15－20 Entitle any person in proper possession of the relevant part of the works to copy, use and communicate the Contractor's documents for the purposes of completing, operating, maintaining, altering, adjusting, repairing and demolishing the works.

"completing, operating, maintaining, altering, adjusting, repairing and demolishing"在这里都使用了现在分词的形式，显然强调的是在本合同中从事这些职业的人。"any"显然是特指而不是泛指。

参考译文：为竣工、操作、维护、改变、调整、修理和拆除项目的目的，赋予适当拥有相关项目部分人的复制、使用和交流承包商的文件的权利。

EG－15－21 In the case of Contractor's documents which are in the form of computer programs and other software, permit their use on any computer on the site and other places as envisaged by the Contract, including replacements of any computers supplied by the contractor.

该"including"显然是特指由承包商提供的计算机，不能对"replacements of any computers"作扩大解释。

参考译文：一旦承包商的文件以计算机程序或其他软件形式形成，应许可使用在工地或其他合同涉及地方的任何计算机，包括更换由承包商供应的计算机。

EG－15－22 They shall not, without the Employer's consent, be copied, used or communicated to a third party by the Contractor, except as necessary for the purposes of the contract.

"other documents" 显然是泛指而非特指，因为后面用 "except as necessary for the purposes of the Contract" 作了限定。

参考译文：除非为合同目的之必要，未经业主的同意，承包商不得复制、使用或用于与第三方的交流。

EG -15 -23 The Employer shall give the Contractor right of access to and possession of, all parts of the site within the time (or times) stated in the particular conditions. The right and possession may not be exclusive to the Contractor. If, under the contract, the Employer is required to give (to the Contractor) possession of any foundation, structure, plant or means of access, the Employer shall do so in the time and manner stated in the Employer's requirements. However, the Employer may withhold any such right or possession until the performance security has been received.

"all parts of the Site" 强调的是整体性，不能对部分开放许可就视为满足了要求。"any foundation, structure, plant" 强调的是基础、结构、装置的可分性。

参考译文：在合同特别条款约定的时间内，业主应赋予承包商进入和占有工地全部区域的权利，享有的权利和占有不得理解为承包独有。依照合同约定，如果业主必须给予承包商对任何基础、构筑物、装置许可进入权或专用通道，业主应按照业主陈述的方式、时间去确保，但是，业主在收到履约保函之前可撤销这一赋予的权利。

EG - 15 - 24 The Employer shall submit, within 28 days after receiving any request from the Contractor, reasonable evidence that financial arrangements have been made and are being maintained which will enable the Employer to pay the contract price (as estimated at that time) in accordance with Clause 14 [Contract Price and Payment]. If the Employer intends to make any material change to his financial arrangements, the

Employer shall give notice to the Contractor with detailed particulars.

本条款中的"any"在这里显然是对具体财务安排的泛指，或者说安排是不确定的，因此不能换成"all"。

参考译文：业主应在收到承包商要求后 28 天内提交有关财务安排的合理证据，能够证明其在估计的时间，根据合同价格和支付条款（第＊＊条＊＊款）之规定有能力向承包商支付合同价款。如果业主想要就财务安排作出任何实质性的变化，业主应给予承包商详细的通知。

EG – 15 – 25 The Employer may deduct this amount from any moneys due, or to become due, to the Contractor. The Employer shall only be entitled to set off against or make any deduction from an amount due to the Contractor, or to otherwise claim against the Contractor, in accordance with this Sub – Clause or with sub – paragraph (a) and/or (b) of Sub – Clause 14. 6 [Interim Payments].

"any moneys due"、"any deduction"显然都是针对金额的可数性。

参考译文：业主可扣减承包商这一任何到期的或即将要到期的金额，业主仅有权对承包商抵消或作出任何抵扣或其他的索赔，根据这一条款和分条款（a）和/或（b）及 14.6 临时支付条款。

EG – 15 – 26 The Contractor shall design, execute and complete the works in accordance with the contract, and shall remedy any defects in the works. When completed, the works shall be fit for the purposes for which the works are intended as defined in the contract.

显然，"design, execute and complete"是由"the works"的三个互相独立的工序类聚而成，不会产生歧义，因此"any defects"是指"design, execute and complete"各个工序都可能存在瑕疵。严格来讲，这里的"design, execute and complete"修改为"design, execute or complete"就不会产生歧义了。

参考译文：依据合同承包商应设计、施工和完工项目，并修补项目的任何缺陷，当竣工时，项目应满足按照合同定义约定的项目目的。

EG - 15 - 27 The Employer shall indemnify and hold the Contractor harmless against and from all damages, losses and expenses (including legal fees and expenses) resulting from a claim under the performance security to the extent to which the Employer was not entitled to make the claim.

"all" 在这里强调的是损失、成本和费用的整体性，在实际过程中不能作严格区分，也没有必要作严格区分。

参考译文：业主应赔偿承包商并使其免受赔偿、损失和费用支出，包括法定费用，导致根据履约保函延长索赔的，业主不能提出索赔。

EG - 15 - 28 Compliance with the quality assurance system shall not relieve the Contractor of any of his duties, obligations or responsibilities under the contract.

Unless otherwise stated in the contract, the contract price covers all the Contractor's obligations under the contract (including those under provisional sums, if any) and all things necessary for the proper design, execution and completion of the works and the remedying of any defects.

"any defects" 显然是指前面四种情况中的任何一种成立则成立。而对于与义务相对应的缺陷修补，所有问题应作为一个整体来考虑，即用 "all" 修饰，并用 "necessary" 来强调，表明任何项的修补都包括在合同价款内。

参考译文：符合质量保证体系不免除承包商的任何本合同约定的职责，除非合同规定，合同价款应包括所有承包商合同项下的义务（包括暂定价，如有）和所有必要的事项，为项目的适当设计、履行和竣工及缺陷弥补。

EG - 15 - 29 The Contractor shall indemnify and hold the Employer harmless against and from all damages, losses and expenses（including legal fees and expenses）resulting from any such unnecessary or improper interference.

"all damages, losses and expenses" 中的 "all" 强调整体性，不可严格区分，只要是发生的损失、损害、费用等都可列入其中之一。

"including legal fees and expenses" 中的 "including" 应属典型列举，无不完全枚举。

参考译文：承包商应赔偿业主涉及不必要、不合适的费用支出，并使其免受损害、损失和费用支出（包括法律费用）。

EG – 15 – 30 The Contractor shall be responsible for packing, loading, transporting, receiving, unloading, storing and protecting all goods and other things required for the works.

参考译文：承包商应负责包装、卸货、运输、接收、卸货、储存和防护所有货物和其他因施工需要的东西。

EG – 15 – 31 "Affiliate" means any person or company that directly or indirectly controls a Party or is directly or indirectly controlled by a Party, including a Party's parent or subsidiary, or is under direct or indirect common control with such Party.

"any" 在这里显然强调 "person or company" 不同类，且可分。

参考译文："关联公司" 指直接或间接控制一方（包括其母公司或子公司）或受一方直接或间接控制，或与该方共同受直接或间接控制的任何人或公司。

EG – 15 – 32 The contract is prevented from executing the Contract in case of force majeure such as war, serious fires, flood, typhoon and earthquake, etc. The time for execution of the contract shall be extended for a period equal to the affect of those causes.

"at any time" 中的 "any" 强调时间的可分性。"such as" 与后面

的"etc"相呼应，属于典型枚举。

参考译文：在合同期间的任何时候，合同任一方，由于受到战争、严重火灾、洪水、台风和地震等不可抗力事件的影响而不能履行合同时，合同履行期应予延长，延长期限相当于事件影响的时间。

第 *16* 章

学会说不：否定性关键词的描述与理解

在人类社会发展过程中，不同民族形成了表达否定情感的多种方式，这些方式在不同的语言中均有具体体现。在商务洽谈活动中，买卖双方因保护自身利益而拒绝对方的条件，经常在合同中使用一些表达否定含义的描述。否定比肯定有时更具有法律的约束性，例如，甲乙双方通过肯定的形式能够形成对甲乙双方具有约束力的条款，但一般来讲，该条款不具有对第三方的约束力，特别是对于排他性约定来讲，就不能当然地约束任何一方授予第三方同样的合同权利。在英美法的判例形成过程中，法官认为肯定式的表述通常被认为不具有可执行力，而否定式则可形成较为明确的警示或禁令作用。因此在涉外合同中，常通过否定形式来直接说明自己提醒或警示对方的意愿：要么是不希望对方过度行使权利，要么是不希望为对方承担合同外的额外责任。在涉外合同中，有关否定的理解与翻译应注意以下四点：一是注意正话反说和反话正说；二是注意结构否定与内容否定；三是注意全面否定与部分否定；四是注意直接否定与婉转否定。

在表达技巧上，英语合同中常用到的否定形式主要分为两种：直接而明显的否定形式与间接而隐含的否定形式。

一、直接而明显的否定形式

1. 直接在句子中用"no"或"not"

（1）在合同条款中直接用"no"或"not"能够明确表达意愿。

（2）静词否定方式常用否定词"no"，在形式上是否定名词、代词和副词。

在对涉外合同中的静态直接否定句进行审核的过程中，要注意以下几点：

第一，全称否定判断必须使用静词否定方式，而不能使用动词否定方式。

第二，静词否定方式的否定口气较重，比较生硬，应根据其谈判的强弱势情形来判断其恰当性。

第三，"no"不用于否定比较级的形容词和数词"one"，因为这时并不一定否定为谓语动词。

（3）动词否定方式用否定词"not"表示，在形式上否定谓语或系表结构的系动词。

在对涉外合同中的动态直接否定句进行审核的过程中要注意以下几点：

第一，全面否定方式情形下，一般将否定词用在主语后，通过助动词完成。

第二，部分否定方式情形下，一般将否定词直接用在谓语前，无须增加助动词。

第三，审核动态否定形式时应注意：动态否定常有逻辑上的混乱；动态否定常会产生歧义，为避免歧义，就要适当增加修饰或分句。

EG-16-1 The termination of this contract shall not in any way affect the outstanding claims and liabilities existing between the Parties hereto upon the expiration of the validity of the contract and the debtor shall continue to be kept liable for paying the outstanding debts to the creditor.

合同终止后，债权人总不希望已经形成的债权也随之终止，因此常用"not affect"关键词来说明其他条款的独立性，以保护"outstanding claims"（未决索赔）和"liabilities existing"（未了债务）。

参考译文：本合同期满时，双方之间发生的未了债务不受合同期满的影响，债务人应向债权人继续支付未了债务。

EG – 16 – 2 The establishment of a limited liability company or a company limited by shares shall comply with the conditions and provisions of this Law. A company complying with the conditions and provisions hereof may be registered as a limited liability company or a company limited by shares. Provided that if a company fails to comply with the conditions and provisions hereof, the company in question shall not be registered as a limited liability company or a company limited by shares.

关键词"not be registered"表示"不得登记为"，具有禁止性作用，权利义务十分清晰。

参考译文：设立有限责任公司、股份有限公司，必须符合本法规定的条件。符合本法规定的条件的，登记为有限责任公司或者股份有限公司；不符合本法规定的条件的，不得登记为有限责任公司或股份有限公司。

2. 直接在句子中用含有否定意义的词缀

在涉外合同中最常用的含有否定意义的词缀是"un – "、"ir – "、"a – "、"ab – "、"anti – "、"de – "、"dis – "、"mal – "、"mis – "、"non – "、"in – "、"ob"、"under – "、" – less"、" – free"等。如：It is duty – free（免税）.

（1）irrevocable.

EG – 16 – 3 By irrevocable, unconditional letter of credit for 90% of the total invoice value of the goods to be shipped, in favor of the Seller, payable at the issuing bank against the Seller's draft at sight accompanied by the shipping documents stipulated in the credit.

"irrevocable"、"unconditional"为"不可撤销"、"无条件"的意思，是见索即付保函必须要的限定条件，表达的意思十分清楚。

参考译文：按货物金额90%开立以卖方为受益人的不可撤销、无条件的信用证，凭卖方汇票跟单向开证行议付。

EG‑16‑4 This agreement and its effectiveness，validity，interpretation，execution and settlement of disputes shall be governed by the laws of the PRC. The parties irrevocably submit to the non‑exclusive jurisdiction of the courts in china as regards any claim or matter arising under this agreement.

参考译文：本合同及其效力、有效性、解释、实施及争议解决应适用中华人民共和国法律。协议双方不可撤销地将因本协议而引发的主张或事件提交中国法院非排他性的司法管辖机构。

（2）non‑delivery.

EG‑16‑5 The Seller shall not be responsible for the delay of shipment or non‑delivery of the goods due to force majeure，which might occur during the process of manufacturing or in the course of loading or transit.

关键词"non‑delivery"意为"不能交货"，对于义务的履行责任十分清楚。如果能够界定原因，那么责任承担也就十分清楚了。

参考译文：凡在制造或装船运输过程中，因不可抗力致使卖方不能或推迟交货时，卖方不负责任。

（3）unforeseen，unpreventable and unavoidable.

EG‑16‑6 Should either of the parties to the Contract be prevented from executing the contract by force majeure，such as earthquake，typhoon，flood，fire and war and other unforeseen events，and their happenings and consequences are unpreventable and unavoidable，the presented party shall notify the other party by a written notice without any delay，and within 15 days thereafter provide the detailed information of the events and a valid document for evidence issued by the relevant public notary organization for explaining the reason of its inability to execute or delay the execution of all or part of the contract. Both parties shall, through consultations, decide whether to rescind the contract or to exempt the part of obligations for implementation of the contract or whether to delay the execution of the contract according to the effects of the events on the performance of the contract.

"unforeseen, unpreventable and unavoidable" 意为"不可预见、不能防止并不可避免"，是界定不可抗力的"三不原则"，用"un –"前缀形成，没有任何含混，意思十分明确，也便于认定。

参考译文：由于发生地震、台风、水灾、火灾、战争及其他无法预见并且对其发生和后果均不能防止或避免的不可抗力事件，致使直接影响合同的履行或者不能按约定的条件履行时，遇有上述不可抗力事件的一方应立即将事件情况书面通知对方，并在其后 15 天内提供事件详情及全部或部分合同不能或需要延期履行的理由的有效证明文件，此项证明文件应由事件发生地区的公证机构出具。按照事件对履行合同影响的程度，由双方协商决定是否解除合同，或者部分免除履行合同的责任，或者延期履行合同。

(4) unable.

EG – 16 – 7 The Party shall suspend its performance of the contract, if it has conclusive evidence that the other party is unable to perform the contract. However, it shall immediately inform the other party of such termination.

关键词"unable to perform"意为"不能履行"，显然是实质上、主观上的不能，因此对于非违约方来讲，就有足够的理由提出中止合同、解除合同或终止合同。

参考译文：当事人一方有另一方不能履行合同的确切证据时，可以中止履行合同，但是应当通知另一方；当另一方对履行合同提供了充分的保证时，应当履行合同。

（5）impossible.

EG – 16 – 8 In case that one or both parties are impossible to perform the duties provided herein on account of force majeure, the party（or parties）in contingency shall inform the other Party（or each other）of the case immediately and may, provided the case is duly verified by the competent authorities, delay in performance of or not perform the relevant duties hereunder and be partially or entirely exempted from the liability for breach of this agreement.

关键词"impossible to perform"意为"不能履行"，这往往表示非主观的不可能，即客观上的不可能，在理解上应结合"unable to perform"加以分析。

参考译文：如因人力不可抗拒之因素，致使一方或双方不能履行合同有关条款，则该方（或双方）应及时向对方通报情况，并在取得合法机关的有效证明之后，可延期履行或不履行有关合同义务，并可根据情况部分或全部免除违约责任。

（6）non – acceptance or non – payment.

EG – 16 – 9 The collection order shall give specific instructions regarding the protest（or shall take other legal process in lieu thereof）, in the event of non – acceptance or non – payment.

"non – acceptance or non – payment"意为"拒绝承兑"、"拒绝支付"，属金融领域的专业术语。

参考译文：如果托收委托书被拒绝承兑或拒绝支付，应就拒付的理由给予解释（或采取其他法律程序），否则就应按照相关条款承兑。

（7）inconsistency.

EG – 16 – 10 This agreement is written in both English and Chinese. In the event of any inconsistency between the two versions, the English version/the Chinese version shall prevail.

"inconsistency"意为"不一致"。

参考译文：本协议由中文或英文做成。两种版本内容出现不一致的，以英文或中文为准。

（8）be disadvantageous.

EG – 16 – 11 The Seller and the Buyer hereby agree to enter into this contract of purchase on the terms and conditions set forth below and on the general terms and conditions attached hereto. the Seller hereby acknowledges that the Buyer has sufficiently called the Seller's liability and responsibility. It is therefore that the Seller has been fully informed of and understood, such provisions and other provisions which may be disadvantageous to the Seller and that the Seller has determined to enter into this contract of purchase. the Seller fully understands that the Buyer, being a trading company, shall enter into this contract of purchase in order to make a resale profit.

参考译文：卖方和买方特此同意签订以下条款的采购合同，包括一般条款和合同附件条款。卖方特此理解买方充分相信卖方的能力和责任，因此，卖方完全知悉与理解，这些条款或其他条款对卖方可能不利，卖方也决定签署本采购合同。卖方完全理解买方，作为一个商贸公司，签署本采购合同的目的是为了获取进销的差额利益。

（9）insolvent.

EG – 16 – 12 This agreement will automatically cease, in the event that the licensee becomes insolvent or bankrupt or goes into liquidation (whether voluntarily or otherwise), or the licensee's substantial assets have been possessed, confiscated, expropriated or occupied by any third party, or the licensee becomes incapable or unable to fully perform its obligations under this agreement.

"solvent" 意为 "有偿付能力的"，其否定意为 "没有偿付能力"。"破产清算" 为法律专业术语。

参考译文：倘若许可方实施清算或破产，或进入清算程序（无论是主动清算或以其他方式清算），或者被许可方的主要资产被任何第三方占有使用、没收、自用或占用，或者被许可方成为无能力或无法充分履行本协议项下的义务，本协议则自动终止。

（10）non – exclusive and non – assignable.

EG – 16 – 13 Subject to the terms and conditions set out in this agreement, the licensor hereby grants to the licensee a non – exclusive and non – assignable and personal right and license to use and exploit the technology to produce, manufacture and/or assemble and process the products during the term hereof.

参考译文：在满足本协议规定的条款或条件的前提下，许可方在此授权被许可方在本协议有效期内使用及开发该技术以便生产、制造以及/或者组装及加工该产品之非独占性的、不可转让的、只限于被许可方本身的权利和许可。

（11）irreparable harm.

EG – 16 – 14 The licensee acknowledges and agrees that a breach of the confidentiality provisions set forth in this agreement will result in serious and irreparable harm to the licensor and that the licensee shall be responsible for any damage, loss or injury to the licensor, caused by any disclosure without the prior written consent by the licensor of any item, part or element of the technology or technical documentation provided by the licensor.

参考译文：许可方确认并同意，如果违反本转文中的保密规定，将对许可方造成无法弥补的严重损害。对于许可方提供的该技术或技术文件的任何项目、部分或要素，任何未经许可方事先书面同意的披露而给许可方造成的任何损害、损失或伤害，均应由被许可方负责。

（12）inadequate remedy.

EG – 16 – 15 The licensee further acknowledge and agree that in any breach of this article by it or its affiliates or any one of them, damages may be an inadequate remedy, and the licensor shall have the right to claim injunctive relief in addition to any other claims for damages which they may have.

参考译文：被许可方进一步承诺或同意，对于因其自身或其任何关联公司违反本条款而作出的赔偿可能是不充足的补救措施，许可方要求对其可能遭受的损害进行赔偿之外，有权要求禁止令救济。

（13）unclear.

EG – 16 – 16 Now that the Seller, with its ability to understand and/or the Buyer's explanation, has fully understood the provisions of this contract of purchase (including the attached general terms and conditions) which may release or mitigate the Buyer's liability and responsibility, and that there is no any other provision which is unclear to the Seller, the Seller hereby for executed this contract of purchase.

参考译文：卖方基于其理解能力及/或买方说明，已充分理解本购货合同（包括所附一般条款和条件）项下可能免除或减轻买方责任的全部条款，且不存在任何其他不明确的条款，故签订本购货合同。

（14）invalidity.

EG – 16 – 17 The invalidity of any provision of this agreement shall not affect the validity of any other provisions herein.

参考译文：本协议任何条款的无效，不影响本协议任何其他条款的有效性。

3. 直接在句子中使用含否定意义的不定代词

如 "none"、"little"、"few"、"neither"、"nobody"、"nothing" 等。

（1）nothing.

EG – 16 – 18 Nothing in Article ＊＊ shall prevent Party A or any of its affiliation from continuing to carry on any of their present businesses.

上述合同条文中用了含否定意义的不定代词 "nothing"。

参考译文：合同第＊＊条规定不得妨碍甲方或其分支机构持续经营现有业务。

（2）neither.

EG – 16 – 19 Each party shall be responsible for its own applicable taxes imposed upon it resulting from its performance of its part of this agreement, neither party shall be responsible for any unpaid taxes of the other party.

在涉外合同中，常用"either party"、"each party"来表示各方都可同等地享有某些权利或承担某一义务，而用"neither party"来表示各方都不得享有某一权利或不得承担某一义务。

参考译文：合同各方应各自承担本合同应适用的税务征缴，任何一方不对另一方没有缴纳税款承担责任。

（3）outstanding.

EG – 16 – 20 With respect to the outstanding ＊＊M/r of low – density polyethylene NY2—11 under Contract ＊＊.

参考译文：关于＊＊号合同项下尚未执行的＊＊公吨 NY2—11 低密度聚乙烯。

EG – 16 – 21 Notwithstanding the issue of the Defects Liability Certificate, the Contractor and the Employer shall remain liable for the fulfillment of any outstanding obligation incurred under the provisions of the contract when the Defects Liability Certificate is issued. To determine the nature and extent of the obligations in question, the contract shall be deemed to remain in force and be binding upon the parties thereto.

参考译文：尽管签发了缺陷责任证书，当缺陷证书签发时，承包商和业主仍应就任何依照本合同项条款未了结的债务承担支付责任。决定延长该义务，合同应被视为维持效力，对双方当事人具有约束力。

4. 含否定意义的介词结构

常用的含有否定意义的介词有："without"、"instead of"、"in place of"、"out of"、"but for"、"beyond"、"except"、"but"、"in the dark"、"at a loss"、"in no respect"、"in no sense"、"by no means"、"under no circumstance"、"in no shape"、"in no way（case）"、"on no condition"、"above"、"behind" 等。

（1）in no event.

EG – 16 – 22 In no event shall the Seller be liable for lost profits, delay, injury to goodwill or any special or consequential damages howsoever any of the same are caused.

参考译文：对于利润损失、延误、商誉损害或任何特别或间接的损害赔偿，不论任何原因引起的，卖方概不承担责任。

（2）without.

EG – 16 – 23 Therefore, executive agrees that the company shall be entitled to an injunction restraining executive from any actual or threatened breach of paragraphs 7, 8 or 9 or to any other appropriate equitable remedy without any bond or other security being required.

参考译文：因此，董事同意本公司无须提供任何保证或其他担保，有权发出申请禁令限制董事任何实际或危及违反7、8 或 9 节的行为或获得任何其他适当衡平救济。（作状语）

EG – 16 – 24 It is agreed that, upon termination of this agreement, the right of the distributor to use the trademarks and any other of the above-mentioned intellectual property rights shall be terminated and all such rights shall thereupon revert to the supplier unconditionally and without considera-tion and the distributor shall discontinue the use thereof.

参考译文：双方同意，在本协议解除时经销商使用指定商标和上述其他知识产权的权利也随之终止，所有这些权利应无条件地无偿返还给供货商，经销商不得继续使用上述知识产权。

（3）in no case.

EG－16－25 In this case, Party B shall refund to Party A the amount which Party A has paid to Party B plus the related interest at the rate of 10% per year immediately, but in no case shall such refunding by Party B exceeds 30 days from receipt from Party A of the notice to terminate the contract.

参考译文：在此种情况下，乙方应立即返还甲方已支付给乙方的款项并按年利率 10% 加算利息，但不论怎样乙方该返还不得超过收到甲方终止合同通知后 30 日。

5. 用具有否定意义的句式

如 "too...to"、"too...for"、"let alone"、"anything but"、"why not"、"not so...as" 等。

（1）neither..., neither...nor....

EG－16－26 Neither the supplier or the distributor is an agent of the other, and neither party shall hold itself out or act as such nor shall the distributor assume or create any obligations or liability expressed or implied on behalf of the supplier, nor bind the supplier in any manner whatsoever except as provided therein. Each party shall indemnify and hold harmless the other party against any liability arising from breach of any representation or warranty made in this agreement.

参考译文：经销商或供货商均不是对方的代理人，任何一方不得自称代理或代表对方；经销商也不得代表供货商承担或者设立任何明示或者默示的义务；除了本协议中另有明确约定外，不在任何方面对供货商具有约束力。倘若任何一方违反本协议中的陈述或保证，应对另一方作出赔偿或者确保其不受损害。

（2）not...nor.

EG－16－27 Failure or delay on the part of any party to exercise any

right, power or privilege under this agreement, or under any other contract
or agreement relating hereto, shall not operate as a waiver there of, nor
shall nay single or partial exercise of any right, power or privilege preclude
any other future exercise thereof.

参考译文：一方没有行使或延迟行使按本协议或与本协议相关的
其他合同或协议规定的任何权利、权力或优先权，不应作为放弃该等
权利、权力或优先权；任何单独或部分地行使任何权利、权力或优先
权，不应妨碍将来另外行使该等权利、权力或优先权。

（3）not...or.

EG - 16 - 28 The general manager or assistant general manager shall
not concurrently hold posts as general manager or assistant general manager
of other economic entities, or take part in commercial competition activities
organized by other economic entities.

"not...or"对并列的前后两分句都具有否定作用。

参考译文：总经理、副总经理不得兼任其他经济组织的总经理或
副总经理，不得参与其他经济组织对本合营公司的商业竞争活动。

二、婉转而隐含的否定形式

汉语中用"非"、"不"、"否"、"没"、"无"、"未"等词语表达
"反对、否认、不认可"等显性的否定意义，也有"禁止"、"拒绝"、
"短缺"、"失败"、"薄弱"、"滥用"、"排斥"、"撤销"等不太显性
或隐性的表达形式。

在翻译成英语时，我们可用显性的英语否定表达方式，如"no"、
"non - not"、"neither"、"never"等；也可用隐性的英语否定表达式，
如"avoid"、"prohibit"、"refuse"、"fail"、"weak"、"misuse"、
"cancel"、"miss"、"lack"、"stop"、"preven"、"impossible"、"hardly"等。

同时，我们需要转换角度，显性的否定形式可以用隐性的形式表达，反之亦然。

1. 非正面肯定的形容词

非正面肯定的形容词主要有"far from"、"short of"、"free from"、"different from"、"last"、"poor"、"absent"等。例句如："It is far from the truth"、"I am short of money"、"This is the last thing that I'd like to do"等。

以"in the absence of"为例：

EG – 16 – 29 In the absence of such specific instructions, the banks concerned with the collection shall have no obligation to provide the protest (or to take other legal process in lieu thereof) when the banks in question experience non – acceptance and non – payment.

参考译文：没有明确的指令，当此行拒收和拒绝支付时，相关接收行没有提出拒付的权力，或采购其他替代方式。

2. 非正面肯定的副词

如"hardly"、"scarcely"、"rarely"、"seldom"、"never"、"no longer"、"can not… any longer (more)"、"not … at all"、"nowhere"、"hardly bear"等。

EG – 16 – 30 Party A has been under liquidation and will no longer have the human resources and other resources to perform all the after – sales service obligations under the sales contracts.

参考译文：甲方已进入清算，将不能继续履行销售合同项下的各项售后服务的义务。

3. 非正面肯定的动词

如"fail"、"neglect"、"miss"、"deny"、"ignore"、"refuse"、"keep from"、"protect from"、"dislike"、"prevent from"、"exclude"、"forbid"、"wonder"、"lack"、"stop"等。例句如："Parents keep their children from smoking."

（1）withdrawal.

EG－16－31 If, as a result of withdrawal or any other reasons, an arbitrator fails to perform his duties as an arbitrator, another arbitrator shall, in accordance with the provisions hereof, be selected or appointed.

参考译文：仲裁员因回避或者其他原因不能履行职责的，应当依照本法规定重新选定或指定仲裁员。

（2）free of.

EG－16－32 Within the validity term of the contract, both parties shall provide each other with the improvement and development of the technology related to the contract products free of charge.

参考译文：在合同有效期内，双方当事人应免费互相提供相关合同产品技术的技术开发与改进。

（3）fails to.

EG－16－33 The Borrower fails to pay any amount payable thereunder as and when such amount shall become payable.

An agent shall bear civil liability if he fails to perform his duties and thus causes damage to the principal.

参考译文：当这一数额成为应付账款，借款方又不支付这一应付款时。

代理人不履行职责而给被代理人造成损害的，应当承担民事责任。

EG－16－34 Either Party who fails to perform its obligations as stipulated in this agreement shall be deemed to be in breach of this agreement.

参考译文：任何一方未能按本协议规定履行其义务的，应视为对本协议的违约。

（4）failure.

EG – 16 – 35 Failure to notify Party A shall be deemed to be a material breach of this agreement.

参考译文：未能按上述要求通知甲方的，则视为构成实质违约。（作谓语）

（5）prohibited.

EG – 16 – 36 The contractor is prohibited from sub – contracting any part of the project to an entity not appropriately qualified. A sub – contractor is prohibited from further sub – contracting its contracted word. The main structure of the construction project must be constructed by the contractor itself.

参考译文：总承包商禁止分包工程的任何工作量到没有资质的企业。分包商禁止再行分包他所承包的工作量。建设项目的主体工程应由总承包商自行建设。

（6）freely.

EG – 16 – 37 In the event that the licensee develops any other improvement of any kind to any item of the technology, the licensee shall grant the licensor the right to use all such improved technology freely during the term of this agreement.

The licensor shall grant the licensee the right to use freely any improvements developed by the licensor to any item of the technology which is listed in the schedule attacted hereto, without imposing additional costs and conditions on the licensee during the term of this agreement.

参考译文：如果被许可方对任何一项该技术作了任何其他改进，被许可方应在本协议的有效期内授权许可方免费使用该技术。

许可方对本协议附件 A 所列的任何一项该技术所作的任何改进，均应授权被许可方免费使用，被许可方在本协议有效期内无须为此负担额外的费用和条件。

（7）adversely affected

EG – 16 – 38 Each of the parties hereto agrees that if it or any of its affiliates or related enterprises decides to establish or otherwise engage in other manufacturing facilities identical or similar to those of the JV company, it shall inform the other party beforehand and consult together to ensure that the business of the JV company is not and will not be materially adversely affected thereby.

参考译文：本协议各方同意，如果其本身或其任何关联公司或有关企业决定设立或另外从事与合营公司相同或相似的其他生产设施，该方应事前通知另一方并共同协商，以确保合营公司的业务不致因此受到严重的不利影响。

（8）prevented from performing.

EG – 16 – 39 If any party is prevented from performing any of its obligations under this agreement due to an event of force majeure, the affected party shall immediately notify the other parties of the occurrence and subsequent termination of the event of force majeure by facsimile or e – mail.

参考译文：如果任何一方由于不可抗力事件而法无法履行其在本协议项下的任何义务，受影响的一方应立即以传真或电邮通知另一方该不可抗力事件的发生以及随后的终止。

（9）be silent.

EG – 16 – 40 This agreement shall be governed by and construed in accordance with the laws of the PRC in the event that PRC law is silent on any particular point in dispute, the parties agree to follow relevant international practice with respect thereto.

参考译文：本协议适用中国法律，并按照中国法律解释。如果中国法律对争议中的特定问题未作规定的，双方同意遵循相关的国际惯例。

4. 非正面肯定的连接词

常用的含有否定意义的连接词主要有以下形式："unless"、"would rather...than"、"other than"、"neither...nor"、"before"、"except that"、"or"、"otherwise" 等。例句如："I would rather die than give in." "The truth is quite other than what you think." "I thanked him before he said anything."

（1）events of default.

EG – 16 – 41 If one or more of the following events of default（hereinafter called "Event of Default"）occurs or occur or continues or continue the agent and the bank shall be entitled to the remedies specified in Sub – Clause 11. 2 of the agreement.

参考译文：如果一个或多个违约事件（以下简称违约事件）发生或持续发生，代理人和银行应有权去修改本合同第＊＊条的规定。

（2）without prior consent.

EG – 16 – 42 Neither party, without prior consent of the other, may assign or transfer to any third party any equity interests held by its side.

参考译文：未经对方同意，任一方不得向任何第三人转让其持有的股权。

（3）at many outlets and many prices levels.

EG – 16 – 43 At this stage, the average – income mass market makes its purchases. A full line of products is made available at many outlets and many prices levels. Promotion becomes very competitive.

参考译文：在此阶段，产品销售主要在一般收入的大众化市场，整个产品系列在不同场合以不同的价格出售，促销具有很强的竞争性。

对于格式合同，不同国家有不同的处理方式，但总的来讲均倾向于对弱者的保护。其主要是说明合同中的不利条款是否对弱势方起到了提示作用，对方是否有不理解、不清楚的地方。

（4）not in conformity with.

EG – 16 – 44 The Buyer shall inspect the goods immediately after delivery. In the event that the Buyer shall discover in the course of any such inspection that all or any portion of the goods is not in conformity with this contract, the Buyer shall make a claim in writing against the Seller within 7 days after the delivery thereof or within the period of time which the Buyer and the Seller may have stipulated on the face of this contract. The Buyer shall assert all claims in writing against the Seller in connection with any latent defect of the goods within 30 days after delivery thereof. In the event that the Buyer does not assert any claim in writing during the above – mentioned period of time, the delivered goods shall be deemed to be in conformity with this contract.

参考译文：买方应在货物交货后立即进行验收。在验收中如发现货物全部或部分不符合本合同规定时，买方应在自货物交付后 7 日以内或在买卖双方或许于本合同正面所规定的期限内以书面方式向卖方提出索赔。货物存在潜在瑕疵时，买方应在货物交付后 30 日以内以书面方式向卖方提出索赔。如买方未在上述期限内以书面方式提出索赔，则视为所交付的货物符合本合同的规定。

三、涉外合同中常用的正面否定实意性关键词

下面摘录一些涉外合同中常用的与否定词配套使用的实意性关键词，以便更好地理解。

（1）not be returned.

EG – 16 – 45 The royalties described in article ＊＊ and all other fees in relation thereto as described in this agreement as the consideration for the technology license and related technical assistance and services shall not be returned in the event of early termination of this agreement.

参考译文：本协议第 ＊＊ 条约定的许可费以及本协议约定的其他

全部相关费用，作为该技术的使用许可费以及本协议约定的其他全部相关费用，作为该技术的使用许可和相关技术援助及服务的对价，即使在本协议提前解除的情况下也无须退还。

（2）not to distribute.

EG – 16 – 46 In consideration of the exclusive right granted herein in respect of the territory, the distributor agrees not to distribute the products outside the territory directly or indirectly, or sell the products to any party which the distributor knows or has reason to suspect who has an intention to export outside the territory. The distributor further agrees that it will not sell any other products of any kind other than the products as provided in this agreement. As for the accessories and products (including, without limitation, glasses, bags, perfumes, etc.), whose production has been licensed by the supplier to third parties, such products shall be purchased by the distributor directly from the supplier's licensed partners.

参考译文：作为本协议中授予经销商在指定地域内独家经销权的对价，经销商同意不直接或间接地将指定商品经销到指定地域以外，或者销售给经销商知道或有理由怀疑任何有意将指定商品出口到指定地域以外的当事人，并且经销商同意不销售本协议约定的指定商品以外的任何其他种类产品。而对于供货商已许可第三方生产的配饰及产品（包括但不限于如眼镜、手袋、香水），经销商应直接从供货商许可的第三方处购买。

（3）not contest.

EG – 16 –47 The distributor hereby acknowledges that the title to and/or the right to use the trademarks vests solely in the supplier as the trademark owner and the distributor shall not contest the ownership or validity of the trademarks. Upon termination or expiration of this agreement, the right to use the trademarks grated by the supplier to the distributor shall be terminated and all such rights shall revert to the supplier unconditionally and without any consideration and the distributor agrees thereupon to discontinue use of the trademarks.

参考译文：经销商在此承认，供货商作为指定商标的所有人，对指定商标拥有唯一的所有权以及/或使用权，经销商不得对指定商标的所有权或有效期提出异议。在本协议解除或者期满时，供货商授予经销商的指定商标使用权亦随即终止，所有该等权利将无条件地、无须任何对价地回归供应商，经销商同意不再继续使用指定商标。

(4) not be challenged.

EG – 16 – 48 The distributor acknowledges that any and all trademarks, trade names, designs, inventions and other intellectual property rights, including the trademarks, used in connection with or embodied in the products are and shall remain the sole property of the supplier, and the supplier shall not in any way be challenged or disputed by the distributor. In the event that the distributor becomes aware that such intellectual property rights of the supplier are claimed or infringed upon by a third party, the distributor shall promptly inform the supplier thereof and, in the event that the supplier decides to take any action in respect thereof, shall render reasonable assistance to the supplier to enable the protection of such rights.

参考译文：经销商确认，用于指定商品或指定商品所包含的任何及全部商标、商品名称、外观设计、发明和其他知识产权，包括指定商标，均属于供货商的专有财产，经销商不得以任何方式对该等知识产权提出质疑或争议。如果经销商获悉供货商的该等知识产权被第三方索赔或侵权，经销商应立即通知供货商，在此种情形下，由供货商决定为此采取何种行动，经销商应向供货商提供合理的协助以保护该等知识产权。

(5) not use.

EG – 16 – 49 The distributor shall not use any other trademarks or trade name in connection with the marketing, promotion or sale of the products.

参考译文：经销商不得将其他任何商标或商品名用于指定商品的市场推广、促销或销售。

(6) not be used.

EG – 16 – 50 The headings within this agreement are used for convenience only and shall not be used to interpret, construe or otherwise affect the meaning of the provisions of this agreement.

参考译文：本合同的标题仅为方便使用而设，不得用于本协议的解释、分析或以其他方式影响本协议条款的含义。

(7) bear no liability.

EG – 16 – 51 The supplier shall bear no liability whatsoever for any alleged infringement or suit with regard to intellectual property rights of a third party which may arise in connection with the sale of the products by the distributor conducted in compliance with this agreement. In the event that such a claim or suit is made against the distributor, the supplier shall be promptly notified thereof, and the distributor, the supplier shall be promptly notified thereof, and the supplier shall furnish the distributor with such evidence and information available to the supplier as reasonably requested by the distributor to assist the distributor in defending such claim. The distributor shall bear the legal cost involved in defending the claim.

参考译文：对于经销商按照本协议规定销售指定商品所发生的第三方声称的知识产权侵权或诉讼，供货商不承担任何责任。如果此种索赔或者诉讼是针对经销商而提起的，经销商应立即通知供货商；在经销商提出合理要求时，供货商应尽可能向经销商提供相关证据和信息，以协助经销商对该索赔进行抗辩。经销商应承担对该索赔进行抗辩所发生的相关法律费用。

(8) not be renewed.

EG – 16 – 52 This agreement shall not be automatically renewed without the parties express consent.

"renewed" 意为 "续期"、"续签"。

参考译文：除非经双方明示同意，本协议不得自动续期。

（9）not due.

EG－16－53 Any indebtedness of either party to the other party not already due shall become immediately due and payable as of the effective date of termination or expiration of this agreement. In no event shall any party be liable for any debts of any other party to pay customers or other creditors.

参考译文：在本协议解除或到期的生效日，任何一方对于另一方的未到期债务均视为到期，并应立即支付。在任何情况下，任何一方均无义务就另一方的债务向其客户或其他债权人进行偿付。

EG－16－54 If no agreement can be reached by the parties, the prices shall be the original prices set forth hereunder.

参考译文：如果双方未能达成一致协议，则按照本协议的原定价格表执行。

（10）not violate.

EG－16－55 The parties hereto hereby undertake that their business activities carry out hereunder does not violate any applicable laws and regulations. In the event that a party commits a breach of this clause and causes any loss or damages to the other party, the defaulting party shall bear all legal liabilities and indemnify the other party for all its losses and damages so incurred.

参考译文：双方在此保证，其在本协议项下所进行的经营活动不违反所适用的法律法规。如因任何一方违反本规定并给对方带来任何损失或损害，违约方须承担所有法律责任并赔偿给对方造成的全部损失。

（11）not participate in.

EG - 16 - 56 Party B shall be solely responsible for any disputes, claims, losses, infringements and liabilities, etc. between itself and its customers. Party A would not participate in such disputes, claims etc. between party B and its customers and shall not be responsible for any losses of party B's customers.

参考译文：乙方应负责自行解决与其客户之间的任何争议、索赔、损失、侵权和违约责任等，甲方不介入乙方与其客户之间的这些纠纷、索赔等，也不对乙方客户的任何损失负责。

（12）no agent.

EG - 16 - 57 No party hereto shall declare itself as the agent of the other party or has any authority to create or assume any obligation of any kind for or on behalf of the other party.

参考译文：本协议任何一方不得声称自己是另一方的代理人或声称其有权代表另一方设定或承担义务。

（13）not include.

EG - 16 - 58 The license is personal to the licensee and, except with the licensor's prior written approval, the grant does not include any right for the licensee to grant any sub - license, concession, right or privilege of any kind relating thereto, or to use the technology in connection with any products manufactured by any third party for the licensee. Such license is indivisible and may not be transferred or assigned in whole or in part, by contract, operation of law or in any manner whatsoever, except with the licensor's prior written approval.

参考译文：该许可权仅授予被许可方本身，除非获得许可方的事先书面批准，该授权并不包括被许可方进行与之相关的任何种类的再授权、特许、权利或优先权，或将该技术用于任何第三方为被许可方生产的任何产品。该许可权是不可侵害的，并且不得全部或部分转让，无论是通过合同、法律的实施或是以任何方式转让，但事先获得许可方书面批准的不在此限。

(14) not to introduce or pursue any such suit or action.

EG – 16 – 59 In the event that the licensor elects not to introduce or pursue any such suit or action, the licensee may take such action in its own name and on its own cost, after receiving prior written consent from the licensor.

参考译文：如果许可方选择不起诉或不采取法律行动，被许可方在事先征得许可方书面同意后，可以自己的名义自费采取上述行动。

(15) not acquire.

EG – 16 – 60 The licensee shall not acquire any right or interest in the technology or the technical documentation except the limited use rights pursuant to the terms of this agreement. Any action by the licensee that challenges jeopardizes or in any way threatens any of the licensor's proprietary rights in the technology or technical documentation shall entitle the licensor to terminate this agreement.

参考译文：除了本协议规定的有限使用权之外，被许可方不得获取该技术或技术文件中的任何权利或权益。倘若被许可方采取行动对许可方在该技术或技术文件中的任何专有权进行质疑、损害或以任何方式威胁，许可方有权解除本协议。

(16) not be disclosed.

EG – 16 – 61 All confidential information of the parties furnished to each other in connection with this agreement shall be kept in strictest confidence shall not be disclosed to any third party and shall be used only for the purpose for which it was originally received. In the event of necessity to disclose such confidential information to its employees, the parties shall take every procedure reasonably required to cause such employees to keep the information in confidence.

参考译文：双方均应对与本协议有关而提交给对方的保密信息严格保密，不得向任何第三方披露，而公用于其接受保密信息的本来目的。如果有必要向其雇员披露保密信息，双方应采取全部必要的合理措施，使接受该等信息的雇员对此保密。

（17）no written objection.

EG – 16 – 62 If no written objection is raised by either party one month before its expiry, the contract will be automatically extended for another year.

参考译文：在期满前1个月，如果合同双方没有提出书面异议，本合同将自动延长1年。

（18）unclear.

EG – 16 – 63 Now that the Seller, with its ability to understand and/or the Buyer's explanation, has fully understood the provisions of this contract of purchase (including the attached general terms and conditions) which may release or mitigate the Buyer's liability and responsibility, and that there is no any other provision which is unclear to the Seller, the Seller hereby for executed this contract of purchase.

参考译文：卖方基于其理解能力及/或买方说明，已充分理解本购货合同（包括所附一般条款和条件）项下可能免除或减轻买方责任的全部条款，且不存在任何其他不明确的条款，故签订本购货合同。

四、双重否定的描述

在涉外合同中，也会出现几个双重否定条款。遇到双重否定条款时，一定要注意否定词的位置假设与翻译的语气表述。

双重否定句是一种非常特殊的句型，能够起到一般否定句和肯定句所不具备的表达功能。由于涉外合同是双方协商的结果，因此在翻译时，为便于双方更好地沟通、理解，不仅要注重双重否定句所需要表述的肯定语气，更要注重强调否定和委婉否定的特殊功能。

EG – 16 – 64　Any waiver of any breach of this contract shall not be deemed to apply to any succeeding breach of the provision or of any other provision of this contract. No failure to exercise and no delay in exercising on the part of any of the parties hereto any right, power or privilege hereunder shall operate as a waiver thereof nor shall any single or partial exercise of any right, power or privilege preclude any other or further exercise thereof or the exercise of any other right, power or privilege. The rights and remedies provided in this contract are cumulative and not exclusive of any rights or remedies otherwise provided by law.

参考译文：任何对本合同违约条款的放弃，不能视为适应于任何其他存续的违约条款或任何本合同的其他条款。双方当事人不实施或延迟实施合同约定的任何权利、权力或特权不得理解为对它的放弃，双方当事人全面实质实施合同约定的任何权利、权力或特权后才可理解为对它的放弃，任何单一或部分地履行任何权利、权力或特权不得阻止任何其他有关权利、权力或特权条款的实施。本合同的权利或弥补是累积的，权利与弥补不因其他法律条文的规定而免除。

"双方当事人全面实质实施合同约定的任何权利、权力或特权后才可理解为对它的放弃"的翻译显然要比"双方当事人不实施或延迟实施合同约定的任何权利、权力或特权不得理解为对它的放弃"婉转。

以下是其英文的类似表达方式：The Receiving Party agrees that no failure nor any delay in exercising on the part of the Disclosing Party any right or remedy under this NDA, shall operate as a waiver thereof (in whole or in part), nor shall any single or partial exercise of any right or remedy prevent any further, future or other exercise thereof or any other right or remedy. The rights and remedies existing by virtue of this NDA shall be cumulative and not exclusive of any rights or remedies provided by law.

"NDA"意为"non disclosure agreement",等同于"confidentiality agreement"。

EG – 16 – 65 Indulgence, Waiver, etc. No failure on the part of any party to this agreement to exercise and no delay on the part of an party in exercising any right hereunder will operate as a release or waiver thereof, nor will any single or partial exercise of any right under this agreement preclude any other or further exercise of it.

参考译文:迁就,放弃等任何一方部分不行使或延迟行使其合同约定的权利将不得理解为解除或放弃其余权利的行使,任何一方全面实质行使合同约定的权利才可理解为对权利的解除或放弃,否则,无论这种放弃是单一或部分行使本合同权利都不得妨碍对其他权利的行使或随后选择去行使。

第 *17* 章

重点强调：合同条款描述
形式上的多样性理解

"形式决定内容，内容通过形式表达。"在涉外合同的阅读过程中，不仅应重视内容的审核，同时也要注重合同条款描述形式上的审核，特别是要注意合同条款重点强调的表达形式。下面重点谈谈涉外合同条款中含有强调意味的表达方式。

一、处于"it is ..."形式表语位置的关键词

在普通英文中，"it is ..."形式是较为突出的强调形式。涉外合同中也不例外，常常用"it is ..."形式作为重点强调。

1. It is duly organided

EG – 17 – 1 It is［an independent legal person］duly organized, validly existing and in good standing under the laws of the place of its establishment.

上述条款中用了一个"it is ..."强调句型，强调其独立法人地位。其后又用了一个强调性单词"duly"，强调

其依法定程序成立、有效存续且手续完备。

参考译文：根据其成立地的法律，该方［为独立法人］依法定程序设立、有效存续且相关手续完备。

2. It is mutually agreed that clause

EG - 17 - 2 It is mutually agreed that the certificate of quality and quantity of weight issued by the manufacturer shall be part of the document for payment with the adopted Letter of Credit.

该句的主旨句是说重量或质量的检验证书是支付文件的一部分，强调的是双方协商的结果。"It is"虽是单数表达形式，但重点强调的是"mutually"，意为"双方"。

参考译文：双方同意制造厂出具的质量、数量或重量检验证明书作为有关信用证项下付款的单据之一。

EG - 17 - 3 It is expressly agreed that Lessee will not, without obtaining prior written permission of Lessor, assert on its behalf, or on behalf of Lessor, any immunity from taxation based on the tax - exempt status, if any, of the Lessor.

该句用了一个"it is..."强调句，重点强调的是"明确"，实质上强调的是承租人不得代表出租方行使免税的权利。分句中的谓语"will not assert any immunity"用了否定形式，具有较强的强调性。

参考译文：双方明确同意承租人未经出租人事先书面同意，不得自行或代表出租人基于出租人的免税身份主张免税（如果出租人有该身份）。

3. It is understood that clause

EG - 17 - 4 It is strictly understood that the Sellers cannot be held responsible for non - delivery of delayed delivery of the goods ordered if the situation is caused by force majeure, such as war, rebellion, fire, strike, new levies imposed by government, mistakes in telegrams, inability of, or refusal by the manufacturers to fulfill this contract or any other causes beyond Seller's control.

该条款用了一个"it is ..."强调句，表面上强调的"strictly understood"，实质上强调的是卖方不应承担某种特定的责任。"not be held responsible"处于子句的谓语部分并用了否定形式，具有较高的强调性，足以引起卖方的重视。

参考译文：严格明确卖方对于自己无法控制的不可抗力，如战争、叛乱、火灾、罢工、政府新征税、电报错误、生产厂商无能力或拒绝按合同生产致使已定货物不能发货或迟延发货概不负责。

4. It is stressed that clause

EG – 17 – 5 It is essentially stressed that the Buyers are requested to sign and return the duplicate of this contract within 3 days from the date of receipt. In the event of failure to do this, the Sellers reserve the right to cancel the contract.

该条款用了一个"it is ..."句型，表面上用"essentially stressed"表达强调什么，实质上强调的是买方有一个引起重视的要求，即"requested to sign and return"。因为子句用的是被动语态，具有较强的强调性。加之随后用一个条件句引出可能需要采取的措施，足以引起"the Buyers"的重视。

参考译文：必须强调买方应于收到本合同之日起 3 天内签字并退还合同的副本，如买方不这样做，卖方保留取消合同的权利。

5. It is strictly necessary for the purposes of

EG – 17 – 6 Unless it is strictly necessary for the purposes of the contract, the drawings, specification and other documents provided by the Employer or the Engineer shall not, without the consent of the Engineer, be used or communicated to a third party by the Contractor. Upon issue of the Defects Liability Certificate, the Contractor shall return to the Engineer all drawings, specification and other documents provided under the contract.

该句虽然不是在主句中采取强调句型，但子句中采取了"it is …"强调句型，表面上是对某事项的绝对需要"strictly necessary"的强调，但实质上是对承包商提出了要求（"not be used or communicated"）并予以强调。谓语部分由于采用了被动语态，且加了否定词"not"，因此具有更强的强调作用，加之后面通过"Upon"引出原因句时要求是"the Contractor shall return to the Engineer"，这些在语气上足以引起"the Contractor"的注意。

参考译文：除非为执行合同的绝对需要，承包商在未经工程师同意的情况下，不得将工程师提供的图纸、规范和其他文件用于第三方或（转送）转达给第三方。在颁发缺陷责任证书时，承包商应将根据合同提供的图纸、规范和其他文件退还给工程师。

二、主旨句的"no"表述的关键词

在涉外合同中，"no"具有"禁止"、"不得"、"不能"之意，由于是通过名词、代词或副词否定的传递作用来达到对动词的否定，因此足以引起法务人员的注意。

对于"no"的位置来讲，"no"在条款中的位置越靠前，其强调的意味越浓，越应引起关注。

例如：No changes can be made on this contract without mutual consent.

该条款中，"no"是对"更改"（"changes"）的否定，强调了合同条款的稳定性，通过条件设置也强调了协商一致的原则；且"no"放在句首，其强调性十分显著。

参考译文：不经双方同意，合同不能作任何更改。

EG－17－7 In no event shall the Seller be liable for lost profits, delay, injury to goodwill or any special or consequential damages howsoever any of the same are caused.

在汉语中，"概不负责"可能是合作双方中最强硬的语气了，在涉外合同中就是通过将"no"提前到关联词"in case"之中，对动词进行否定。本条款采取了倒装句的形式来突出责任的重要性，因此是合作双方最强硬的语气，也就相当于汉语中的"概不负责"。

参考译文：对于利润损失、延误、商誉损害或任何特别或间接的损害赔偿，不论任何原因引起的，卖方概不承担责任。

EG－17－8 The Company has no legal obligation, absolute or contingent, to any other Person to sell any material portion of the assets of the Company, to sell any material portion of the capital stock or other ownership interests of the Company or any of its Subsidiaries, or to effect any merger, consolidation or other reorganization of the Company or any of its Subsidiaries or to enter into any agreement with respect thereto.

本合同条款采取"no"形式对法律责任进行了否定，加之插入了"absolute or contingent"句外类聚词，使得"no legal obligation"的强调作用十分明显，这就足以引起法务人员的注意。

参考译文：本公司没有完全或随时的任何法律义务向任何他人出售公司任何重要的资产部分，出售任何重要的股本部分或本公司或其任一子公司的其他所有权权益，或实现本公司或任一子公司的并购、合并或其他的重组或签订有关以上事项的协议。

三、使用对副词的否定，达到对谓语的否定

在涉外合同条款中，有很多不是直接对谓语进行否定的，而是通过对副词的否定来达到对谓语的否定。

EG－17－9 In case part of or all know－how of the above－mentioned technical contents have been published by Party B or Third Parties. obtains evidence of such publication, then Party A shall no longer be responsible for keeping secret and confidential the part already published.

该条款用"no"对副词"longer"进行否定,达到了对"be responsible"的否定。而"be responsible"本身就是较为突出强调的系表形式,加之有"then"的提醒,构成较为强烈的强调,足以引起资料提供方的重视。这对甲方来讲也是一种保密责任的释放。

参考译文:一旦获得足够证据证明,全部或部分上述技术内容的专有技术被乙方或第三方出版,则甲方不承担已出版部分的保密责任。

EG–17–10 Neither this agreement, nor the disclosure of information under this agreement, nor the ongoing discussions and correspondence between the parties, shall constitute or imply a commitment or binding obligation between the parties or their respective affiliated companies, if any, regarding the subject matter. If, in the future, the parties elect to enter into binding commitments regarding the subject matter, such commitments shall be explicitly stated in a separate written agreement executed by both parties, and the parties hereby affirm that they do not intend their discussions, correspondence, and other activities to be construed as forming a contract regarding the subject matter or any other transaction between them without execution of such separate written agreement.

该条款用"neither... nor...nor..."的并列形式强调了保密的范围,实质上想表明双方之间不形成承诺或义务的情形,加之随后的条件句的约束,不难理解双方对于形成相关合约、交易关系的担心,足以引起双方的重视。

参考译文:该协议、该协议项下资讯的提供以及正在进行的磋商和双方信函往来都不构成或意指对标的物的承诺或关于标的物的约束双方及其相关的下属公司的义务。如果将来双方选择对标的物达成约束性的承诺,必须以书面形式单独订立由双方签署的协议以明确说明该义务。双方据此认定无意将他们的磋商、往来信函和其他活动视为形成有关标的物的合约。在没有另行书面协议的情况下，也不得视为其他任何彼此间的交易。

四、对谓语否定的情形

在涉外合同条款中，对谓语的否定主要有两种形式：一是直接用"not"，二是利用隐含形式达到对谓语的否定。

1. 直接使用"not"达到否定谓语的目的

在涉外合同中，除了用"no"外，还有通过"not"对谓语进行直接否定的情形。

EG – 17 – 11 The invalidity of any provision of this contract shall not affect the validity of any other provision of this contract.

本条款用一个前缀否定形式加一个否定谓语词"not"来强调合同条款的效力，足以引起合同各方对于合同条款相对独立性的重视。

参考译文：本合同某一条款的无效不影响本合同其他条款的效力。

EG – 17 – 12 Failure or delay on the part of any of the parties hereto to exercise a right under this contract shall not operate as a waiver thereof, nor shall any single or partial exercise of such a right preclude any other future exercise thereof.

参考译文：如果一方未行使或迟延行使其在本合同项下的某项权利，不构成该方对此项权利的放弃，如果该方行使过某项权利或者部分行使过某项权利，并不妨碍其在将来再次行使此项权利。

2. 通过隐含的否定，达到对谓语的否定

在涉外合同条款中还有一种比直接用"not"形式更有效的方法，那就是使用含有隐含意思的名词或动词来达到对谓语的否定。

（1）fail to.

EG – 17 – 13 Should the Seller fail to make delivery on time as stipulated in the contract, with the exception of force majeure causes specified in Clause of this contract, the Buyer shall agree to postpone the delivery on the condition that the Seller agree to pay a penalty which shall be deducted by the paying bank from the payment under negotiation. The rate of penalty is charged at _____% for every _____ days, odd days less than _____ days should be counted as _____ days. But the penalty, however, shall not exceed _____% of the total value of the goods involved in the delayed delivery. In case the Seller fail to make delivery _____ days later than the time of shipment stipulated in the contract, the Buyer shall have the right to cancel the contract and the Seller, in spite of the cancellation, shall nevertheless pay the aforesaid penalty to the Buyer without delay.

The Buyer shall have the right to lodge a claim against the Seller for the losses sustained if any.

该条款采取倒装的否定句强调了按时交货的重要性。在该条款中用两个"fail to"比用"not"否定谓语更有强调作用。因为"not"可能只理解为不能按照数量交货,而用"fail to"隐含否定则可能还包括质量、时间、地点要求的不相符合或存在瑕疵。这更能够引起交货方的重视,否则就可能招致承担罚款、承担损失甚至被撤销合同的严重后果。

参考译文:罚款可由议付银行在议付货款时扣除,罚款率按每_____天收_____%,不足_____天时以_____天计算。但罚款不得超过迟交货物总价的_____%。如卖方延期交货超过合同规定_____天时,则买方有权撤销合同,此时,卖方仍应毫不迟延地按上述规定向买方支付罚款。

买方有权对因此遭受的其他损失向卖方提出索赔。

(2) failure of.

EG-17-14 Any failure of the engineer's representative to disapprove any work, materials or plant shall not prejudice the authority of the engineer to disapprove such work, materials or plant and to give instructions for the rectification thereof.

该条款用了一个隐含否定词 "any failure of" 以及两个前缀否定词和一个 "not" 否定词，足以强调工程师指令的重要性。

参考译文：因为工程师代表失误，未曾对任何工作、材料或工程设备发出否定意见，不应影响工程师对该工作、材料或工程设备提出的否定（意见）权力，（并）他仍可为此发出进行（改）纠正的指示（的权力）。

（3）free from.

EG - 17 - 15 On the transfer date New Company shall transfer to B, free from any lien or encumbrance created by New Company and without the payment of any compensation, all its right, title to and interest in the infrastructure project, unless otherwise specified in the agreement or any supplementary agreement.

参考译文：新公司应在转让日转让给乙方，概不承担新公司设定的质押或担保并概不支付基础设施工程中的赔偿、全部权利、所有权和权益，除非本协议另有规定或补充协议。

五、主旨句中处于系表位置的关键词

一般来讲，处于英文系表位置的关键词具有较好的强调作用。

1. become

EG - 17 - 16 If the shipment can not be made within three month as stipulated, the contract will become void.

该句的主旨句的意思是 "合同成为无效"，使用了系动词 "become"。

参考译文：如果不能在规定的 3 个月内出货，则合同视为无效。

EG - 17 - 17 Upon expiration of such term of contract, the contract shall automatically become void and null.

参考译文：合同一经届满则自动失效。

2. be

EG – 17 – 18 The Seller shall not be responsible for the delay of shipment or non – delivery of the goods due to force majeure, which might occur during the process of manufacturing or in the course of loading or transit. The Seller shall advise the Buyer immediately of the occurrence mentioned above and within _____ days thereafter the Seller shall send a notice by courier to the Buyer for their acceptance of a certificate of the accident issued by the local chamber of commerce under whose jurisdiction the accident occurs as evidence thereof. Under such circumstances the Seller, however, are still under the obligation to take all necessary measures to hasten the delivery of the goods. In case the accident lasts for more than _____ days the Buyer shall have the right to cancel the contract.

"be" 在这里表明一种状态，属于动态的固化。

参考译文：凡在制造或装船运输过程中，因不可抗力致使卖方不能或推迟交货时，卖方不负责任。在发生上述情况时，卖方应立即通知买方，并在_____天内给买方特快专递一份由当地民间商会签发的事故证明书。在此情况下，卖方仍有责任采取一切必要措施加快交货。如事故延续_____天以上，买方有权撤销合同。

EG – 17 – 19 The information shall be deemed the property of the disclosing party and, upon request; the other party shall return all information received in tangible form to the disclosing party or shall destroy all such information at the disclosing party's direction. If either party loses or makes an unauthorized disclosure of the other party's information, it shall notify such other party immediately and use reasonable efforts to retrieve the lost or wrongfully disclosed information.

"be deemed" 是一种比较婉转的状态描述方式，意为"视为"。

参考译文："资讯"应被视为资讯披露方的财产，一旦该方要求，另一方应以载体的形式把所有"资讯"归还给披露方，或者按照资讯披露方的指示销毁该资讯。如另一方丢失了资讯或者在未经授权的情况下披露了资讯，应立即通知对方并作合理的努力来追回丢失或错误地泄露的资讯。

3. have

EG - 17 - 20 The supervision personnel appointed by Party A and its representative shall have the authority to supervise the progress of work and give instruction.

"have"在这里具有强调作用。

参考译文：甲方任命的监管人员及其代表应有权监督工程进度并发出指令。

EG - 17 - 21 The conditions or consequences of force majeure（as hereinafter defined）which have a material adverse effect on the affected Party's ability to perform continue for a period in excess of six（6）months and the Parties have been unable to find an equitable solution pursuant to Article ＊＊. 2（c）（Consequences of Force Majeure）hereof...

"have a material adverse effect"具有较强的强调作用。

参考译文：不可抗力产生的后果对受影响方履约能力造成实质影响持续超过 6 个月以上的，双方当事人根据合同第＊＊条不能得到公平解决的⋯⋯

六、主旨句中处于谓语位置的关键词

除了系表结构外，主谓结构中处于谓语位置的关键词也具有较好的强调作用。

1. agrees

EG - 17 - 22 Licensee agrees that it will not during the term of this agreement, or thereafter, attack the title or any rights of Licensor in and to the name or attack the validity of this license.

该条款显然用主谓结构进行了强调。其子句用否定谓语的形式强调了不要侵害许可方的所有权或许可效力。"Licensee agrees"强调的是受让方的"同意"。

参考译文：受许可方同意在本协议期间及其后不以或对许可方名义侵害许可方的所有权或任何权利或侵害该许可的效力。

2. expire

EG－17－23 The term shall expire automatically on the expiration date, unless extended for an additional term of _____ years through a written contract signed by the authorized representatives of the Parties at least sixty (60) days prior to the expiration date.

该句用主谓结构形式强调了合同期满。"signed"为过去分词，属被动式。

参考译文：本合同于到期日自动终止，除非在到期日之前双方授权代表至少提前60天签署书面协议，续展本合同期限为＿＿年。

3. terminated

EG－17－24 This contract may be terminated at any time prior to expiration of the term by the mutual written contract of the Parties.

该条款用一个被动的主谓结构强调了合同有效期限。这里的"be"不属于系表结构。

参考译文：本合同期限届满之前，双方可通过书面协议随时终止本合同。

EG－17－25 At any time prior to the expiration of the term, a Party ("Notifying Party") may terminate this contract through notice to the other Party in writing if...

"terminate" 处于主旨句的谓语位置，具有较好的强调作用。

参考译文：本合同期限届满之前，如果发生以下情形之一，一方（"通知方"）可随时向对方发出书面通知后终止本合同……

4. breaches

EG – 17 – 26 The other Party materially breaches this contract, and such breach is not cured within the cure period granted pursuant to Article. (a) (Remedies for Breach of Contract) ...

该句用了一个主谓结构，"breaches" 处于谓语位置。"materially breaches" 具有较好的强调作用，强调的是违反合同项下的某项义务的情形。

参考译文：对方违反本合同项下某一主要义务，且未在通知方根据 (a) 条 (违约救济) 规定发出的书面违约通知中规定的补救期内对违约予以补救……

5. refer

EG – 17 – 27 If the Contractor questions any communication of the engineer's representative he may refer the matter to the Engineer who shall confirm, reverse or vary the contents of such communication.

该条款用一个条件句作引导，用一个主谓结构句强调了可以提交的情形，及要求工程师的反馈。

参考译文：如果承包商对工程师代表传达的 (信函) 信息有任何质疑，他可将该问题提交给工程师，工程师应对该信息 (此信函的内容) 给予确认、否定或更正。

6. settled

EG – 17 – 28 All disputes arising in connection with this contract or in the execution thereof, should be settled amicably through negotiations.

该句使用一个被动语态的形式强调了争议解决的重要性。

参考译文：所有与本合同或合同履行有关的争议，应通过友好协商解决。

七、使用倒装句型引起重视或起到强调作用

和基础英语一样，涉外合同中如果不必知道行为主体或不知道行为主体，而又想强调行为结果时，就会使用被动语态。被动结构往往作为后置定语、状语或者句子的谓语。

EG – 17 – 29 The existence of this contract, as well as its content, shall be held in confidence by both Parties and only disclosed as may be agreed to by both Parties or as may be required to meet securities disclosure or export permit requirements. Neither Party shall make public statements or issue publicity or media releases with regard to this contract or the relationship between the Parties without the prior written approval of the other Party.

参考译文：双方应对本合同的存在及其内容保密，只有在双方均同意的情况下（或者根据有关证券市场规定须披露或为获得出口许可证须披露的情况下）方可向有关方披露。未经对方事先书面同意，任何一方均不得就本合同或双方的关系发表公开声明或发布宣传或新闻稿。

EG – 17 – 30 In no event shall the Seller be liable for lost profits, delay, injury to goodwill or any special or consequential damages howsoever any of the same are caused.

参考译文：对于利润损失、延误、商誉损害或任何特别或间接的损害赔偿，不论任何原因引起的，卖方概不承担责任。

EG – 17 – 31 Where Party B fails to provide equipment or techniques under the terms and conditions herein or in the agreement of assignment of technology or is found fraudulent, Party Bshall be liable for the direct losses of joint venture caused hereby.

参考译文：如乙方未按本合同及技术转让协议的规定提供设备和技术，或发现有欺骗或隐瞒之行为，乙方应负责赔偿合营公司的直接损失。

EG - 17 - 32 Licensee agrees that it will not during the term of this agreement, or thereafter, attack the title or any rights of Licensor in and to the name or attack the validity of this license.

参考译文：受许可方同意在本协议期间及其后不以或对许可方名义侵害许可方的所有权或任何权利或侵害该许可的效力。

EG - 17 - 33 Each party shall formulate rules and regulations to inform its directors, senior staff, and other employees, and those of their affiliates of the confidentiality obligation set forth in this articles.

参考译文：每一方应制订相应的规章制度，告知该方（以及该方的关联机构）董事、高级职员以及其他雇员本条规定的保密义务。

八、采用动名词形式进行强调

EG - 17 - 34 The design, production skills, technological process, examination and inspection methods, etc of _____ provided by Party B must be complete and integrated, accurate, reliable, fit for the requirements of the business of joint venture and keeping of the quality of products and ascertaining of the production capacity herein provided.

"keeping"、"ascertaining" 采用了动名词形式，起到强调作用。

参考译文：乙方保证为合营公司提供的_____（注：要写明产品名称）的设计、制造技术、工艺流程、测试和检验等全部技术是完整的、准确的、可靠的，是符合合营公司经营目的的要求的，保证能达到本合同要求的产品质量和生产能力。

EG - 17 - 35 Judgment upon any arbitral award may be entered in any court having jurisdiction over the Party against which the award has been rendered, or application may be made to any such court for judicial acceptance of the award and an order of enforcement, as the case may be. In the event of judicial acceptance and an order of enforcement, each Party expressly waives all rights to object thereto, including any defense of sovereign immunity and any other defense based on the fact or allegation that it is an agency or instrumentality of a sovereign state.

"having jurisdiction" 强调现在有管辖权，体现了法律对管辖权的时效性要求。

参考译文：仲裁胜诉方可请求对仲裁败诉一方有管辖权的法院作出相应判决，或者向该法院申请对仲裁裁决予以司法承认并发布强制执行令（以适用者为准）。在法院对仲裁裁决予以司法承认并发布强制执行令的情况下，双方特此明确放弃其提出抗辩的所有权利，包括以主权豁免作为抗辩事由，以及基于其是一个主权国家的机构或部门的事实或主张的其他抗辩事由。

EG - 17 - 36 Establishing between the Parties hereto any partnership or any other form of relationship entailing joint liability...

"establishing" 用现在分词形式作了强调。

参考译文：合同双方之间形成合伙关系或其他导致共同责任的关系……

EG - 17 - 37 Constituting either of the Parties hereto as the agent of the other Party (except with the other Party's prior written consent); or...

参考译文：使任何一方成为另一方的代理人（对方事先书面同意的除外）；或者……

"constituting" 用现在分词形式作了强调。

EG - 17 - 38 Authorizing either Party to incur any expenses or any other form of obligation on behalf of the other Party (except with the other Party's prior written consent).

"authorizing" 用现在分词形式作了强调。

参考译文：授权一方为另一方招致费用或其他任何形式的义务（对方事先书面同意的除外）。

九、采用无主句的形式强调行为

EG – 17 – 39 Its execution of this contract and its performance of its obligations hereunder:

(i) will not violate any provision of its business license, articles of incorporation, and articles of association or similar organizational documens;

(ii) will not violate any applicable law or any governmental authorization or approval; and

(iii) will not violate or result in a default under any contract to which it is a party or to which it is subject.

上述合同条款采用了较为典型的无主句来作强调。该种描述方式一般用于责任、义务的集中表述。

参考译文：该方签订本合同以及履行本合同项下的义务：

不会违反其营业执照、成立协议、章程或类似组织文件的任何规定；

不会违反有关法律或任何政府的授权或批准；并且

不会违反其作为当事人一方（或受之约束）的其他任何合同，也不会导致其被认定在该合同项下未履约。

EG – 17 – 40 Give written notice to the breaching party describing the nature and scope of the breach and demand that the breaching party cure the breach at its cost within a reasonable time specified in the notice ("Cure Period"); and

If the breaching party fails to cure the breach within the cure period, then in addition to its other rights under Article. 1 (c) (I) (Termination) or applicable laws, the aggrieved parties may claim direct and foreseeable damages arising from the breach.

"give written notice" 采用无主句的形式强调了发出书面通知的重要性。

参考译文：除本合同其他条款另有规定外，如果一方（"违约方"）未履行其在本合同项下的某项主要义务，则对方（"受损害方"）除享有有关法律赋予的权利外，还可选择采取以下救济措施：向违约方发出书面通知，说明违约的性质以及范围，并且要求违约方在通知中规定的合理期限内自费予以补救；并且如果违约方未在该书面通知中规定的补救期内予以补救，则受损害方可就违约引起的可以预见的直接损失提出索赔。

十、主旨句中本身含有强调、突出意思的关键词

英文条款中存在很多本身含有强调、突出意思的关键词，应引起相关人员的重视。

1. 在以时间、金钱等作为主语的系表语句中直接使用 "essence" 以起到强调作用

EG – 17 – 41 Time is of the essence in respect of any of your obligations under this agreement.

参考译文：本合同中你方的义务中相关时间是至关重要的。

EG – 17 – 42 The delivery date is of the essence of this agreement.

参考译文：交货日期对于本合同来讲是至关重要的。

EG – 17 – 43 Time is of the essence of this agreement and each of the terms and conditions of this agreement, including, without limitation, in the completion of the work in the manner set forth in the contract.

Whenever action must be taken under this agreement during a period of time that ends on a Saturday, Sunday or federal or state holiday, then such period of time shall be extended until the next day which is not a Saturday, Sunday or such holiday.

Time of payment shall be of the essence of the contract.

参考译文：本合同的每一个条款和本合同对于时间来讲是至关重要的，包括但不限于合同中以说明方式对项目完成的说明，在本合同下无论什么时候采取行动，当遇到星期六、星期日或联邦或州等公共假日时，那么这一时间应该顺延至非公共假日。

支付时间对于本合同来讲是至关重要的。

2. 用"sole"表示强调

EG – 17 – 44 The drawings shall remain in the sole custody of the Engineer, but two copies thereof shall be provided to the Contractor free of charge. The Contractor shall make at his own cost any further copies required by him.

"sole"在这里起强调作用，强调图纸不得外传的重要性。

参考译文：图纸应由工程师单独保管，但应免费提供给承包商两套复印件。承包商需要更多的复印件时，其费用自行负担。

EG – 17 – 45 Restrict disclosure of the information solely to those directors, officers, employees and/or agents/consultants with a need to know and not disclose it to any other person.

"solely"在这里意为"仅仅"，起强调作用。

参考译文：把资讯的披露范围仅仅局限于董事会、公司高级职员、职员和/或有必要知道的代理/顾问，不得将资讯披露给其他任何人。

3. 用"any"或"all"表示强调

EG – 17 – 46 The Engineer may from time to time delegate to the

Engineer's representative any of the duties and authorities vested in the Engineer and he may at any time revoke such delegation. Any such delegation or revocation shall be in writing and shall not take effect until a copy thereof has been delivered to the Employer and the Contractor.

"at any time" 强调时间的随时可选择性。

参考译文：工程师可以一次又一次地将赋予他自己的职责和权力委托给工程师代表并可随时撤回这种委托，任何此类委托或撤回均应采取书面形式，而且只有在其副本送达业主和承包商之后才可发生效力。

EG – 17 – 47 The Buyer shall make a claim against the Seller (including replacement of the goods) by the further inspection certificate and all the expenses incurred therefrom shall be borne by the Seller. The claims mentioned above shall be regarded as being accepted if the Seller fail to reply within _____ days after the Seller received the Buyer's claim.

"all the expenses incurred" 意为"所有发生的费用"，同时起强调作用。

参考译文：通过进一步的验收，买方应向卖方提起索赔（包括替换货物），所有因此发生的费用应由卖方承担。若卖方收到上述索赔后 _____ 天未予答复，则认为卖方已接受买方索赔。

4. 用 "duly" 表示强调

在涉外合同中常用 "duly" 表示强调，其中最常见的是在签字时出现的用以强调签字是经授权或有法定权力这一形式要件。如 "position of duly authorized representative" 意为 "签字人职务和部门"，"signature of duly authorized representative" 意为 "签字人签名"。

EG – 17 – 48 At all time during the term of the agreement of assignment of technology, Party B shall report and supply information to Joint venture duly with respect to any innovation made by Party B in the transferred technology, and no extra fee shall be charged hereof.

显然，本条款使用"duly"强调的是"any innovation"，有时可译为"即"。

参考译文：在技术转让协议有效期内，乙方对该项技术的改进，以及改进的情报和技术资料，应及时提供给合营公司，不得另收费用。

5. in whole or in part

EG – 17 – 49 This contract may not be assigned in whole or in part by the Party without the prior written consent of the other Party hereto.

显然，"in whole or in part"在这里强调的是被转让合同的整体性。

参考译文：未经对方事先书面同意，任何一方不得部分或全部转让本合同。

6. entire

EG – 17 – 50 This contract and the schedules and annexes hereto constitute the entire agreement between the Parties hereto with respect to the subject matter of this contract and supersede all prior discussions, negotiations and agreements between them.

"entire"在这里强调整体性。

参考译文：本合同及附录（和附件）构成双方就本合同标的达成的全部协议，并且取代双方之间此前就该标的进行的所有磋商、谈判以及达成的协议。

EG – 17 – 51 This agreement constitutes the entire understanding between the parties with respect to the information provided hereunder. No amendment or modification of this agreement shall be valid or binding on the parties unless made in writing and executed on behalf of each party by its duly authorized representative.

"entire"强调理解的完整性。

参考译文：本协议构成各方对本协议下提供的"资讯"的完整理解。本协议的任何修改或变动应以书面形式由协议双方各自正式指定的代表签署，否则均为无效或对双方不产生约束力。

7. integral part

EG – 17 – 52 The schedules and annexes hereto are made an integral part of this contract and are equally binding with the main body of the contract. In the event of any conflict between the terms and provisions of the main body of the contract and the schedules or annexes, the terms and provisions of the main body of this contract shall prevail.

"integral part"强调整体性，在具体翻译时可采用"正话反说"的翻译技巧。即英文表述的是正说，强调整体性；翻译为汉语时则为反说，即"不可分割"。

参考译文：本合同的附录（以及附件）为本合同不可分割的部分，并且与本合同正文的条款具有同等效力。如果全合同正文的条款与附录（以及附件）的条款有冲突，以本合同正文条款为准。

8. in witness whereof

EG – 17 – 53 In Witness Whereof, each of parties hereto has caused this contract to be executed by its duly authorized representative on the date first set forth above.

"in witness whereof"短语本身属强调，在这里还通过大写来进行了强调。涉外合同中有很多地方采用全大写的形式进行强调，一般如"免责条款"、"额外承担责任条款"、"侵权条款"等，应引起足够重视。

参考译文：双方已于本合同首页所载日期通过其正式授权的代表签订本合同，以资证明。

9. intact

EG – 17 – 54 Except as contemplated by this agreement, from the date hereof through the closing date, ＊＊ company shall cause each ＊＊ subsidiary to use commercially reasonable efforts to conduct its business in the ordinary course in all material respects, and shall use commercially reasonable endeavors to preserve intact its business relationships, keep available the service of its employees and maintain satisfactory relationships with its suppliers and customers.

"intact" 正说为 "完整性"，也可在翻译时 "正话反说" 而译为 "不受损害"。

参考译文：除非本协议预期，从本协议日期到成交日，＊＊公司应促使＊＊子公司竭尽全力在所有实质方面按通常程序进行交易，并应尽力来保持其商业关系完整，可获得其员工的服务并与供应商和客户维持良好的关系。

10. best

EG – 17 – 55 Promptly following the effective Time, the shareholders of tunes who are employed by J ＊＊ or M ＊＊ Sub shall exert their best efforts to cause all employees of tunes and M ＊＊ Sub to execute in favor of M ＊＊ Sub proprietary rights agreements substantially similar to J ＊＊'s existing employee proprietary rights agreement.

"best" 在这里起强调作用，意为 "竭尽"。

参考译文：生效时间后，被 J ＊＊公司或 M ＊＊ Sub 公司所聘的 M ＊＊公司股东应立即竭尽全力促使 T ＊＊公司和所有员工执行 M ＊＊ Sub 公司的控股权协议，该协议实质上与 J ＊＊公司现有的员工控股权协议类似。

11. respectively responsible for

EG – 17 – 56 Party A and Party B shall be respectively responsible for the following matters.

"respectively" 在这里强调责任的独自性，译为 "各自的"。

参考译文：甲乙方应各自负责完成以下各项事宜。

12. immediately/forthwith

EG – 17 – 57 The Seller shall, immediately upon the completion of the loading of the goods, advice the Buyer of the contract No. , names of commodity, loading quantity, invoice values, gross weight, and name of vessel and shipment date by _____ within _____ hours.

"immediately/forthwith" 意为 "立即"，也可采用正话反说，译为"毫不延迟地"。"forthwith" 一般比 "immediately" 正式。

参考译文：待装载完毕，卖方应在_____小时内以_____式立即通知买方合同编号、品名、已发运数量、发票总金额、毛重、船名/车/机号及启程日期等。

EG – 17 – 58 The Buyer shall accept the bill of exchange immediately upon the first presentation of the bill of exchange and the required documents and shall effect the payment on the maturity date of the bill of exchange.

"immediately" 可不直接译出。

参考译文：汇票一经承兑交单，买方应在汇票到期时完成支付。

EG – 17 – 59 Seller shall forthwith make full payment of the balance.

"forthwith" 意为 "立刻"，比 "immediately"、"at ante" 要正规、严谨，能够较好地起到强调作用。

参考译文：卖方应立刻支付这些余额的全部。

13. only

EG – 17 – 60 The parties are only establishing an independent contractor relationship with each other by entering into this contract. Nothing in this contract shall be construed or implied as...

"only" 意为 "仅仅"，起强调作用。

参考译文：合同双方签订本合同仅仅在他们之间产生独立合同关系。本合同任何条款均不得被解释为……

EG－17－61 Each party is liable for the joint venture company only up to the limit of the capital subscribed by it.

"only up to" 在这里具有强调作用，译为"仅以"。

参考译文：各方对合营公司的责任以各自认缴的出资额为限。

EG－17－62 Whereas the Purchaser inquiry for certain goods and ancillary services, viz., low pressure special regulator and has accepted a bid by the Supplier for the supply of those goods and services in the sum of USD 306, 556. 00 (Three hundred and six thousand five hundred and fifty-six Dollar only) amend to the sum of USD 305, 665. 00 (Three hundred and five thousand six hundred and sixty－five Dollar only).

上述条款用"only"作为货币大写的结尾，有点如人民币大写后"整"的意思。

参考译文：鉴于采购方要求提供某一货物设备即低压规格的校准仪并已接受供应方为此提供的货物和服务，总金额为306556.00美元整变更为总金额305665.00美元整。

14. directly

EG－17－63 Neither Party shall directly solicit for employment the other Party's personnel who are engaged in the performance of this contract, during the term of this contract and within one (1) year after the expiration Date, without the prior written consent of the other Party.

"directly" 意为"直接的"，起到强调作用。需要说明的是，"直接"在这不能仅仅理解为间接招聘就可以了。

参考译文：在本合同有效期内以及本合同终止 1 年内，任何一方均不得直接向另一方参与本合同执行的雇员发出招聘要约，经另一方书面同意的除外。

15. full

EG－17－64 That we hereby give and grant to the said (name of

Trading Company) full power and authority to do and perform all and every act and thing whatsoever, requisite, necessary and proper to be done in the premises, as fully, to all intends and purposes as we might or could do, with full power of substitution and revocation, hereby ratifying and confirming all that (name of Trading Company) or its duly authorized representative shall lawfully do, or cause to be done by virtue hereof.

"full"在这里可译为"全部"。全权授权在有些国家的司法实践中是不被承认的，一般应表述为"extraordinary power and authority"（特别授权），并列出具体的授权事项，而不能笼统地表述为全权授权。全权授权会被理解为一般授权，受权人只能对程序性权利进行代理，而无权对实质性权利进行代理。

参考译文：我方兹授予（贸易公司名称）全权办理和履行我方为完成上述各点所必需的事宜，具有替换或撤销的全权。兹确认（贸易公司名称）或其正式授权代表依此合法地办理一切事宜。

16. including but not limited

EG – 17 – 65 The time for the performance of the Seller's obligations set forth in this contract shall be automatically extended for a period equal to the duration of any nonperformance arising directly or indirectly from force majeure events including but not limited to fire, flood, earthquake, typhoon, natural catastrophe, and all other contingencies and circumstances whatsoever beyond the Seller's reasonable control preventing, hindering or interfering with the performance thereof.

"including but not limited"意为"包括但不限于"，由于对于"不可抗力"的描述采取了概括与枚举相结合的综合方式，因此其属于一种不完全枚举，相当于"such as"。为避免双方对"包括但不限于"产生理解上的争议，实质上可以用"such as"来替换。

参考译文：本合同规定卖方履行义务的时间应自动延长等同于由于直接或间接不可抗力事件导致的不能履行的期间。不可抗力事件包括但不限于火灾、洪水、地震、台风、自然灾害和卖方无论怎样也无法合理控制的阻止、妨碍、干扰本合同履行的其他风险和情形。

17. then

EG - 17 - 66 Except as otherwise provided herein, if a Party ("breaching party") fails to perform any of its material obligations under this Contact, then the other Party ("aggrieved party") may at its option.

显然，这里用"then"通过其转折意思说明了"the other Party"可采取的进一步措施。"then"在这里起强调作用，如果是口语，也可通过重读"then"来表明强调。

参考译文：除本合同其他规定外，如果违约方不履行本合同的实质义务，那么另一方（受损害方）可以按照以下他认为适当的方式选择。

18. said

EG - 17 - 67 The Party B shall deliver his certificate of fixed deposits of USD ＊＊ to the Party A for possession and take the said fixed deposits as pledge of the obligatory right.

"said"意为"前面所说的"，译为"该"，起强调作用。

参考译文：乙方应移交固定存款额为＊＊美元的存折到甲方，作为履行义务的质押凭证。

19. in question

EG - 17 - 68 After an application for share listing obtains consent from the stock exchange, the listed company shall, five days prior to the listing, announce the verified documents relating to the said share listing and make documents in question available at designated places for the public to consult.

"in question"意为"该"，起强调作用。

参考译文：股票上市交易申请经证券交易所同意后，上市公司应当在上市交易的5日前公告经核准的股票上市的有关文件，并将该文件置备于指定场所供公众查阅。

20. regarding

EG – 17 – 69 If any change is required regarding the terms and conditions to this agreement, both parties shall negotiate in order to find a suitable solution, provided however, that any change to this agreement shall be subject to the approval by the Chinese govemment.

"regarding" 在这里译为 "对" 十分贴切，以分词形式起强调作用。

参考译文：如果要求对本合同相关条款进行变更，双方当事人应通过谈判找到一个适当的解决方式，但是，本合同的任何变更应经中国政府的批准。

21. with respect to

EG – 17 – 70 The franchiser is to make available to the franchisee advice, guidance and know – how, with respect to management of this franchise.

"with respect to" 意为 "有关的"，在这里起强调作用。

参考译文：特许权拥有人应就有关本项特许的经营管理问题向特许经销代理人提供意见、指导和技术诀窍。

22. as to

EG – 17 – 71 The Contractor shall be deemed to have satisfied himself as to the correctness and sufficiency of the contract price.

"as to" 可译为 "就……而论"，在这里起强调提示作用。

参考译文：承包商应视为自己就合同价格的充分性和正确性而言感到满意。

第 *18* 章

双刃性评估：降低法律风险的有效手段

合同条款总是具有双刃性，对一方来说是机会，对另一方来讲可能是风险；短期可能是机会，长期可能是风险；对单一条款来讲是机会，从整体来讲可能是风险。因此，法务人员要重点关注己方的需求所在、利益所在与风险所在，学会变换角度分析问题，学会换位思考风险所在，这样才可以全面把握合同条款的机会与风险，从而使客户的法律风险降到可以接受的程度。

一、涉外合同阅读的思维顺序

合同是公司商事交往中规避法律风险的有效手段，通过签订合同，双方当事人能够很好地达成一致的意见，并能够将双方意见和谈判内容很好地记录下来。书面合同不仅是对商务条款的确认，更重要的是在双方发生争议时可作为解决问题所引用的依据。条理井然是提高工作效率的有效方法，理清思维是做好风险双刃性分析的前提。因此，合同审核人员应从法律风险规避的角度做好合同的起草与审核工作，并重点从理清思维着手。

（1）先了解双方的基本情况，是否属同一法系。不同的法系涉及不同的法律术语，相同的法律术语在不同的法系中具有不同的解释。

（2）了解合同优先适用的语言。由于涉外合同双方存在较大的文化、社会和法律差异，对于语言的理解也不尽相同，因此，在适用的语言上应尽量选择双方都较为熟悉的语言，这样可减少对于一些术语的解释，对于存在歧义的语言，一定要事先通过定义进行消歧。

（3）了解合同所适用国家的法律。无论是合同阅读者还是审核者，一定要在阅读合同之前了解合同所适用国家的法律。只有清楚了适用的法律，才能对定义、术语、概念等的适当性进行分析。

（4）了解双方当事人是否有优先解释适用的顺序。

（5）在了解合同主要条款的基础上熟悉定义与附件部分。对于与法言法语或通俗理解有歧义的定义要重点了解。

（6）在理解一般条款的基础上重点了解特殊约定条款。对于特殊条款，一定要结合通用条款进行分析，重点要分析其是否会对其他条款的效力产生影响，虽然特殊条款不会对明示的担保否定产生实质性的影响，但必然会因此而产生矛盾或歧义，从而造成纠纷。

（7）对于嵌入式引导条款要重点理解。在合同阅读与审核中，一定要注意嵌入式引导条款的实质意义，学会还原联系被嵌入的条款的适当性与合意性。特别要关注被嵌入后对被嵌入条款前后条款的影响。

（8）在了解违约责任的基础上重点理解免责条款。违约责任约定的目的是为了让承担违约责任方能够忠实履行义务，如果约定好了的违约责任被免责条款冲淡或清洁消毒了，就会失去违约责任条款设置的意义。

（9）在了解权利义务的基础上重点理解担保条款。涉外合同的担保与国内的担保存在一定的差异，重点关注当事方的陈述性担保、默示担保与第三方担保的差异。

二、涉外合同的解释原则

合同是签约双方的一种意思表示，但难免产生争议，这时就需要对合同条款进行解释。由于解释人的文化背景与职业经历不一样，因而会产生不同的理解，这时就需要在合同条款中提前设置对合同进行解释的规则。

英美法官在合同解释方面一般遵循以下几点规律：

（1）按照通常语义（nature and ordinary meaning）对合同进行解释。

（2）依照合同本身进行解释。

（3）整体地解释合同。

（4）特殊优于一般。

（5）非格式优于格式。

（6）明示优于默示。在合同中如果出现了明示的担保，那么就不得在免责条款中推翻自己的承诺；如果是默示担保，则可以通过免责条款排除。

（7）不利地位的辩解优于强势。法律总是以保护弱者为己任，因此，处于强势地位的一方尽量不要在合同中强加于人，否则可能成为法官偏袒弱势方的理由。

（8）善意优于恶意。无论合同条款如何达成，法官总要考虑双方是基于善意还是出于恶意，善意的行为总会受到法律保护，恶意的行为总会受到法律的抵制。

（9）自己认为合理的其他方式解释。

以下为《联合国国际货物买卖合同公约》第 8 条、第 9 条有关解释的阐述，现摘录于此。

EG - 18 - 1 Injunctive Relief

Notwithstanding the foregoing, the Parties agree that each Party has the right to seek injunctive or other similar relief in any court of competent jurisdiction in respect of any claims of breach of confidentiality or IPR infringement.

参考译文：申请禁制令的司法救济权利

无论本合同前述条款有何规定，双方同意如果一方提出对方违反保密条款或侵犯知识产权的指控，则提出指控一方可向任何一个有管辖权的法院申请发布制止侵权、违约行为的禁制令或采取其他类似救济措施。

EG - 18 - 2 For the purposes of this convention statements made by and other conduct of a party are to be interpreted according to his intent where the other party knew or could not have been unaware what that intent was.

If the preceding paragraph is not applicable, statements made by and other conduct of a party are to be interpreted according to the understanding that a reasonable person of the same kind as the other party would have had in the same circumstances.

In determining the intent of a party or the understanding a reasonable person would have had, due consideration is to be given to all relevant circumstances of the case including the negotiations, any practices which the parties have established between themselves, usages and any subsequent conduct of the parties.

参考译文：为本公约的目的，一方当事人所作的声明和其他行为应依照他的意旨解释，如果另一方当事人已知道或者不可能不知道此意旨。

如果上一款的规定不适用，当事人所作的声明和其他行为应按照一个与另一方当事人同等资格、通情达理的人处于相同情况中所应有的理解来解释。

在确定一方当事人的意旨或一个通情达理的人所应有的理解时，应适当地考虑到与事实有关的一切情况，包括谈判情形、当事人之间确立的任何习惯做法、惯例和当事人其后的任何行为。

EG - 18 - 3 The parties are bound by any usage to which they have agreed and by any practices which they have established between themselves.

The parties are considered, unless otherwise agreed, to have impliedly made applicable to their contract or its formation a usage of which the parties knew or ought to have known and which in international trade is widely known to, and regularly observed by, parties to contracts of the type involved in the particular trade concerned.

参考译文:双方当事人业已同意的任何惯例和他们之间确立的任何习惯做法,对双方当事人均有约束力。

除非另有协议,双方当事人应视为已默示地同意对他们的合同或合同的订立适用双方当事人已知道或理应知道的惯例,而这种惯例,在国际贸易上,已为有关特定贸易所涉同类合同的当事人所广泛知道并为他们所经常遵守。

三、法理审核的重点是确保合同效力不被否定或撤销

合同法理性审核的目的是保证合同的效力性。合同必需具备生效的一般条件,有时它也可能成为合同发生效力的基本前提。

法理审核的重点是确保公平,树立合同的对价意识。"对价"是英美合同法中的重要概念,但在中国司法实践中,一些理论素质较高的法官也会用对价理念来引导案件裁判。对价原则与中国合同法的公平原则基本意思一致。根据中国《合同法》规定:"当事人应当遵循公平原则确定各方的权利和义务。"合同条款如果违背了公平原则,合同或相关条款就有可能被判无效或被撤销。因此,法务人员应做好合同条款的公平性审核,确保合同效力不被否定或不被撤销,主要是做好以下几点:

(1)要避免霸王条款。在合同审核中,法务人员一定要注意各方责任分担的合理性,切忌侵害多数人利益的"霸王条款"出现。在合同约定中,若各方责任分担不合理,不仅有违基本的商业道德,而且一旦产生纠纷,此类条款很容易成为众矢之的,从而毁坏公司信誉,且容易被法院或仲裁机构确认为无效条款。尤其是要审核是否存在"造成对方人身伤害的"或"因故意或者重大过失造成对方财产损失的"免责条款,该类免责条款注定是得不到法律保护的。

(2)依照中国《合同法》第52条的规定,合同条款中出现一方

以欺诈、胁迫的手段订立合同，损害国家利益；恶意串通，损害国家、集体或者第三人利益；以合法形式掩盖非法目的；损害社会公共利益；违反法律、行政法规的强制性规定等情形时，会被认定为无效。因此，法务人员要重点审核可能导致合同无效的条款。

（3）依照中国《合同法》规定，一方以欺诈、胁迫的手段或者乘人之危，使对方在违背真实意思的情况下订立的合同，受损害方在一定期限内有权请求人民法院或者仲裁机构变更或者撤销。因此，审核人员要重点分析对分担责任方显失公平的条款与容易让相对方产生误解的条款。

（4）依照中国《合同法》规定，行为人没有代理权、超越代理权或者代理权终止后以被代理人名义订立的合同，未经被代理人追认的，对被代理人不发生效力，由行为人承担责任。因此，法务人员要重点审核对方提交的授权委托书中的期限、授权范围、授权目的等，确保签订合同人员有相应授权。

（5）对于附期限、附条件的合同条款，法务人员一定要引起重视，充分与商务人员及执行人员进行沟通，确保合同能够在所附期限及所附条件内得到切实履行，如果认为存在风险，就应当对期限或条件进行适当修订，确保法律风险降低到可接受的程度。

（6）重点审核涉及多方利益的"格式合同"时，一定要注意各方责任分担的合理性。由于《合同法》规定当"格式条款"出现争议时，适用不利于格式合同制订方的解释规则，因此，制订方在约定各方责任时用词要严谨，概念要明确，权利义务要分明，各方责任分担要公平，避免产生歧义，否则就可能被法院或仲裁机构判定为有利于接受格式合同条款的解释。

（7）在合同公平性审查过程中，还要重点关注双方达成的合同条款是否能够被实质履行。不能明知是不能履行的合同而出于某种目的仍友好签订，特别是对于标的物不存在或针对国家禁止交易的标的物仍签订合同的更要坚决杜绝，防患于未然。

四、涉外合同逻辑性审核的关注重点所在

在审核过程中，法务人员在结合语义、结构进行审核时，还要注意合同条款的逻辑性审核。合同条款的逻辑性是合同审核的精髓，它决定着一份合同是否科学、严谨，是衡量合同完美与否的基本要求。逻辑性审核主要是分析合同定义、概念、条款结构、标的物的子项划分等是否符合逻辑的内涵、外延规则及逻辑的基本原理。这就要注重审核合同条款内容的语言表达是否精确，对于权利义务的解释是否唯一。同一事项、同一术语不能在同一合同中出现不同的解释方式或解释语境；同时，任何前置条件或但书条款都不得与合同签订、成立、履行所要求的条件相冲突。该等条件不会在合同履行期间因环境条件发生较大变化而影响合同的实质履行，对于因预期变化较大而严重影响合同的实质履行的，一定要有双方可接受的变更接口条款，以确保条件变化时双方能够容易达成一致意见。

合同条款的逻辑性审核不仅是保护自己利益、防范法律风险的基础，也能让当事人初步了解企业法务人员的水平和素质。合同条款的逻辑性问题是合同的精髓问题，一份前后条款相互抵触甚至相互矛盾的合同不仅会给公司经营带来风险，也会让对方当事人感受到己方法务人员的水平和素质欠佳，进而会使当事人产生忧虑感，当事人会因此丧失对法务人员的信任，并很难在短时间内摆脱对法务人员工作水平的质疑。

1. 逻辑性审核重点关注以下 5 点

（1）概念明确。涉及合同标的构成的子项要划分完整，能够构成不重叠、不缺块的完整拼盘，尤其是要注意审核合同总额、合同分项计价与结算金额之间存在严格的衡等关系或相互的勾稽关系。

（2）思维严谨。任何违约都没有借口或机会可以逃避制裁，任何理由都不可借此随意对义务不予履行。

（3）是否存在非法律用语，是否存在容易产生歧义的语句。如果存在，就要作出精确的定义，且定义的内涵与外延应符合逻辑性规则。

（4）违约责任的可能性和必然性。要审核违约责任的设计是否源于双方的权利义务，违约责任的承担与权利义务是否具有紧密的逻辑关系，否则就要对双方的权利义务重新进行明确。

（5）审核合同的内容是否存在冲突、矛盾之处，是否违反逻辑的一般规律。特别是使用类聚词来表达己方应承担义务时更要严格，防止外延过大。

2. 权利义务相匹配的审核要点

权利义务相匹配的实质涉及合同条款的均衡。所谓合同条款的均衡就是指合同条款针对合同一方权利与义务要相对平衡。这主要是指一方享受了权利，就必须承担相应的义务。权利与义务必须"匹配"，不应出现有权利而没有义务主体或有义务而没有权利主体的情形，一方当事人的权利内容应与另一方当事人的义务相对应。过分强调一方的权利、忽略合同相对方的利益的合同，要么得不到签署，要么会变成有失公平。同时，在责任追究方面必须设定相对方有什么样的可供检验的过错，或者说没有按照约定履行合同时的处理方式。也就是说，要承担相应的责任，就必须有追究其违约责任的条款依据。

一般来讲，在考虑合同的均衡性时一般要注意以下几点：

（1）权利义务的平衡。权利义务要对等，主要注意风险分担上不能出现一边倒的不公平现象。

（2）违约责任的平衡。合同应当有双方违约的责任追究条款，在条款的设计上不能只对一方的违约责任进行限定。

（3）变更条款的平衡。对于合同变更的前置条件，不能只授予单方面变更合同的权利。变更须经双方协商达成，或者设置双方都可接受的假设性条件。

（4）结算条款的平衡。合同的结算必须与合同标的物的交付相适应，不能与交货期、服务期和其他合同约定的期间不相适应。为保证交易的安全，支付货款的一方要注意合同的对价。

（5）重点关注"对价"原则。在合同是否符合"对价"原则的审核中，要注意合同要约与承诺是否一致，合同条款的依据是否充足。合同要约与承诺必须一致，否则就可能形成新的要约和承诺。特别要审核合同标的物的技术参数是否与需求方的要求相一致。

（6）与其他支撑性文件的平衡。合同审核中要注意确保主合同与辅合同（如担保协议、三方协议、框架协议下的具体协议等）、主合同与补充协议、主合同与技术协议、主合同与合同附件（如标的物清单、到货通知形式、工程结算清单等）的接口条款明确并便于实施。

五、特别条款审核的重点所在

对于特别约定条款的审核，应重点关注以下 8 个方面：

（1）注意合同内容的前后一致性。合同作为对当事人各方都非常重要的一项法律文件，在内容上必须讲求逻辑严谨、前后一致，不能前后内容相互矛盾、主合同内容和附件内容相互抵触。所以，在起草或审核合同时，一定要注意合同内容的前后一致性，注意对合同前后内容产生矛盾或冲突时的处理原则作出约定，如是"以主合同内容为准"还是"以合同附件内容为准"等必须在主合同中约定清楚。对于较重要的合同，最好用专门的条款确定协议书、通用条款、专门条款、招投标文件、澄清文件、技术协议等的优先适用的顺序。

（2）注意考虑合同订立后的可变更性。在订立合同时，必须考虑到合同订立后履约过程中所可能发生的一些影响合同正常履行的因素。对影响合同变动的因素考虑得越周密细致，就越能避免纠纷，合同权益也就越容易得到保障。特别是在约定性条款审核中，要仔细分析是否有对于合同的实质性条款的变更，特别是通过招投标形成的合同文本，如果在谈判后又进行了修订，一般该修订不得对实质性条款进行变更，对于此点更要细致审核，以防出现差错。

（3）注意专业条款的技术成熟性和可验证性。双方特别约定的合同条款往往涉及技术专业性问题，法务人员在审核时一定要结合技术附件进行审核，以防合同正本与合同附件不相一致，必要时应与相关技术人员进行有效沟通。

（4）注意接口条款的审核。比较重要或专业的合同一般都会出现较多的接口条款或引用指向条款，对于这些条款一定要结合全文进行审核，防止错号、漏号，避免出现引用指向错误或者出现与其他条款相互矛盾的地方；更要防止合同条款的相互引用，一般引用指向不得超过一次，否则就可能存在循环引用问题。

（5）注意不同国家和不同文化背景下的双方对合同条款或术语可能产生的不同理解。法务人员要学会用自己的文化、法律背景草拟出反映对方文化背景的条款，以便于双方的理解。以此可反映出对于对方文化背景的深刻理解，更重要的是哪些与自己所掌握的不同，以确保双方的意思一致。特别是转换成其他国家的语言时，更要注意与对方术语、行话的一一对应，与之尽量保持一致。如果意思不能充分表达，就可能造成纠纷或执行上的困难，特别是在不同文化背景下更要注意这一点。

（6）在阅读和审核合同时，法务人员应判断所持立场方所处的地位是否有利。往往存在谁起草合同就考虑对谁有利的问题。而发生纠纷时法官的解释倾向是对非起草方有利。还有一点就是对于合同标的物所涉业务的熟悉程度，一般来讲，谁越对所涉及行业熟悉，合同就越对谁有利，当然这也要求熟悉业务的一方有提供行业技术规范、标准的义务。

（7）要注意国内条款惯性思维对涉外合同条款的影响。阅读者由于对国内法的熟悉，会产生一种惯性思维，而这种思维拿到涉外合同中去理解会产生很大的差异。因此，在英文合同的审核中还要克服国内合同法所产生的惯性思维，以保证对涉外合同的正确理解。

为便于合同的执行，强势的一方应尽量规避不公平的优势，签订合同的目的是各方当事人更好地行使权利、更好地履行义务。

（8）是否满足己方的采购需求，是否能够避免风险。所谓风险就是未来支出的不确定性。这一不确定性可能使企业陷入纠纷或债务危机，甚至引发经营危机而不得不申请破产。在争议发生前就要预料如何去解决，这是涉外合同最首要的原则，也是最后的原则。只有这样，在发生纠纷时才会有双方可接受的处理方法。如果合同签订前没有预料到，那就是法务人员的水平不到位了。

六、合同风险控制的重点所在

一般来讲，合同最可怕的就是履行中的风险，其中比较重要的一个原因就是花很大精力签订的合同条款缺乏可操作性。这具体表现在合同各方权利义务、交易程序的规定过于抽象、含混或原则，或虽作了详细规定，但没有违约责任条款加以保障。

合同的可操作性是达到交易目的、预防风险的具体保证，尤其是履行周期长、风险大的合同更需要注意。当事人往往碍于情面，不愿意对权利义务、交易程序进行细化，不愿意提及违约责任或轻描淡写，这些都是要不得的。

如何通过特殊条款达到控制风险的目的是法务人员全盘考虑合同风险的重点所在。因此，应从合同风险控制角度对合同进行整体性审核，一般应注意如下事项：

（1）注意交易实施的安全。在审核合同时应特别注意能够保障交易顺利实现的条款内容。在对价明确的情况下，除对当事人进行必要的信誉评估外，还应通过银行等金融机构的担保来确保交易安全。随着市场环境的变化，为有效防范合同风险的发生，买方为确保资金安全，往往通过在合同中设置要求卖方提供合同履约保函、质量保证金保函、预付款保函等条款来确保合同的实质履行，以降低履约风险。对此法律审核人员要特别关注，因为保函条款往往会涉及合同的效力及违约责任问题，这就要重点审核相关附期限或附条件条款、违约责任与履约保函的内容的一致性，防止出现担保瑕疵。

EG – 18 – 4 Agent of buyer upon receipt from the Seller of the delivery advice specified in Clause 7. 1 of the contract, shall, sixty (60) days prior to the date of delivery, open an Irrevocable Letter of Credit (L/C) through the AGENT OF BUYER's bank in favor of the SELLER covering one hundred percent (100%) of the total Contract price. The L/C shall be valid until twenty – one (21) days after time of delivery specified in Clause 6. 1.

参考译文：买方代理依照合同＊＊条的规定从收到卖方发货通知时起，于交货60天前在买方代理银行开出一张以卖方为受益人，额度为合同总价100%的不可撤销的信用证。该信用证按照合同条款＊条在交付后21天内一直有效。

（2）注意合同纠纷发生的可能。审核合同必须具备"法律"和"商业"两种意识，充分考虑到发生合同纠纷的法律风险，在合同中尽可能将双方的权利义务及违约责任条款约定清楚。

（3）综合判断合同标的物的检验是否有双方认定的执行标准，对于质量验收不符合标准的补救措施是否切实可行，是否存在乱用标准的情形。特别要注意对于质量担保条款的例外约定。

（4）分析是否有开口条款。关于合同价款，重点应审核合同价款的构成和计价货币。此时应注意汇率风险和利率风险，以及双方对汇率风险和利率风险的分担比例或办法。

（5）对于经过招投标程序的，应审核合同的实质性条款是否有重大修改，审核合同的价格组成是否唯一。结合合同价款构成审核结算条款是否可行，相互是否形成勾稽关系，同时还要分析合同实质性条款发生变动后是否会影响到双方权利义务的重新分配问题，以及评估双方对合同风险的分担是否合理。

（6）审核"包括但不限于"条款。为了说明合同价款或权利享有，权利的享有方一般都要求约定"包括但不限于"条款，这对于义务的承担方就可能会形成开口性责任。开口性责任是法务审核人员十分敏感的问题，对此应高度警觉。

（7）审核违约责任是否大于合同标的额，义务方是否有相应的履约能力。在违约责任的设定上一定要考虑违约的最大可能。因此，对于违约责任一定要有较为客观的兜底条款。

（8）审核但书条款。合同的但书条款往往是该条款在合同履行过程中环境因素发生变化后的处置方案。

（9）审核假设性条款。假设性条款一般是在合同实际履行中容易形成法律纠纷的条款。这种假设性存在的可能性在60%以上，因此应当作为对标的额的实质变更条款，还要分析其他条款是否也有相应的变动方案。

（10）审核合同履约期间是否合理。合同的履约期间对于合同标的价格构成具有十分重要的影响，有时履约期间可能涉及市场价格的变动，这就要区别违约责任与市场激烈变化所带来的履约不能。对于能够预料的市场变动风险，双方应约定好相应的风险分担方案，或设定价格调整方案，如以国家统计部门发布的国民生产总值或物价指数的增幅标准作为调价依据，或以某一市场价格发布机构发布的原材料价格作为调价基准等。

（11）审核合同履约的前置性条件。在合同的签订中，处于强势的一方会在合同中规定：对于某些信息的准确性己方不承担责任，承接方有义务自己解读、分析并核实这些信息。因此，应重点分析附条件或附期限条款对于条件与期限的责任界定。

（12）审核专业技术性很强的特别约定条款。对此主要是审核合同条款与技术附件是否一致。尤其是对于涉及合同成果交付范围和技术性比较强的合同，必须首先审核合同文件是否规定了明确的合同成果交付范围，注意双方的责任范围，明确界限划分与分包合同及其他相关合同的接口是否准确。

（13）审核合同中有关标的物的物权转移条款。重点分析标的物的物权的转移时限是否符合合同法及物权法有关物权的规定，特别是当合同条款涉及留置权、优先受偿权时，更要加以足够的重视。

综上所述，合同审核是多方位的法律思考过程，无论是对于合同的起草还是合同的审核，法务人员都要结合已有的资料和法律规定，对未来履约风险进行评估。可以说，合同风险性审核是合同审核的重中之重，如果其他审核思路清晰，并且做到了认真仔细，是完全可以降低合同风险的，但并不能说所有风险都已排除，还要站在风险性角度进行专门审核，这样才可确保合同条款的风险降至可控制的程度。如果在审核中认为可预测的法律风险是必须保留的，最好请法务人员或自己的法律团队进行专门的法律风险评估，并附有针对性的法律意见。这样，对于风险控制才能够做到心中有数、防范有力。

参考文献

［1］兰天. 国际商务合同翻译教程［M］. 北京：北京财经大学出版社，2011
  （4）.

［2］王道庚. 新编英汉法律翻译教程［M］. 杭州：浙江大学出版社，2006（6）.

［3］KARLA C. SHIPPEY, JD. 国际商务合同［M］. 上海：上海外语教育出版
  社，2009（1）.

［4］白慧林. 英美合同法律实务［M］. 北京：北京大学出版社，2008（8）.

［5］［美］陶博. 法律英语（中英文以及法律文书中的语义歧义）［M］. 上海：
  复旦大学出版社，2010（8）.

［6］范文祥. 涉外合同阅读与分析技巧［M］. 北京：法律出版社，2007（12）.

［7］林克敏. 中英商务合同精选与解读［M］. 北京：中国人民大学出版社，
  （3）.

［8］刘川，王菲. 涉外合同阅读与翻译［M］. 北京：国防工业出版社，2010
  （6）.

［9］严明. 应用法律英语写作［M］. 长春：吉林出版集团，2010（1）.

［10］张今，陈云清. 英汉比较语法纲要［M］. 北京：商务印书馆，1981（8）.

［11］雷彦璋. 民商诉讼博弈与律师技能突破［M］. 北京：知识产权出版社，
  2008（8）.

［12］雷彦璋. 非诉博弈与企业法务精要［M］. 北京：中国法制出版社，2012
  （6）.

［13］王金玲. 法律英语导读［M］. 上，下. 英汉对照. 北京：西宛出版社，
  1999（5）.

［14］帅建林. 国际贸易惯例案例解析［M］. 北京：对外经济贸易大学出版社，
  2006（11）.

后 记

《民商诉讼博弈与律师技能突破》、《对风险说不！非诉博弈与企业法务精要》这两本书相继与读者见面后，经过数月的伏案深思，终于完成了其姊妹篇《对风险说不——涉外合同关键词导读与解析》。这是笔者对实用法学的热爱，也包含了领导、同事和朋友们对笔者创作与工作总结的理解与支持。

如果说《民商诉讼博弈与律师技能突破》从提升律师执业技能角度讲述了民商诉讼的技巧与素质要求，《对风险说不！非诉博弈与企业法务精要》侧重于提升企业法务人员或企业法律顾问处理企业非诉事务能力的话，那么，本书旨在提升涉外商务谈判人员、企业法务人员及有志于涉外事务的法律人员涉外合同的谈判、起草、审核与应用能力。

本书内容新颖，理念独特，多是笔者的切身感受与善于思考的智慧结晶。特别是对于行为经济学理论在批判吸收的基础上提出了情感类聚这一独特理念，并将这一理念应用于企业的涉外合同谈判、文本起草与审核的法律事务之中，这对于指导企业涉外法务工作或涉外商务谈判工作具有较高的实务性意义。

当然，懂得英文合同条款之中所蕴含的辩证关系，也是读者能够很快熟悉本书的捷径。

读者在学习本书的过程中，一定要用辩证思维的观点来分析相关问题，并掌握好相关关系：

（1）强与弱。无论您处于什么立场，无论您站在什么角度看问题，一定要注意谈判各方所处地位的强弱，不同的合同条款对所处地位不同的当事人在风险测试时其评估值是有所偏重的。

（2）实与虚。合同条款有虚实之分。虚属于合同的格式或形式要求，实属于权利义务的设定。虚并非作用不大，实并非作用就一定强，这主要看虚实之间的结合与合理配置。必要的格式或形式条款不可少，过于繁琐的权利义务也可简洁与省略，其前提还要结合法律的一般规定，以及是否有商务习惯等。

（3）动与静。合同条款也有动静之分。动是用发展与动态的眼光看待权利义务；静是从相对静止的角度看待事物属性与行为特征。静主要用于描述可定量的事物，如陈述与保证、交付验收标准等；动主要用于权利义务的行使描述，如违约责任、不可抗事件的处置等。在涉外合同中动与静的描述方式也是有显著区别的。

当然，对于合同条款的理解还有"因与果，固与变，损与益，正与反，精与略"等辩证关系的区别，这些本书都会有所体现，希望读者能够在阅读中感悟。限于篇幅，这里不再赘述。

读了笔者的《民商诉讼博弈与律师技能突破》之后，民商诉讼的技能会得到有效提升，让当事人的满意度也会大为增强，《对风险说不！非诉博弈与企业法务精要》一书在手，则让您能够对企业较为复杂的法务事务处理起来是得心应手，而《对风险说不——涉外合同关键词导读与解析》则让您很快熟悉涉外合同文本的关键所在，风险控制所在，让领导对您的涉外合同谈判、起草与审核能力的提升惊讶不已。

在写作本书前，笔者吸吮过众多名家大作之精髓，并没有一一在引文或参考文献中标注，包括一些未署名的网络博客文章，当然还有同事与谈判对手在涉外商务谈判中的智慧奉献，值此一一表示感谢。

我之所为，您之所欲。

我之所苦，您之所乐。

能力提升，与大家共享，才是我们共同的心愿！

雷彦璋

2013 年 3 月 18 日于泉州